POLITICAL
TRIALS

POLITICAL TRIALS

edited by
THEODORE L. BECKER

The Bobbs-Merrill Company, Inc.
Indianapolis and New York

TO POLITICALLY UNTRIABLE RADICALS:
the unco-optables in every system
who fight the system in themselves,
yet find themselves within it

contents

FOUR: "POLITICAL" TRIALS

FIVE: A "POLITICAL TRIAL"

the contributors

THEODORE L. BECKER is professor of political science at the University of Hawaii. During 1969–70 he was visiting professor of politics at New York University.

CARROL W. CAGLE, editor and free-lance journalist who has contributed to several national publications, is press secretary to Senator Clinton P. Anderson of New Mexico.

DAVID J. DANELSKI is professor of government at Cornell University. He previously taught at Yale University and during 1968–69 was a Fulbright lecturer and Guggenheim fellow at Tokyo University.

KENNETH M. DOLBEARE is professor and chairman of the department of political science at the University of Washington in Seattle. He spent 1969–70 at the Law and Society Center in Berkeley on a Guggenheim fellowship.

WILLIAM G. FLEMING is associate professor of politics at New York University. A former associate with the East African Institute of Social Research, he completed a research tour of Nigeria and Great Britain in 1967.

GEORGE H. GADBOIS, JR., is associate professor of political science at the University of Kentucky. Recipient of two grants from the American Institute of Indian Studies, he spent 1969–70 in New Delhi.

JOEL B. GROSSMAN is associate professor of political science and director of the Center for Law and Behavioral Science at the University of Wisconsin.

WILLIAM B. HARVEY is professor of law and political science and dean of the faculty of law at Indiana University. He held similar positions in law at the University of Ghana from 1962 to 1964, and was director of legal education in Ghana during that period.

DONALD P. KOMMERS is associate professor of government and international studies at the University of Notre Dame. He spent 1967–68 in West Germany engaged in research on the Federal Constitutional Court.

SAMUEL KRISLOV is professor and chairman of the department of political science and adjunct professor of law at the University of Minnesota. He is the editor of *Law and Society Review*.

FRANCISCO JOSÉ MORENO is associate professor and chairman of the department of politics at New York University. He holds a law degree from the University of Havana, Cuba.

HARRY P. STUMPF is associate professor of political science at the University of New Mexico. During 1967–68 he directed a project which studied Legal Service Programs of the Office of Economic Opportunity in the San Francisco bay area.

JOHN E. TURNER is professor of political science at the University of Minnesota. Since 1965 he has served as a member of the editorial board of the *American Political Science Review*. He recently returned from a research tour in the USSR.

introduction

Marat in the courtroom Marat underground
sometimes the otter and sometimes the hound*

In a sense, *all* trials are political. Since courts are government agencies and judges are part of "the system," all judicial decisions can be considered political. Judges, who are usually lawyers, are politicians too, and every judicial decision, whether in contract or divorce, has the heavy hand of government upon it. Still, to call a case involving a traffic accident a political trial would rob that phrase of its usual meaning.

Criminal cases are closer to the usual notion of what political trials are all about. In such trials, regardless of offense, the state is directly involved (*People of the United States* v. *Smith,* etc.). And no matter how trivial the crime, it is clear that the government seeks to remove the defendant from circulation, either temporarily or permanently. So, on the one hand, such trials are political trials; the polity is the active agent. But, on the other, criminal proceedings are considerably removed from more commonplace ideas about political trials. When Lightfinger Lester is hauled before the bar of justice for picking pockets, no one would call this a political trial, even though (1) the public interest is involved; (2) the judge might be a political hack; and (3) Lester's freedom may soon be curtailed by the government.

What makes the trials of such various individuals as Jesus, Captain Dreyfus, Socrates, Joan of Arc, Tom Mooney, and Sir Thomas More political is something else. In each case, men in power believed the defendant to be threatening them in some way. This is not to say that Jesus or Sir Thomas More broke no laws. Rather, that perception of a direct threat to established political power is a major difference between political trials and other trials.

If members of a ruling elite believe a particular individual or group to be imminently hostile to the prevailing pattern of value distribution, and if they

*From *Marat/Sade* by Peter Weiss. Copyright © 1965 by John Calder Ltd. English version by Geoffrey Skelton. Verse adaptation by Adrian Mitchell. Reprinted by permission of Atheneum Publishers.

xi

activate the criminal process against him (or them) for that reason, what results is a political trial. Additionally, if members of the ruling elite feel someone seriously intends to alter the *way* in which the government distributes those values, and if the elite activates the criminal process against them for that reason—that, too, constitutes a political trial. In each instance, powerful men decide, wisely or unwisely, that the regular courts offer a reliable way of eliminating what they consider to be pesky irritants or deadly challenges.

It is easy to attribute such motives to a government when the defendants are charged with breaking a law explicitly prohibiting such action: treason, conspiracy to overthrow the government by force, attempted assassination of a ruler. In this sense, political trials are as endemic to the American system as to any other.

Yet many Americans get ruffled when someone suggests seriously that political trials occur regularly in the United States—even though the law is well known as a stabilizer of the status quo, and courts enforce the law by means of trials. In order to bring about necessary but drastic changes in any society, some men feel it necessary to ignore or flout existing laws. According to the rules of *all* contemporary governments, such individuals must be tried; more often than not, they are found guilty. They are enemies of whichever system happens to be legally established at the time, and they are judged accordingly. It is not astonishing to find this occurring in the United States—past or present.

No system ever devised has been reluctant to face some of its foes in court. In fact, the court trial is one of the more humane ways of dispensing with an intractable opponent. Why, then, all the public blushing, stammering, and denial when an obvious political trial is called a political trial? Even the most diehard revolutionaries, once victorious—and beyond the judicial clutches of the losers—set up their own courts and run their own trials. It is a natural cycle in many political dramas—first the otter, then the hound.

In order to redeem further the concept of political trial, consider another "good" point about political trials: they are frequently begun by people *out* of power in order to protect themselves *against* the government. Counterelites, rebels, and protesters (foreign and domestic) know that a court can be a sanctuary, if not a fortress, against impending tyranny from potentates, presidents, police, princes, and prelates. Thus, a realistic conception of the political trial should emphasize the fact that such a trial involves the calculated use of the court-forum by *any* party to a political struggle in order to damage or destroy the other party's potential or actual power position. The important distinguishing factor is the motive triggering such a trial.

Neither the propriety of the trial itself (or its impropriety) nor the outcome (since political defendants often go scot-free) can tell us whether or not a trial is political. The motivation must be political and the procedure must be judicial, as well as judicious. An event fulfilling these conditions, then, may be considered a political trial.

These requirements square with the views of the preeminent writer in this field, Otto Kirchheimer, who believes that a political trial swells "the area of political action by enlisting the services of courts in behalf of political goals.

It is characterized by the submission to court scrutiny of group and individual action. Those instrumental in such submission seek to strengthen their own position and weaken those of their political foes."*

Although this definition seems almost a truism, it is not, even though it does not go far enough, and fails to explain why so many people get upset over the attribution of a political trial character to certain cases. It does not go far enough because the English language has not yet to come to grips with certain important differences among distinctly dissimilar *types* of political trials.

The problem can be overcome by distinguishing obvious political trials (as I have just described them) from those which (1) camouflage the political nature of the case by cover charges and those in which (2) the hearing itself fails to meet minimum standards of judicial impartiality and independence. What actually rankles people about political trials are the connotations of deception or unfairness that attach to them—at the same time, there is not sufficient discrimination between dubiously nonpolitical trials, unfair trials, or dubiously nonpolitical *and* unfair trials. Yet many Americans today are sophisticated enough to realize that governments resort to a wide variety of devices to hide their political motivations behind "routine" actions. And they have become cosmopolitan enough to recognize the many shabby facades, commonly called courts of law, which governments erect in order to assure a "proper" disposition of their enemies. For such reasons writers frequently employ quotation marks, referring to this or that political trial, as a "political trial." They are being noticeably skeptical about what is actually going on.

I propose a systematic clarification of this simple grammatical convention: we should take more advantage of quotation marks to designate the particular kinds of political trials we are talking about. Whether a writer uses such marks, and when and where he uses them, can indicate whether he believes there has been duplicity on the part of the party bringing the action (usually the government), or whether there has been a breakdown in the judicial nature of the trial proceedings—either at its start or during its operation. Thus, it seems possible and desirable to identify and distinguish among (1) political trials, (2) political "trials," (3) "political" trials, and (4) "political trials."

The political trial sans quotation marks has already been defined: the nature of the crime is clearly political and the impartiality of the judge applying the law is not called into serious question. Four essays in the following collection describe political trials in this sense.

First is the *Der Spiegel* case, instituted by the government for that newsmagazine's alleged violation of the internal security laws of West Germany—clearly a political crime. The subsequent trials were conducted under impeccably fair and impartial judicial scrutiny.

The second is the bizarre proceeding against Keshav Singh, in India, for contempt of legislature; it ended as a fantastic crisis which called into question the nature of federalism, dissent, democracy, and separation of govern-

Political Justice: The Use of Legal Procedure for Political Ends (Princeton: Princeton University Press, 1961), p. 419.

mental powers in Indian society. The crime was clearly political and the independence of the judiciary so steadfast that this very independence became one of the major political issues of the trial.

The third is a famous Philippines case which developed during the presidential election in 1965 when forces behind candidate Ferdinand Marcos sought to enjoin a government ban of a Marcos campaign movie. The plaintiffs accused the government of political motivation in banning the film. The reader will come to agree that no one could doubt the fierce independence and stubborn impartiality of the Philippine judiciary.

The fourth and final example of a political trial is that of Nigeria's Chief Enahoro. Initially the issue of his extradition from England to Nigeria revolved largely around the legal question of his political status—the objectivity of the courts was not in question, at least while he remained in England. When he arrived back in Nigeria, however, doubts increased as to how detached and unprejudiced the judges were—which comes close to the situation in which a political trial can turn into a political "trial." It might be instructive to note that in three of these four classic political trials, the government (as political protagonist) lost in court.

Two other famous political trials which did turn into political "trials" occurred in Ghana and Cuba. Upon learning that despised political enemies had been freed by the courts (in other words, that the legal system had really done its thing), two political strong men (Kwame Nkrumah and Fidel Castro) belatedly undid the legal system of their countries and established more compatible (to them) tribunals to re-hear the cases. Being conveniently stacked with judges more sympathetic to the Nkrumah and Castro points of view, the courts delivered new verdicts of "guilty"—as charged. On the basis of such obvious absences of impartiality and independence at the hearings, we are justified in identifying the emergence, in each instance, of a "trial." However, it should be noted that in five of six political trials described in this collection, the defendants were acquitted—two cases had to be transformed into "trials" before those who had incurred the wrath of the dictators could be removed from circulation.

Sometimes, however, the phrase political "trial" must be taken to refer to a situation wherein the indictment is clearly political but the impartiality and independence of the court is questionable at the very beginning of the proceedings. Sometimes this state of affairs is permanently built into the judicial system; sometimes it comes about because of a single judge. A good example of the former is the notorious trial of Soviet writers Andrei Sinyavsky and Yuri Daniel for the essentially political offense of circulating literature that weakened governmental authority and libeled the state. The "trial" was held in the duly constituted courts of the Soviet Union. However, as John Turner observes in the article which follows, no political crime tried in these courts has ever ended in acquittal. This would seem to offer substantial evidence of the nonimpartiality or nonindependence of the Soviet judicial system in clearly political cases. Additional circumstances surrounding the "trial" support the view that the conviction was predetermined.

An illustration of how such partiality can inhere in an individual rather than a system is to be found in the political "trial" of a small band of assorted radicals in Chicago during 1969–70. The charge against the Chicago Eight was that of crossing state lines with intent to incite a riot at the 1968 Democratic National Convention. The political nature of the charge is obvious enough. The "trial" was not a "trial" in the same way as in the Soviet Union—since many American political trials *do* end in acquittal and there is no explicit party line compelling judges to decide in a specific manner. The "trial" seemed to demonstrate quite clearly, however, the possibility that the American judicial system could collapse under the pressure of a judge exercising great bias and prejudice against political defendants and their attorneys. When a judge follows this course, any trial procedure becomes a sham and a "trial" in name only. Political "trials" almost always end in conviction at the lower court level.

In proposing the phrase "political" trial I am suggesting that a charge can be quite unpolitical or apolitical in nature—and still be, rather simply, a subterfuge. The real political aspects of the case are disguised and hidden. This happens frequently in America, as elsewhere, and the formal charges can vary from extremely minor ones—such as impeding traffic—through minor felonies —such as possession of marijuana—on up to major felonies—such as murder. This volume includes an excellent example of an overtly political situation which, in effect, came to trial under non-political pretensions in New Mexico in 1968. Reies Tijerina was accused of three crimes: leading an attack on a jail, kidnapping, and false imprisonment. The political reasons for his actions —and those of the government—were masked by the wording of the indictment. However, the trial was meticulously fair and Tijerina was acquitted.

Another essay discusses the much less obvious set of political motivations behind the trials and tribulations of Teamster leader Jimmy Hoffa, who had incurred the special disfavor of John and Robert Kennedy. According to Samuel Krislov, the pattern of indictments for mail fraud, tax evasion, and other business-oriented crimes gives strong indication that political considerations lay behind the "persecution" of Hoffa—hence, his case can be designated a "political" trial. Men who seek to challenge governmental power—directly or indirectly—must be careful to abide by all the laws, for "political" trials can frequently be as fatal as political "trials."

Deception, then, is a chief ingredient contributing to the eventual discreditation of political trials—or, more accurately, "political" trials and political "trials." The latter two varieties are particularly offensive because they indicate that the system itself—and those who control it—is behaving dishonestly. But perhaps even worse—possibly worst of all—is the trial which combines hoked-up charges with a simultaneous implosion of judiciousness in the legal proceeding. This situation adds up to a "political trial"; though rarer than the other types, it is the most reprehensible of the genre, having, perhaps, the most pernicious effects. I have included a study of one recent case which occurred in the United States.

Kenneth Dolbeare and Joel Grossman describe the extremely shaky charges brought against the well-known black writer, LeRoi Jones, for carry-ing concealed weapons in his Volkswagen microbus during the Newark riots. The authors also treat at even greater length the question of whether or not the Jones "trial" was prejudiced. Although Jones was convicted, it is hearten-ing that the decision was reversed on appeal, for reasons described by the authors. Furthermore, the American system being what it is, there remains little likelihood that the governor of New Jersey will set up a special ad hoc tribunal to reverse the action of the superior court.

This book, then, is basically an outline and a detailing of the wide assort-ment of political power plays to be found in courtrooms, real and makeshift, around the world. My classification system was not imposed on any of the contributors; in the essays that follow, many of the individual authors develop their own definitions of the political trial. In my opinion, however, calling *all* the various cases political trials tends to muddle the play and befuddle the audience. My system is offered in the hope that it will help others grasp some of the elusive subtleties in future political prosecutions in the United States as well as elsewhere.

I also hope that this book will generate objective interest in the tangle of problems concerning causes and consequences of political trials, "political" trials, and so on, for intensive research into all such aspects has been nearly nil. For example, when books are written about individual political prosecu-tions, the defendant, almost inevitably, is cast into the role of St. Sebastian (slings, arrows and all), while the courtroom scene is presented as an episode fit for encyclopedias of infamy. The reason for such lopsided accounts is that they make for better melodrama. But good melodrama is not necessarily good theatre, for melodrama need not lend an accurate appraisal of reality, nor stimulate thought and concern after the curtain has fallen. The eleven acts in this book are, I hope, dramatic rather than melodramatic; realistic rather than sentimental.

To be more realistic, then, a fuller portrayal of the political trial should include all of its types, examine all elements of its composition, and stimulate issues worthy of additional investigation beyond the confines of the particular accounts. Thus a secondary emphasis of this book is on the politics preceding and following the triggering of the legal mechanism. As the reader will ob-serve, the trial (or "trial") is only a piece of the action; it is simply a middle act in a far longer tragicomedy in the theatre of the political absurd. We should try to understand it much better than we have in the past; otherwise we may either bore or laugh ourselves to death.

T.L.B.
New York
July 1970

POLITICAL
TRIALS

one:

political

trials

DONALD P. KOMMERS*

1

THE *SPIEGEL* AFFAIR

a case study in judicial politics

On Friday night, 26 October 1962, squads of West German Federal Criminal Police and Hamburg state police mounted a coordinated attack on the main offices of the weekly newsmagazine, *Der Spiegel*.

Editors Johannes K. Engel, Claus Jacobi, and Hans Dieter Jaene, jolted by the sudden appearance of men in uniform, were arrested before they could rise from their chairs. Sixty *Spiegel* employees preparing a forthcoming issue were ordered from their places of work and promptly questioned. Filing cabinets and desk tops were rifled for anything that looked like incriminating evidence. Outside communications were forbidden.

In Hamburg, following the protest of editor Jacobi, ten *Spiegel* employees were permitted to proceed with the next edition of the magazine under the surveillance of eleven policemen. Meanwhile, silently and methodically, security police from the Federal Criminal Police Office converged on the homes of *Spiegel* publisher Rudolf Augstein and military affairs editor Conrad Ahlers, as well as on the private residences of Engel, Jacobi, and Jaene. Though Augstein and Ahlers were not at home, reams of papers and personal letters were carried off to the Federal Ministry of Justice.

By midnight on Friday neither Augstein nor Ahlers had been found. Prior to this time there had been only one serious slipup—the false arrest, around 7:30 P.M., of Erich Fischer, an advertising man in *Der Spiegel*'s Düsseldorf of-

*I wish to thank the American Philosophical Society and the Program of West European Studies, University of Notre Dame, for funds which helped to make possible the preparation of this chapter. The generous assistance of Dr. Josef Mackert, who allowed me unrestricted access to the archives of the West German Federal Constitutional Court, is also gratefully acknowledged.

fice; he was mistaken for Augstein who, along with Ahlers, was the principal target of the evening's police maneuvers. Fischer was nevertheless detained under virtual house arrest for several hours, to preclude him from alerting his co-workers of the impending seizure. Officials pulling the strings at the command post in Bonn were beginning to fidget, however. Everything seemed to have gone as planned, but the chief culprits were still at large.

Shortly after midnight, to the complete surprise of the hunters, word came that one of the hunted—Conrad Ahlers—was vacationing with his wife in Spain. Upon discovery of this embarrassing circumstance, Volkmar Hopf, secretary of state in the Defense Ministry, ordered the security police to arrange for Ahler's immediate arrest and extradition. At this point officials in the Ministries of Defense, Justice, and Interior fell to quarreling among themselves about the legality of Ahler's arrest on foreign soil, since he was wanted for a political crime. The Defense Ministry, however, under the stewardship of Franz-Josef Strauss, was not about to permit the scruples of an attorney general, or the police, to obstruct its solemn mission.

Hopf bluntly informed the Federal Criminal Police that the Defense Ministry would find a way of apprehending Ahlers if the police would not. At thirty minutes past midnight Strauss himself telephoned the German ambassador in Madrid and ordered him to instruct Colonel Ochim Oster, military attaché, to return his call immediately. Thirty minutes later Oster was on the telephone to Bonn. Strauss asserted that he had just seen Chancellor Adenauer; and, intimating that the safety and security of the Federal Republic were involved, Strauss ordered the colonel to arrange Ahler's arrest.

A few hours later Spanish police, at the request of West German authorities, sped to a hotel in Torremalinas. At 3:30 A.M., Ahlers and his wife were suddenly awakened, arrested, and immediately dispatched to nearby Malago. Shortly afterwards Ahlers boarded a plane back to Germany, and upon his arrival was taken into custody. Before noon of the same day Augstein, having heard of the warrant for his arrest, voluntarily turned himself over to the Hamburg police.

With the initial mission of the police accomplished, news of the previous night's mysterious doings began to trickle out of Bonn. Official and unofficial Germany buzzed with whispers of the event. The daily newspapers, which in Germany do not appear on Sunday, carried the story to the country under banner headlines on Monday morning. News of the event loosened tremors which jolted West German citizens, rocked the Federal Republic to its political foundations, and alarmed the rest of the world.[1]

[1]Details of the *Spiegel* affair as recounted in this narrative have been drawn mainly from the following sources: *Bericht der Sozialdemokraten über die Behandlung der "Spiegel" Affäre durch die Bundesregierung* (Bonn: Neue Vorwarts Verlag, 1963); "Spiegel Bericht des Bundesministers der Justiz an den Bundeskanzler der Bundesrepublik Deutschland," *Bulletin des Presse und Informationsamtes der Bundesregierung*, 5 February 1963, pp. 195–204; Alfred Grosser and Jürgen Seifert, *Die Staatsmacht und Ihre Kontrolle*, Die Spiegel-Affäre: Texte und Dokumente zur Zeitgeschichte, vol. I (Olten and Freiburg: Walter-Verlag, 1966); and Thomas Ellwein, Manfred Liebel, and Inge Negt, *Die Reaktion der Öffentlichkeit*, Die Spiegel-Affäre: Texte und Dokumente zur Zeitgeschichte, vol. II (Olten and Freiburg: Walter-Verlag,

It was an affair that reminded Germany of its past. The police raid against an established publication was bound to evoke memories of Nazi bootstrap justice, and to raise questions concerning the vigor of West German democracy.

BACKGROUND OF THE AFFAIR

The *Spiegel* affair happened at a time when Christian Democrats were in a coalition government with Free Democrats. As a result of the 1961 national parliamentary election the Christian Democratic Union (CDU), together with its Bavarian affiliate, the Christian Social Union (CSU), had lost their absolute majority in the German Bundestag. The CDU-CSU won 242 seats, the Social Democratic Party (SPD) acquired 190, and the Free Democratic Party (FDP), holding the balance of power, received 67. Christian Democrats considered forming a coalition government with Social Democrats, but the idea was torpedoed by elements within the SPD. Free Democrats, under the leadership of Dr. Erich Mende, agreed finally to enter a coalition with the CDU-CSU, but only on condition that Adenauer step down as chancellor. Adenauer, facing opposition within his own party from those who wanted to replace him with Economics Minister Ludwig Erhard, refused.[2]

As a compromise, the FDP agreed to enter a governing coalition with the CDU-CSU in exchange for Adenauer's promise to retire as chancellor by the end of 1963. A further price paid for this coalition was a cabinet not altogether to Adenauer's liking. Gerhard Schröder replaced Heinrich von Brentano—a hard liner, like Adenauer, on East-West relations—as foreign minister, while the FDP was awarded five ministries, among them the Ministry of Justice. But Franz-Josef Strauss, head of the Bavarian Christian Social Union and a trusted lieutenant of Adenauer, continued as minister of defense. What made Strauss's appointment interesting was the fundamental disagreement between him and the FDP over defense policy. The government crisis that followed the Spiegel affair must be evaluated against this background, and against the alignment in the cabinet.

The proximate cause of the affair was *Der Spiegel's* 8 October 1962 cover story on the NATO Fall Exercise (Fallex 62), a military "practice session" which had been executed a few weeks earlier. The article constituted the most vigorous condemnation of West German military and defense policy that had appeared during the seven years the Federal Republic had been a member of the North Atlantic Treaty Organization.[3] Fallex 62 was the first NATO maneuver

---

1966). For other treatments of the *Spiegel* affair see Ronald F. Bunn, *German Politics and the Spiegel Affair* (Baton Rouge: Louisiana State University Press, 1968); Otto Kirchheimer and Constantine Menges, "A Free Press in a Democratic State: The Spiegel Case," in *Politics in Europe,* edited by Gwendolen M. Carter and Alan F. Westin (New York: Harcourt, Brace & World, 1965), pp. 87–138; and David Schoenbaum, *The Spiegel Affair* (Garden City: Doubleday, 1968).

[2]See Egon Klepsch, Günther Müller, and Rudolf Wildenmann, *Die Bundestagswahl 1965* (Munich-Vienna: Günter Olzog Verlag, 1965), pp. 10–13.

[3]*Der Spiegel,* 10 October 1962, pp. 32–53. An English translation of this article appears in Bunn, *German Politics and the Spiegel Affair,* pp. 186–216.

actually designed to test both the survival response of the civilian establishment and the retaliatory striking power of Atlantic Pact countries in a simulated Third World War suddenly unleashed by a Soviet atomic attack upon Western Europe.

The mock war, reported by *Der Spiegel,* was nothing less than a catastrophe for West Germany. On the civilian front everything broke down logistically, from provision for proper sanitation facilities to mobilization of the reserves; militarily, *Der Spiegel* reported, the NATO high command awarded West Germany the lowest rating for its battlefield performance. These devastating conclusions were supported by an astoundingly detailed account of the tactics and strategies that spelled military impotency for the German armed forces establishment. *Der Spiegel,* moreover, had no doubt as to where the blame lay for West Germany's deplorable defense posture. It was resolutely and brutally flung at the feet of Defense Minister Franz-Josef Strauss.

Personalities and Issues

This was not the first time that Strauss and Augstein had tangled over West German defense strategy. The antagonism between the two men actually ran much deeper than any single issue of military policy. The feud began in 1955 when Strauss entered Adenauer's cabinet as minister of atomic affairs; gradually, feelings between Strauss and Augstein evolved into a political hatred without parallel in postwar German politics. It would not be true to assert that the root of the *Spiegel* affair lay wholly in the Strauss-Augstein rivalry. Nevertheless, the affair is linked to the personalities of the two antagonists and the fervor with which each has executed his self-appointed mission in the Federal Republic, Strauss from his position of power as head of the Bavarian Christian Social Union (CSU), and Augstein through the pages of his magazine.

One would be hard pressed to imagine antagonists more different in background, manner, and political outlook than Augstein and Strauss—the former, Protestant, liberal, cynical, and doleful; the latter, Catholic, conservative, confident, and buoyant. Together they largely personify the differences between Hanover and Munich, their places of birth, or between the states of Hamburg and Bavaria, their places of work, or between northern and southern Germany. In addition, with regard to the issue of national security, the two men symbolize the deepest division which today afflicts the German nation. Their single point of political agreement seems to be a mutual suspicion of—in Augstein's case, antagonism toward—United States military policy in Europe; but the two men proceed from irreconcilable estimates, or assumptions, concerning the existing state of world affairs.

Strauss is one of West Germany's most ardent proponents of Atlantic union. He regards Europe's political integration as a means of giving Germany a more meaningful role in European affairs—of allowing it to develop a new variant of German nationalism—and of negotiating a European solution to problems left unresolved by World War II. He defends the NATO alliance as essential to the security of the West, but he does not like the terms of the partnership; he resents American insistence upon retaining a monopoly over the production and use of atomic weapons while the European countries are obligated to raise and maintain conventional military forces.

Strauss believes that American nuclear hegemony within NATO constitutes as much a danger as a safeguard to German security. American reliance on massive retaliation, he reasons, renders large land armies obsolescent. At the same time he doubts that a Soviet conventional attack on Germany would meet with an American nuclear response. This would be fatal to Germany, since it could not begin to match Russia's conventional forces, particularly at a time when the United States appears to be contemplating withdrawal of its own ground forces from Europe.[4] Hence Europe and West Germany need their own nuclear deterrent. As defense minister, Strauss dedicated himself to equipping the German army with tactical nuclear weapons and to redefining Germany's role in NATO.[5]

Augstein, on the other hand, tends toward a neutralist posture in foreign affairs, but it is a neutralism that seems fed by another kind of nationalism. Whereas Strauss finds the key to German security, independence, and reunification in the West—in the military alliance with the United States and in West European union—Augstein finds it in the East. He regards the post-war dismemberment of Germany as a national catastrophe and believes that reunification should be relentlessly pursued. In his view this requires disengagement from the Western alliance, reconciliation with the Soviet Union, and a friendly disposition toward East Germany.[6] By no means do these attitudes spell pacifism on his part. In fact, Augstein's views seem to converge with the neutralism found among certain German military leaders antagonistic toward the United States.[7] In any case, he has never opposed a limited conventional military establishment for the purpose of defending West Germany's borders.

Beyond defense policy and German reunification it is extremely difficult to define Augstein's political philosophy. It would not be entirely appropriate to place him on the left wing of German politics, at least where economic issues are concerned. He has been a member of the Free Democratic Party (FDP), political home of a large number of industrialists, liberal Protestants, professional people, and middle-class intellectuals. Clearly in the tradition of nineteenth-century German liberalism, the FDP is marked by its opposition to a planned economy and by its anti-clericalism. In matters of foreign policy, however, the party has been rent by disagreement over Adenauer's defense policy and the question of German reunification.

Perhaps the most accurate mirror of Augstein himself is the magazine he publishes. Its dominant characteristic is a fierce independence; its awesome

[4]See Franz-Josef Strauss, *The Grand Design* (New York: Frederick A. Praeger, 1966), esp. pp. 51–60.

[5]These events are described in *Der Spiegel*, 10 October 1962, p. 38.

[6]See Schoenbaum, *Spiegel Affair*, p. 36.

[7]See Hans Speier, *German Rearmament and Atomic War* (Evanston, Ill.: Row, Peterson, 1957), pp. 66–68.

reputation is built on the virtual certainty that with its appearance each Monday morning some public scandal or human frailty will be exposed to public view. Modeled after *Time* in the United States, *Der Spiegel* offers highly literate and comprehensive news stories—sprinkled with much more pepper than even *Time* would think of giving its readers—on foreign and domestic affairs in Germany and in the world.[8]

Though *Der Spiegel* has enjoyed an astounding success in West Germany—its circulation has escalated from around ninety thousand in 1950, to over half a million in 1963, one year after the affair, to nearly a million in 1968—it would not suit the tastes of those looking for a positive program of political action. Reflecting Augstein's personality perhaps as much as his reading clientele, *Der Spiegel* is largely uncommitted. Its forte is opposition—often, it appears, for the sake of opposition—and the political exposé. This role *Der Spiegel* has played with a classic voltairean contempt of most things held dear by the West German establishment. *Der Spiegel* perceives itself primarily as the scourge of the regime, consciously poised to lash out at the first sign of official malfeasance, ineptitude, or incompetence, not excluding the private moral shortcomings of public figures.

No individual or institution is exempt from *Der Spiegel*'s flailings. Every sacred icon before which the Federal Republic has worshipped—for example, the Schuman Plan, the Common Market, NATO, the French-German Treaty, even the Basic Law itself—has been assailed in its pages. The German people themselves have been repeatedly stung by its verbal lash. From the beginning *Der Spiegel* has reminded Germans of their Nazi past, exploiting every incident, however trivial, that somehow recalls it; it is difficult to determine whether Augstein wishes simply to taunt his countrymen or to hasten their regeneration.

On the other hand, there is hardly a politician or important public figure left in Germany who has not countered with his own attack on *Der Spiegel*. The magazine has been assaulted for occupying the reactionary right, the radical left, or the nihilistic middle, and sometimes all three at once. At least one book published in Germany attempted to show that *Der Spiegel*'s position on most issues affecting the nation parallels Soviet foreign policy and the Communist Party line.[9] *Spiegel* editors have spent a fair portion of their time defending themselves in libel suits; on at least two occasions before the affair of 1962, individual copies of the magazine were seized on government orders. Yet the magazine is a factor to be reckoned with in the public life of West Germany. *Der Spiegel* is widely read—occasionally in fear—by men of public affairs. Its stories have caused the resignation of more public officials in West Germany than any other political force, including the opposition parties.[10]

---

[8]For a description of the organization and style of *Der Spiegel* see Grosser and Seifert, *Die Staatsmacht und Ihre Kontrolle*, pp. 40–47; Paul Sackarndt, *Der Spiegel Entzaubert: Analzse eines deutschen Nachtrichtenmagazines*, 2nd ed. (Essen: Dreiwer, 1961); and Martin Löffler, *Der Verfassungsauftrag der Presse: Modellfall Spiegel* (Karlsruhe: Verlag C. F. Müllen, 1961).

[9]Gert Bergner, *Rudolf Augstein und die "Spiegel Affäre"* (Berlin: Stoedtner, 1964). See also Kurt Zeisel, *Der deutsche Selbstmord* (Frankfurt: Bild Verlag für politische Bildung, 1963).

[10]See, generally, Schoenbaum, *Spiegel Affair*, pp. 37–42.

Most observers concede that *Der Spiegel* often furnishes the only opposition voice to policies of the regime. Even its enemies are prepared to admit that this has been one of the important roles that *Der Spiegel* has played in the politics of the Bonn Republic.

Der Spiegel's Offensive Against Strauss

Since becoming minister of defense in 1956, Strauss has been attacked repeatedly by *Der Spiegel*. Even his drinking and driving habits were subjected to its verbal jabs. It seemed as though *Der Spiegel* were testing his mettle and his capacity to strike back, and giving due warning that these attacks were only the beginning. Finally, with its Strauss cover story of 5 April 1961, *Der Spiegel* let loose. No fewer than fifteen pages, spiced with uncomplimentary photographs and cartoons, were devoted to Strauss's political and moral disembowelment.[11] He was pictured as a beer-barrel Bavarian politician drunk with power, the most dangerous man in Europe, a genuine threat to democracy, a man eager to trample on the rights of others in order to realize his ambitions —the most burning of which was to become chancellor of West Germany. *Der Spiegel* concluded the story by saying that it no longer made any difference whether the CDU or the SPD won the forthcoming national parliamentary election; the only matter of importance facing Germany at that time was to stop Strauss's march toward the chancellorship, an office he was determined to get, said *Der Spiegel*, even at the risk of war or internal rebellion.[12]

Nevertheless, with its 5 April cover story, *Der Spiegel* had declared war on Strauss. Augstein virtually said as much in a subsequent issue. In a letter to his readers he announced *Der Spiegel*'s intention to carry the battle forward. He deplored the fact that radio, television, and influential national newspapers were either incapable or unwilling to expose the machinations of Strauss. The FDP and the SPD did not fare any better in his estimation. He charged that the Social Democrats, following the "non-partisan Brandt line," were actually bartering their souls in exchange for a partnership in the new government to be formed after the September 1961 elections. He believed that nothing less than a national crusade was necessary to drive out of the land the devil who came to entice her into a moral and material abyss.[13]

Several articles in 1962 which implicated Strauss in a variety of scandals nearly forced him to resign and accept the office of prime minister that the CSU seemed ready to offer him in Bavaria; but Strauss elected to fight on in Bonn. As testimony to its further resourcefulness, *Der Spiegel* then published

[11]*Der Spiegel*, 5 April 1961, pp. 14–30.
[12]Ibid., p. 30. *Der Spiegel*'s fear of Strauss was based on his selection in March 1961 as chairman of the Christian Social Union. Given the strength of the CSU in the Bundestag, no Christian Democratic government could be formed without his cooperation. Actually, *Der Spiegel*'s fears seemed exaggerated, for there was little chance that the Bundestag would elect Strauss as chancellor. First, he had too many enemies among CDU leaders. Second, Adenauer was determined to cling to the chancellorship awhile longer. Finally, under no circumstances would the FDP have entered a coalition government under Strauss.
[13]Ibid., 12 April 1961, p. 12.

the most damaging article yet, involving him in another scandal—the so-called "Uncle Aloys" affair. In this story, published one week prior to that which led to the *Spiegel* affair itself, Strauss was accused of enriching himself by passing out luscious defense contracts to party associates and old friends.[14]

Der Spiegel's preoccupation with Strauss's alleged malefactions was not accompanied by any relaxation in its attack upon his defense policies. Throughout 1962 several articles sought to dissect these policies. Considerable copy was devoted to his conflict with American officials within NATO, and to his iron-fisted control over the Defense Ministry; the latter involved some rather serious rows with high-ranking German army officers. On 13 June 1962 *Der Spiegel* ran an article on the Bundeswehr which focused on the fight that was shaping up in NATO between Strauss and American officials.[15]

The Kennedy administration, on the verge of negotiating an agreement with the Soviet Union to limit membership in the atomic club, was about to reverse a decision, approved by the Eisenhower administration, to go forward with a plan to equip NATO forces with nuclear weapons. The article pointed out that the Federal Republic was financially incapable of supporting both American demands for more conventional forces and Strauss's plan for atomic weapons. It also described the extent of Strauss's opposition within the German army general staff.

This article turned out to be the forerunner of the famous Fallex 62 story. West Germany's military unpreparedness, so starkly disclosed by Fallex 62, was attributed to Strauss's deliberate policy of holding back on civil defense preparations and conventional military forces in his single-minded determination to secure for Germany a nuclear deterrent.

FROM POLITICS TO POLITICAL JUSTICE

Resort to the legal process in the *Spiegel* affair was facilitated by the convergence of certain political and legal realities indigenous to Germany. These realities stem largely from the division of Germany and its pivotal position in the cold war between the Western and Soviet power blocs. They also derive from the precarious way in which West Germany has sought to insure itself against any repetition of the events which led to the collapse and destruction of the Weimar Republic. Finally, they are a product of certain operations and procedures of governmental institutions whose behavioral roots lie deeply embedded in Germany's political culture.

The Political Setting

Politics in Bonn throughout the 1950s and well into the 1960s were largely motivated by a crusading anti-communism. German anti-communism was

---

[14]Ibid., 3 October 1962, p. 28.
[15]Ibid., 13 June 1962, pp. 16–20.

rooted in the country's partition and in the refusal of the western sector to recognize the legitimacy of the East German government. It was also rooted in the conviction that the German Democratic Republic was a perpetual source of danger to West Germany. It is not surprising, therefore, that opposition to German reunification became a political dogma, and in time was linked to and supported by related articles of faith such as the Hallstein Doctrine, the European Defense Community, NATO, and Atlantic union. These policies constituted the deposit of faith that Adenauer and his Christian Democrats swore to defend against all enemies, external and internal.

Anti-communist sentiment in Germany was easily transposed by the governing regime into an instrument of cold war strategy. The regime also employed it as a means of stigmatizing the opposition. For example, in the 1957 national election campaign, Social Democrats were repeatedly accused, on the hustings and in the pulpit, of following the Soviet Communist line, especially with regard to the issue of Germany's division.[16] Anti-communism was elevated virtually into an ideology, one that largely came to be identified with Adenauer's foreign and defense policies. This was one measure of the limits on free speech in West Germany.[17] When other ingredients of the West German system are considered, such as Adenauer's authoritarian leadership, the passivity of Parliament, and the political lassitude of the general population, it is not difficult to appreciate the extent of the government's leverage against those who would question the dominant ideology.

The Legal-Constitutional Setting

The West German political system is a constitutional democracy. But its base is fragile. It could hardly be otherwise in a system erected out of the ruins of military defeat, whose Constitution—the Basic Law—was a child of the cold war; and in a country whose population less than a generation earlier had succumbed to totalitarian appeals. The Basic Law does secure the fundamental rights of man, but the exercise of these rights is severely limited by competing provisions of the Constitution.

Above all, the Basic Law demands loyalty to the established political order. Freedom to associate, for example, is protected so long as its purpose is not "directly against the constitutional order or the concept of international understanding." Any person who attacks the "free democratic basic order" risks forfeiting his fundamental rights to press, speech, and association. Even political parties may be declared unconstitutional if they threaten the "free democratic basic order" or endanger the existence of the Federal Republic.[18] These appeals to order and authority undoubtedly conformed to the erstwhile con-

---

[16]See U. W. Kitzinger, *German Electoral Politics* (London: Oxford University Press, 1960), pp. 224–26.

[17]See Grosser and Seifert, *Die Staatsmacht und Ihre Kontrolle*, pp. 17–33.

[18]The Basic Law of the Federal Republic of Germany (23 May 1949), Articles 9 (2), 18, and 21 (2).

servative instincts of the German people. But West Germany's constitution-makers were also influenced by the memory of Hitler. In any case, the result of their efforts was a constitutional order in which the right to political expression was bracketed by a consuming vigilance over dangerous speech originating both inside and outside of the Federal Republic.

In a constitutional regime, defamation of the government's foes in the open political arena—what Kirchheimer calls the "derivative political trial"—is not always sufficient to suppress literature deemed injurious to the security of the state.[19] The West German political establishment thus resorted to the criminal process as its principal weapon for keeping criticism of the regime within bounds. In 1951, against the backdrop of the Korean War and Communist revolutionary activity in Eastern Europe, West Germany enacted a far-reaching set of internal security laws designed to insulate its citizens against subversive "propaganda" and promptly to nip in the bud any conspiracy, remote or imminent.[20] Among these laws were provisions which prohibited the dissemination or publication of printed matter attacking the constitutional principles upon which the Basic Law of 1949 was based.[21] A further regulation, still in effect, bans the sale or distribution of East German newspapers in the Federal Republic.[22]

These laws have been enforced with vigor, for the number of criminal proceedings under the security provisions of the German Penal Code is staggering.[23] Yet cases which never reached the trial stage may have been as important in curtailing unorthodox political speech as the political trial itself. One cannot discount the significance of the preliminary inquiry or pretrial investigation—a process which in Germany is under the exclusive control of the public prosecutor—as a potential instrument for intimidating the dissenter.

Because of the political climate in West Germany, Communists and leftists have been the chief victims of the security laws.[24] Nearly all of the reported cases of the Federal Supreme Court in this field have involved such persons.[25] A large number of them were accused of being linked to East German

[19]Otto Kirchheimer, *Political Justice: The Use of Legal Procedure for Political Ends* (Princeton: Princeton University Press, 1961), p. 46.

[20]See "Strafrechtsänderungsgesetz," *Bundesgesetzblatt*, I, 739 (30 August 1951).

[21]See, for example, "Sechstes Strafrechtsänderungsgesetz," *Bundesgesetzblatt*, I, 478–79 (30 June 1960).

[22]For a discussion of the laws and cases relating to this and similar regulations see Gunther Willms, "Zum Verbot der Einfuhr Verfassungsfeindlicher Schriften," 18 *Neue Juristische Wochenschrift* 2177–2179 (25 November 1965).

[23]Between 1953 and 1959, according to reports of the Federal Criminal Office in Wiesbaden, 56,955 proceedings were initiated in internal security matters. These cases were instituted under sections 100–100b (treason against the state), sections 89–97 (treason against the Constitution), and sections 128–129 (formation of secret and criminal societies) of the German Penal Code. Although official publication of these figures was discontinued in 1959, an authoritative article recently disclosed that public prosecutors handled more than 57,000 cases from 1960 through 1966; in addition, 3,679 cases were disposed of by courts, and roughly 450 persons were convicted and sent to prison each year. See Hans Luttger, "Staatsschutzverfahren," 21 *Monatschrift für Deutsches Recht* 260–261 (1967). See also Kirchheimer, *Political Justice*, p. 90, n. 74.

[24]See Lutz Lehmann, *Legal und Opportun: Politische Justiz in der Bundesrepublik* (Berlin: Voltaire Verlag, 1966), pp. 46–60.

[25]A selection of these cases appears in *Hochverat und Staatsgefährdung: Urteile des Bundesgerichtshofes*, 2 vols. (Karlsruhe: Verlag C. F. Müller, 1957).

agents or conspiratorial organizations in West Germany. Contributing to the legitimacy of these acts of official repression was the 1956 decision of the Federal Constitutional Court which banned the Communist party as unconstitutional and forbade the formation of substitute organizations.[26] The decision seems actually to have increased the tempo of official activity in the security field. In 1956, for example, the number of preliminary inquiries initiated by public prosecutors was 7,975; in 1957 it shot up to 12,600; in 1958 it climbed to a figure well over 13,000.[27] It seems reasonable to relate all this to the unhappy history of free speech in Germany. It was, of course, totally abolished in the Third Reich, and not fully restored until the ratification of the Basic Law in 1949. But constitutional guarantees of free speech do not insure a courageous press or a politically articulate public. This depends upon a system's political tradition, and basic popular attitudes within it toward democracy. On this score most students of the Federal Republic seem to agree with Leonard Krieger's observation that "democracy in Germany is still not so much a matter of active faith as a system of formal law and that its current liberal interpretation is the effect of Allied power, economic prosperity, and anti-totalitarian resentment operating in a political vacuum."[28]

At the level of constitutional theory, the limits of freedom of speech and press are somewhat narrower in Germany than in the United States. These freedoms are expressly limited, according to the Basic Law, not only by provisions of the general statutes, but also by the obligation to tell the truth and to preserve the honor of the individual person. Truth and personal honor are not so highly valued in the American theory of free *political* speech.[29]

In Germany defamation suits by public officials against their political foes, the press, or even private citizens are a common occurrence. German law, moreover, provides a harsher penalty for defamation of a public official than of a private citizen.[30] Special legislation protects certain governmental institutions, such as the armed forces, against defamatory speech.[31] What is more, the Bundesgerichtshof ("Federal Supreme Court"), the highest court of appeals for ordinary criminal and civil matters, has liberally construed the internal security laws to cover even the most generalized verbal assaults upon West

[26]Decision of 17 August 1956, *Entscheidungen des Bundesverfassungsgerichts* (Tübingen: J. C. B. Mohr [Paul Siebeck]), Volume V, p. 85. (Hereinafter cited as BVerfGE.)

[27]See Lehmann, *Legal und Opportun*, p. 125.

[28]Leonard Krieger, *The German Idea of Freedom* (Boston: Beacon Press, 1957), p. 468.

[29]In the United States, speech must be malicious to be punishable. Americans tend to regard free speech primarily as a method of settling controversies and arriving at decisions; *what* is said is secondary. Germans tend to value speech primarily for the substantive result it produces. The theoretical difference between these two notions may be one merely of emphasis, but the practical consequences are substantial. American politicians expect to be battered and torn by their political enemies, including the press; resort to legal process to recover damages because of verbal assaults upon them is a rare occurrence. For an American view see *New York Times Co. v. Sullivan*, 376 U.S. 254 (1964). For the German view see Gerhard Leibholz and H. J. Rinck, *Grundgesetz: Kommentar an Hand der Rechtsprechung des Bundesverfassungsgerichts* (Cologne-Marienburg: Verlag Dr. Otto Schmidt KG, 1966), pp. 121–24.

[30]This law, passed by the Nazi regime, is still in the statutes. See *Reichsgesetzblatt*, I, 597 (26 May 1933) and, currently, section 164 of the German Penal Code.

[31]See "Viertes Strafrechtsänderungsgesetz," *Bundesgesetzblatt*, I, 597 (11 June 1957). It also appears as section 109d in the German Penal Code.

Germany's political institutions or the principles enunciated in the Basic Law.[32] Indeed, editors have been convicted and sent to jail under the provisions of these statutes. It takes little imagination to perceive how all this leads to cautious journalism.

The Bureaucratic Setting

The regime's policy of using law to suppress the activities of its internal enemies has been facilitated even further by the support of the judiciary; West German courts have been no obstacle to the daily enforcement of the internal security laws. It is reasonable to suggest that the deferential attitude of courts toward the regime in these matters is attributable to the deep-seated conservatism of the German judiciary. At the same time the rather mechanical processing by the courts of government action in internal security affairs seems as much a manifestation of the German judiciary's customary deference to the executive establishment. It should be noted in this connection that the very organization of the German judiciary lends itself to rather mindless collaboration between prosecutor and judge.

A prosecutor's office is attached to every court in Germany, and though the functions of judge and prosecutor are clearly separate under the law, both work in close cooperation. Both are members of a career service, versed in the art of bureaucratic administration; both are appointed by the same Ministry of Justice. Civil service values such as adherence to formal rules and obeisance to superior authority run deep within the German judiciary and are shared by public prosecutors. One consequence of this is that judges are often inclined to grant search and arrest warrants as a matter of course, without really making an independent assessment of the basis of the prosecutor's application.[33]

Germans have traditionally trusted their professional civil servants far more than their political leaders. The German civil servant, unlike his American counterpart, enjoys a position of honor and respect in the society. He is a highly trained, tenured, and well-paid professional with a long tradition of faithful service to the state. The civil servant commonly regards himself as the expert in statecraft as well as the state's instrument for the implementation of its will. He prizes his expertise and political neutrality, and resents interferences from politicians, interest group leaders, and political parties.[34]

Many important political decisions are in fact made by civil servants, often at the lower echelons of administration, and under a veil of secrecy. That is one difficulty with German democracy, for the lines of political responsibility are not always clear. The attack on *Der Spiegel,* for example, was conducted

---

[32]For example, see Decision of 11 December 1958, *Entscheidungen des Bundesgerichtshofes in Strafsachen,* vol. 12 (1959), pp. 174–77 and Decision of 28 February 1964, 19 BGH St. 246–58 (1964). See also documentation of Kirchheimer, *Political Justice,* pp. 42–43.

[33]Interview with Professor Horst Ehmke, Parliamentary State Secretary, Ministry of Justice, Bonn, 11 July 1968.

[34]See generally Arnold J. Heidenheimer, *The Governments of Germany,* 2nd ed. (New York: Thomas Y. Crowell, 1966), pp. 143–55.

without the knowledge of certain politically responsible cabinet members whose ministries were deeply implicated. Responsibility for the raid was not clarified until after months of investigation.

The Decision to Investigate

Many of the factors mentioned above—involving the drift of events as well as conscious behavior—converged to move the *Spiegel* affair into the courts. The political effects of legal action against *Der Spiegel* seem not to have been fully taken into account by the prosecution. German criminal procedure actually forbids prosecutors to consider the political implications of a case; they are required to investigate criminal complaints from whatever source, and to bring charges when it appears that a crime has been committed. The values of the bureaucracy frequently incline public servants to act as if they were not functioning in a political environment. In this antiseptic atmosphere even an issue as politically hot as the *Spiegel* investigation seemed to have been regarded as ordinary business.

The German tendency to base important decisions on expert opinions rather than on political judgments also manifested itself in this case. When subordinate officials in the attorney general's office received the complaint against *Der Spiegel,* they proceeded rather routinely to secure the assistance of the Defense Ministry. Not even the attorney general himself was informed of the matter until the investigation was well underway. The decision to invoke the law against *Der Spiegel* seemed largely based on an expert opinion by a lawyer in the Defense Ministry who concluded that the magazine had published military secrets to the detriment of the security of the Federal Republic.

But more than bureaucratic procedures were involved in the final decision to move against *Der Spiegel.* The first accusation that the magazine was revealing state secrets came from a private citizen, Dr. Friedrich August Freiherr von der Heydte, a law professor at the University of Würzburg, and a man well known in Germany for his right-wing affiliations.[35] A Catholic rightist newspaper carried an article by him alleging that *Der Spiegel* had been playing fast and loose with the fatherland's military secrets. *Der Spiegel* then sued for a restraining order against Heydte. In his defense Heydte made a formal complaint to the attorney general in Karlsruhe, asserting that several articles published by *Der Spiegel* in previous weeks had dealt with state secrets. He wrote a second letter to the attorney general, repeating the charge, after the appearance of the Fallex article.[36]

Whether Heydte's letters to the attorney general were the real reason for the preliminary inquiry in this case is difficult to say. It is known that on the

[35]*Deutsche Tagespost,* 6 July 1962, p. 1.
[36]*Deutsche Tagespost, Sonderdruck,* n. d., p. 3. This special edition, published in November 1962, included selected articles and letters on the *Spiegel* affair which appeared in *Tagespost* between 30 October and 17 November 1962.

day after the Fallex story appeared, Albin Kuhn, an official in the attorney general's office, asked the security division of the Defense Ministry for an advisory opinion—a *Gutachten,* as it is called in Germany—on whether or not *Der Spiegel* had disclosed state secrets. Before preparing his report, Heinrich Wunder, a high-ranking lawyer and civil servant attached to the security division, conferred with several officials in the Defense Ministry, including State Secretary Hopf.

Strauss himself, returning to Bonn from a vacation, entered the picture here. At this point Strauss and his aides, particularly Hopf, appeared to snatch the initiative from the attorney general's office. Federal prosecuting attorneys were, of course, formally responsible for starting the investigation and bringing charges against *Der Spiegel.* But the record in the case, including the transcript of the proceeding before the Federal Constitutional Court,[37] compels the conclusion that the Defense Ministry was the driving force behind the action. Convinced of security leaks within his own organization, Strauss was determined to track down *Der Spiegel*'s informants. He had personal enemies in the military establishment and had grounds for suspecting that some of them would release military information to discredit him. Yet a politician as astute as Strauss could not have been unaware of the opportunity now in his grasp to discredit *Der Spiegel* and the reputations of its editors. Whether motivated by revenge or by the conviction that acts of treason had been committed, or both, Strauss must also have been aware of the calculated risk involved in bringing *Der Spiegel* to the bar of political justice.

But the risk might have seemed at the time well worth taking. Strauss's strategy appeared to depend upon two things: first, he would have to conceal his own role in the affair; second, the government would have to keep the ensuing public controversy under control. The latter would be accomplished by confining the controversy to the judicial forum and insisting upon the observance—or creating the image—of due process of law throughout the trial. Popular admiration for Adenauer, public belief in the objectivity of the courts, and general trust in the good sense of West German officials constituted a substantial reservoir of community support upon which the regime could expect to draw in its action against *Der Spiegel.*

Moreover, the *Spiegel* affair occurred at a time when the government needed to bolster confidence in its foreign policy, and when Strauss's leadership in the defense establishment was under fire. With the Cuban missile crisis in the background, it seemed as good an occasion as any to warn those opposing the regime of the limits of public discussion in certain critical areas. The law of treason was the most effective legal weapon with which to punish and discredit the opposition. Existing constitutional arrangements were more than adequate for the achievement of this objective by lawful means. The relevant laws were on the books; the courts, which had vigorously enforced these laws so many times before, seemed available and willing to oblige.

Strauss apparently realized that the most damaging argument against *Der Spiegel* and its editors would be tangible evidence of treasonable activity.

---

[37]See Grosser and Seifert, *Die Staatsmacht und Ihre Kontrolle,* pp. 573–98.

Plans to acquire this evidence were carefully laid by the attorney general's office, with the close collaboration of the Defense Ministry. On 22 October representatives of both agencies held a secret meeting in Karlsruhe with officials of the security division of the Federal Criminal Police and a judge of the Bundesgerichtshof. All hands accepted the recommendation of Wunder's *Gutachten* which advised legal action against *Der Spiegel.* Shortly afterwards, prosecuting officials petitioned the Bundesgerichtshof—that is, the investigating judge present at the meeting—for search and arrest warrants. The warrants, carrying the unusual provision that they could be executed at night, were immediately signed. On the night of 26 October, the day after the Bundestag had cleared Strauss of any wrongdoing in the Fibag affair,[38] the historic blitz against *Der Spiegel* took place.

The sense of urgency which surrounded the planning of the affair was demonstrated by Strauss's attempt to keep the circle of informed persons as small as possible. Interior Minister Hermann Höcherl, the cabinet official ultimately responsible for the Federal Criminal Police, was first informed of the action and the role of his subordinates in it four days before it occurred. The Ministry of Justice was informed only upon the insistence of officials in the attorney general's office; but it was State Secretary Walter Strauss, not Justice Minister Wolfgang Stammberger, who was given the news. In fact, Hopf appears to have ordered Strauss not to inform Stammberger, his superior, of the impending seizure. Moreover, Foreign Minister Schröder was apparently unaware of Defense Minister Franz-Josef Strauss's attempt to obtain the extradition of Conrad Ahlers until the matter became a source of embarrassment to the governments of both Spain and West Germany.

State authorities in Hamburg and North Rhine-Westphalia were also kept in the dark, despite a federal law which requires the notification of local officials before federal police are employed in their jurisdictions. Indeed, both states involved were actually confronted with a federal fait accompli.[39]

A Mighty Array

Police examination of thousands of documents, including the personal correspondence of *Spiegel* editors, disclosed that Ahler's Fallex story was the product of a complex network of personal contacts that reached high into government circles. These discoveries were followed by the subsequent arrests of editor Hans Schmeltz; Hans Detlev Becker, director of the Spiegel Corporation; Colonel Adolf Wicht, an officer in the Bundeswehr; Colonel Alfred Martin, a military officer attached to the Ministry of Defense; Paul Conrad, a businessman whom Strauss had offended; and Josef Augstein, friend of Conrad and brother of Rudolf. All were arrested on suspicion of being accomplices to treason.

[38] See *Der Spiegel,* 31 May 1961, pp. 40–44.
[39] These events, once again, have been reconstructed from the official and unofficial reports cited in note 1.

It was an interesting roster. For one thing, several of these men were members of the FDP. For another, nearly all had personal grievances or policy disagreements with Strauss. All of them had close personal friends among high government officials, some of whom were in Adenauer's cabinet. One link even extended to Reinhard Gehlen, head of the Federal Intelligence Service. It was a mighty array. But whether anyone had committed treason was not certain at all. What *was* certain was that some of those arrested had contrived to discredit Strauss. In the process, personal confidences may well have been betrayed and information generally regarded (but never officially classified) as confidential may have been disclosed.

AFTERMATH OF THE AFFAIR

Since the founding of the Bonn Republic, West Germany had never witnessed anything like the outrage which greeted the affair. Officials in Hamburg and North Rhine-Westphalia fumed. Paul Nevermann, prime minister of Hamburg, threatened to refuse federal agents the use of state facilities and the cooperation of local police for the continuation of their searches. The SPD demanded an immediate parliamentary investigation. The party's chairman, Erich Ollenhauer, called for a confidence vote against the government; one by one, party members rose in the Bundestag to demand Strauss's resignation. The most damaging protests, however, came from the FDP.

Stammberger, along with the four other members of his party holding ministerial portfolios, threatened to resign unless Adenauer offered a satisfactory explanation of the affair. But the government was caught in a morass of contradictory statements; the version of the affair differed from agency to agency. The Defense Ministry deepened the suspicions of almost everyone by saying nothing. State Secretary Hopf refused to answer questions while Strauss himself solemnly announced to reporters on at least three different occasions that he had absolutely nothing to do with the matter. Subsequent disclosures of the ministry's very substantial role in the affair simply added fuel to the fire that was engulfing the regime.

The CDU-CSU struck back with fury, and the parliamentary rhetoric became increasingly venomous; debate in the Bundestag was reduced to a shouting match. Christian Democrats saw red in all opposition to the government's action in the *Spiegel* case. Adenauer, losing his composure, at one point banged the rostrum and publicly accused Augstein of committing treason. Christian Democrats, stung by the taunts and jeers of their opponents, described the SPD as "the Spiegel Party," equivalent to calling it the "party of treason."[40]

In some cases punitive action was threatened. The CDU-controlled German Press Agency, for example, announced that Wolfgang Döring (FDP) and Gerhard Jahn (SPD), both prominent members of the Bundestag, were under sus-

[40]See *Verhandlungen des Deutschen Bundestages*, 4. Wahlperiode, 45. Sitzung, 7 November 1962, p. 1984.

picion of having passed secret information to *Der Spiegel*. It was reported that Adenauer even demanded the arrest of the head of the German Intelligence Service because of his association with one of the persons who allegedly fed information to Ahlers.[41] In fact, the disclosure of the relationship between certain government officials, prominent members of the Bundestag, and *Spiegel* editors, all of whom were associated with or friendly to the FDP and SPD, almost looked like a conspiracy against the CDU-CSU and Strauss. Many Christian Democrats, Adenauer included, appeared to interpret this as a conspiracy against the fatherland itself. The government's critics, of course, looked upon the entire affair as a violation of a free press: a blatant attempt to crush the opposition with heavy-handed methods.

Meanwhile, the intellectual community—artists, writers, professors, students, and journalists—was in an uproar. All of its previously bottled-up political emotions seemed to surge forth. Except for its extreme right wing, the German press was highly critical of the affair. The president of the German Society of Newspaper Publishers protested, as did the German League for Human Rights. Radio and television commentators were preoccupied with the affair, generally deploring it. University students demonstrated in the streets of nearly every major German city, while their professors sent a steady stream of signed protests to newspapers, members of the Bundestag, and other public officials.[42]

The reaction abroad was equally critical. The foreign press saw the attack on *Der Spiegel* as a restoration of Gestapo practices. Foreign statesmen had second thoughts about the stability of German democracy. The International Federation of Jurists, meeting in Brussels at the time, issued a statement deploring the circumstances of the affair. The depth of the political crisis facing West Germany was indicated by Adenauer's talk before the National Press Club in Washington on 14 November 1962, and his radio-television address to the German nation on 23 November, when he sought to assure Germans and foreigners alike that the rule of law and freedom of the press were still cherished constitutional principles in the Federal Republic.[43]

The public crisis, however, soon evolved into a genuine governmental crisis. The CDU-CSU saw its image tarnished, Adenauer's authority diminished, and the government on the verge of collapse. CDU losses in the Hessian state election of 11 November 1962, widely interpreted as a by-product of the affair, did not help matters. From 1 November to about 11 December, Bonn was the site of bids for power that would rival the machinations of an oriental oligarchy. The first heads to roll were those of Volkmar Hopf and Walter Strauss; this was the FDP's initial price for remaining in the coalition. But soon the FDP and the SPD united in a further demand for Franz-Josef Strauss's resignation. He refused, and was bolstered by Adenauer's ardent defense of his conduct in the *Spiegel* affair.

---

[41]See Grosser and Seifert, *Die Staatsmacht und Ihre Kontrolle,* pp. 150–51.

[42]For a discussion of the reaction of these and other groups to the affair see Ellwein, Liebel, and Negt, *Die Reaktion der Öffenlichkeit,* pp. 150–217.

[43]On the foreign press reaction to the *Spiegel* affair see ibid., pp. 485–505.

On 19 November 1962 the five FDP ministers resigned from the Adenauer cabinet, precipitating a major governmental crisis. It appeared to be FDP strategy to force a new coalition cabinet without Strauss. At first Strauss tried to hang on, but he could not resist the pressures against him now beginning to build up within the CDU itself. The SPD saw the situation as a golden opportunity to enter a ruling coalition after thirteen years of opposition, and perhaps even to maneuver Adenauer out of the chancellorship. The FDP shared the latter objective, which now seemed a realistic possibility, even to Adenauer's enemies within the CDU-CSU.

The SPD first negotiated with the FDP on the question of forming a coalition government between them. Leading Social Democrats also entered into bargaining negotiations with the Christian Democrats. But the Christian Democratic price for a CDU-CSU-SPD coalition was the passage of a single member district election system—a long-standing objective of the CDU-CSU—which would have done away with proportional representation, and, interestingly, the FDP. The SPD's thirst for a share of the state's power, however, did not go that deep; its executive committee accordingly voted against a coalition with the Christian Democrats.[44] On 30 November, Strauss, with Adenauer's approval, finally resigned to pave the way for the cabinet's reconstruction. On 7 December, the CDU-CSU parliamentary party announced Adenauer's promise to resign as chancellor in October of 1963—a concession Adenauer made in response to pressures from the FDP and within his own party, attendant to reconstructing the old coalition. On 11 December, the coalition was reconstituted, with Strauss, of course, put out to pasture.

While all this was taking place, Rudolf Augstein, from his prison cell, was issuing apocalyptic warnings about the future of German democracy. Supplied with a typewriter, books, paper, and other comforts, Augstein was allowed to write and to publish, a fact that some government spokesmen mentioned with pride as proof that freedom of the press was not being denied.

As Augstein awaited indictment and trial, he filed a complaint with the Federal Constitutional Court of West Germany, claiming that *Der Spiegel*'s right to freedom of the press had been violated by the arrest of its editors, the seizure of its files, and the police occupation of its premises, which were not relinquished until 29 November 1962. The documents sequestered by the government were not returned until September 1963. Most of the editors arrested by the regime were released within a few weeks after their apprehension. Augstein himself was finally set free on 17 February 1963, three-and-a-half months after his arrest, and three days after the release of the official government report on the *Spiegel* affair.

Phase Two

The second phase of the affair began shortly after Strauss resigned. The principal questions which now confronted CDU-CSU powerholders in Bonn

---

[44]Grosser and Seifert, *Die Staatsmacht und Ihre Kontrolle*, pp. 279–80.

were whether they could reestablish the ruling coalition under Adenauer and in the process recover the losses they had sustained because of the affair. A two-pronged counterattack was evident from the actions and rhetoric of the Christian Democrats. One prong sought to extend the debate (which, up to this time, had focused upon the circumstances of the affair) to the broader issues of reunification, the division of Germany, and the continuing threat from the East. The executive committee of the CDU chose the embattled city of Berlin in which to assemble and from which to release a statement saying that because "our country is a focal point of the East-West conflict, every act that even suggests the commission of treason must be taken seriously and thoroughly investigated."[45] Adenauer, as a result, very easily shifted the emphasis of the affair to a defense of his long-standing stewardship of the Federal Republic.[46]

The second prong of the attack was to manipulate the symbols of law, including the tradition of an independent judiciary, so as to confine the affair itself and the specific issues it generated—such as the free press and treason questions—to the courts. This was the regime's way of "depoliticizing" the affair, which reminds one of Duverger's observation that "depoliticization" of an event always tends to favor the established order.[47]

Both offensive tactics gave Adenauer room for political maneuvering. He was also assisted by the convergence of certain institutional, political, and cultural factors favorable to the regime in a time of crisis. First, the constructive vote of no confidence—a constitutional arrangement which permits the chancellor to remain in office until his successor is chosen by a majority of the Bundestag—saved Adenauer and partially accounted for the FDP's willingness to reestablish the coalition under his leadership. The FDP, holding the balance of power in the Bundestag, was unwilling—for strong political and psychological reasons—to form a coalition with the SPD. At the same time Free Democrats could ill afford, out of consideration for West Germany's political stability and international prestige, to stand aloof and let Adenauer rule the country with a minority government. Against the backdrop of the affair this would have handed West Germany's enemies a propaganda weapon of immense value. What is more, with the Ministry of Justice again under the control of the FDP, the party would be in a position to influence the course of any future proceeding against *Der Spiegel*.

A related factor was the remarkable cohesion of the CDU-CSU. The initial vehemence of the attack on the regime by the SPD and the FDP seems to have propelled Adenauer, his cabinet—even those ministers with reason to be chagrined at Strauss's tactics—and his party into an equally vehement defense of the regime. Another reason for the virtual unanimity among Christian Democrats was the involvement of *Der Spiegel*. Most CDU-CSU politicians could take invidious delight over Augstein's predicament; in the opinion of many,

[45]Ibid., p. 270.
[46]This thesis is ably argued in John Gimbel, "The Spiegel Affair In Perspective," *Midwest Journal of Political Science* 9 (August 1965): 282–97.
[47]Maurice Duverger, *The Idea of Politics* (Indianapolis: Bobbs-Merrill, 1966), pp. xii–xiii.

he had finally gotten what he deserved. After all, he thrived on political sensationalism, and was willing to publish damaging evidence of the nation's military weakness in order to discredit a personal enemy. Much of the debate was over the general merits of Der Spiegel and the character of Augstein, a factor which also had the effect of dividing the opposition and deflecting consideration from the legal and constitutional issues in the case. Adenauer himself delivered the most damaging blow by openly accusing Augstein of having committed treason for money.[48]

Lastly, Germany's civic culture—with its long-standing trust in the objectivity and competence of the experts—proved receptive to the regime's attempt to confine the affair to the courts, and to leave its outcome to trained prosecutors and judges. The regime's spokesmen attacked the press more than once for meddling in a matter concerning which they were considered to be amateurs. This attitude was forcefully expressed by Dr. Max Güde, a leading CDU member of the Bundestag and a former attorney general, who wrote: "In the battle between the bureaucracy and the press the bureaucracy should remember that the press is nothing but an incompetent intruder into the area of internal security."[49] After its original outcry against the government, the press itself appeared to concede that a judicial solution was the only way out of the crisis. Newspapers which continued to upbraid the government were greeted with remarks like those of Kurt Kiesinger (CDU)—at the time prime minister of Baden-Württemberg—who, after blandly observing that "no state is more observant of the rule of law than West Germany," indignantly charged that "public opinion is poisoned by press assertions that the proceeding against Der Spiegel has violated basic constitutional principles."[50]

The attitude of the general population appeared to be one of noninvolvement. Germans interviewed at random on the street preferred not to comment on the affair, asserting that it was a matter for the police and the government to handle. There was a general tendency to believe that if a judge sanctioned an investigation of Der Spiegel, this had to be in accordance with law.[51] Thus a good measure of diffuse public support appeared to lie beneath the government's decision to bring Augstein and his cohorts to trial.

Yet the regime had to proceed with caution. The press, now more vigilant than ever, and highly suspicious of governmental activity impinging on its freedom, closely followed the course of investigation. Der Spiegel, sales of which had zoomed to well over a half million copies per issue, continued with

[48]Verhandlungen des Deutschen Bundestages, 4. Wahlperiode, 45. Sitzung, 7 November 1962, p. 1984.

[49]Grosser and Seifert, Die Staatsmacht und Ihre Kontrolle, p. 256.

[50]Ibid., p. 259.

[51]Sunday Times (London), 11 November 1962, quoted in Ellwein, Liebel, and Negt, Die Reaktion der Öffentlichkeit, p. 493. A more systematic survey showed that twenty-two percent of West Germans felt that the arrest of Der Spiegel's editors was wrong, compared with thirty-one percent who approved of the arrest; forty-three percent had no opinion regarding the government's conduct of the arrest; forty-three percent had no opinion regarding the government's conduct of the affair. (Four percent of the responses were rejected by the computer as nonusable.) See Elisabeth Noelle and Erich Peter Neumann, The Germans: Public Opinion Polls 1947–1966 (Allensbach: Verlag für Demoskopie, 1967), p. 93.

its usual zest to attack the regime, repeatedly charging it with the violation of a free press. In March 1963 the SPD released a comprehensive documentary on the *Spiegel* affair, designed in part as a rebuttal to the official report drawn up a month earlier by the Ministry of Justice in cooperation with the Foreign, Interior, and Defense Ministries.[52] German intellectuals, moreover, had not abandoned their suspicions of the regime. Finally, the attention of much of the Western world was focused upon West Germany, and the regime knew it.

Phase Three

This phase of the affair, marked by quiet efforts to prepare a legal case against *Der Spiegel*, spanned a period of nearly three years. By the end of the period the *Spiegel* controversy had almost totally receded from public attention.

During this time the defense committee of the Bundestag held an investigation in the hope of tracing the leaks that led to *Der Spiegel*'s revelations about the state of West Germany's military preparedness. (At the same time, Strauss's conduct was being investigated by the Bonn district attorney.) This and parallel investigations by the Justice Ministry and the attorney general's office resulted in the lodging of formal charges against Colonel Martin, Ahlers, and Josef Augstein. The attorney general received a setback, however, when the Third Penal Division of the Bundesgerichtshof ordered him to show certain records, upon which the charges were based, to the defendants. This the attorney general refused to do, on the grounds that they contained secret information critical to the country's defense. It was becoming increasingly clear also that the Federal Supreme Court was unwilling to accept as a basis for trial the *Gutachten* prepared by Wunder in the Defense Ministry.

In December 1963 the attorney general announced, with the court's approval, that a new *Gutachten* would be drafted by Brigadier General Kurt Gerber, commander of the Combat Troop School in Hammelburg. Not too surprisingly, Gerber's *Gutachten*, completed in December 1963, supported the earlier findings of the Defense Ministry that secrets had been disclosed. Another pretrial investigation was ordered on this basis; it lasted several months, and was accompanied by indications that the attorney general was beginning to tire of the whole matter.

In October 1964, however, the attorney general brought formal charges against Ahlers, Martin, and Augstein, and requested that a trial be held. A procedural rule worth mentioning here is that the court, not the attorney general, decides whether or not to hold trial. If, under German procedure, the court feels that a prima facie cause of action has not been presented by the prosecutor, it may dismiss the case without trial. Colonel Martin was charged with disclosing, while Ahlers and Augstein were charged with accepting and

[52]See *Bericht der Sozialdemokraten*.

publishing, military information that endangered the security of the Federal Republic, in violation of sections 99 (2) and 100 (1) of the German Penal Code. Paul Conrad and Josef Augstein were formally charged with being accomplices to treason.[53]

As the case was being readied for trial a strange episode took place, involving Judge Heinrich Jagusch of the Bundesgerichtshof. Jagusch was president of the Bundesgerichtshof's Third Penal Division, the chamber with exclusive jurisdiction over cases involving treason. The jurisprudence that had sanctioned such harsh treatment of political defendants in West Germany was developed substantially under Jagusch's leadership. Toward the end of 1962, however—shortly after the *Spiegel* affair arose—East German officials dredged up details of Jagusch's Nazi past. Perhaps to avoid embarrassment to the regime, Jagusch requested a transfer; he was forthwith appointed president of the traffic division. Some two years later, in November of 1964, *Der Spiegel* carried an article, under the pseudonym "Judex," that was highly critical of West German security legislation.[54] The author charged that the original intent of the internal security laws had been perverted for the purpose of prosecuting innocent people in disagreement with the regime's policies, and concluded that a *Spiegel* prosecution would revive memories of the Ossietzky trial of 1931.[55] Who did "Judex" turn out to be? In keeping with the bizarre character of the affair, it was none other than Jagusch himself. This became known in an exposé and shortly thereafter Jagusch retired from the court.

The press reaction to "Judex" appears to have prompted former Attorney General Dr. Max Güde to suggest a postponement of the *Spiegel* trial until after the 1965 national election campaign. Some CDU politicians were fearful of the impact of an actual trial upon the forthcoming Bundestag elections, for the SPD was certain to make an issue of it. Judge Günther Willms, press secretary of the Bundesgerichtshof, rejected the suggestion, asserting with indignation that the scheduling of trials is not done for political convenience.

Nevertheless the trial was put off for several more months, as more evidence was accumulated. The attorney general's efforts, however, proved futile; four months prior to the national elections, the Bundesgerichtshof, without trial, dismissed the charges against Ahlers and Augstein for lack of proof that treason had been committed.[56] By August 1965 charges against all defendants

<hr/>

[53]See statement released by the Federal Prosecutor's Office, 16 October 1964 in Grosser and Seifert, *Die Staatsmacht und Ihre Kontrolle*, pp. 305–6.

[54]"Droht ein neuer Ossietzky-Fall?" *Der Spiegel*, 4 November 1964, pp. 34–38.

[55]Carl von Ossietzky was the pacifist editor of the well-known radical weekly, *Die Weltbühne*, which opposed German rearmament and exposed secret violations of the Versailles Treaty by the Weimar government. He was arrested, tried, and, on 23 November 1931, sentenced to eighteen months in prison for high treason by the Reich Supreme Court. After Hitler's accession to power he was arrested again and sent to a concentration camp where he remained until his death in 1938. See Kurt R. Grossman, *Ossietzky* (Munich: Kindler Verlag, 1963).

[56]On 13 May 1965 the Third Senate of the Bundesgerichtshof dismissed the case against Augstein and Ahlers for lack of proof. But Colonel Martin's case was still pending. See *Der Spiegel*, 19 May 1965. The decision of the Bundesgerichtshof was published in *Der Spiegel*, 26 May 1965, pp. 83–86.

except Colonel Martin had been dropped for the same reason. But the court was far from convinced of the defendants' innocence. There is good reason for believing that the judges were as concerned with a public trial's harmful effect upon the nation's security as with the evidentiary question. (Security reasons were in fact given by the judges for their final dismissal of the case against Colonel Martin in October of 1966.)

Few government officials cared to comment on the court's decision. The minister of justice at the time, Karl Weber, simply averred that in view of the decision the federal government had no further reason to comment on the case. But Press Secretary Karl-Günther von Hase, taking a most sanguine view of the matter, announced that the whole affair helped to clarify and improve the relationship between the press and government in the sensitive area of internal security.

THE LITIGATION CONTINUES: AT THE CONSTITUTIONAL COURT

The *Spiegel* affair still did not come to an end. Although charges were dismissed, clouds of suspicion continued to hover over Augstein's head; he was neither acquitted of the charge of treason nor vindicated, and his right to publish still remained in question. Also, the organization of the West German judiciary gave him an option and right to continue his legal fight against the regime in yet another forum—the Federal Constitutional Court. This court, at the apex of the German judiciary, was established to deal exclusively with constitutional disputes. German law holds that a person whose rights under the Basic Law are violated may file a constitutional complaint with the court.[57] *Der Spiegel* filed several such complaints, alleging that the original search and arrest warrants, together with Bundesgerichtshof decisions upholding their execution, violated Articles 5, 13, and 14 of the Basic Law. These articles guaranteed, respectively, freedom of the press, the inviolability of the home, and the rights of property.[58] Actually, *Der Spiegel* had been in the Constitutional Court for years, and a series of decisions had already come down. In essence, *Der Spiegel* had not fared well with its contentions concerning violated rights, while the government had not done much better with its contentions of treason.

The Federal Constitutional Court received the case in a different setting from that which prevailed in 1962. Adenauer was no longer chancellor, West Germany was beginning to make overtures to the East, emotions over the affair had cooled a great deal, and *Der Spiegel*'s case was being pressed by some of West Germany's best lawyers, among them Dr. Horst Ehmke (SPD) and Dr. Fabian von Schlabrendorff (CDU). Moreover, the case was now before a group

[57]"Gesetz über das Bundesverfassungsgericht," *Bundesgesetzblatt*, I, 243 (12 March 1951), section 90.
[58]See 20 BVerfGE 162–63 (1967).

of judges far different in background and attitudes from the judges of the Bundesgerichtshof. The judges of the Constitutional Court, men of wide experience in political affairs, were more disposed than the career judges of the Bundesgerichtshof to hand down an anti-government decision. The Court is composed of two chambers, the First and Second Senates. A federal statute confers on the First Senate jurisdiction over basic civil liberty matters. This statutory requirement was of enormous consequence to the final outcome of the *Spiegel* case because the First Senate divided rather sharply between liberals and conservatives.[59]

The ideological cleavage within the First Senate was evident in the judges' questioning of government witnesses in the public hearing. The chief antagonists were Judge Herbert Scholtissek, the Reporter in the case, and Judge Gebhard Müller, the president of the Federal Constitutional Court and the presiding officer of the First Senate. Scholtissek, who recommended a decision in favor of *Der Spiegel*, is known for his libertarian views in the area of speech. President Müller, a former prime minister of Baden-Württemberg, takes an expansive view of the government's authority to curb speech in internal security matters.[60]

The *Spiegel* affair did not appear to split the eight-member Senate in the same way that it did the Bundestag, for the division was not along partisan lines. Both Müller and Scholtissek are former members of the CDU. Judge Erwin Stein, also a former member of the CDU, frequently expresses off-the-bench views which identify him as the most outspoken civil libertarian on the Court. One could have assumed that Stein would support Scholtissek within the First Senate. Informed observers also calculated that Judge Karl Haager, identified with the SPD, would vote for the government in the *Spiegel* case while his Social Democratic colleagues, Judges Wiltraut Rupp-von Brünneck and Hugo Berger, would vote for *Der Spiegel*. Thus it appeared likely that at least four judges—Scholtissek, Stein, Rupp-von Brünneck, and Berger—would vote against the government. The outcome of the case would depend, therefore, on the votes of the two remaining judges—Theodore Ritterspach and Werner Böhmer—whose views on free speech, as they relate to the problem of internal security, could not be obtained from off-the-bench speeches or writings. It seemed clear that President Müller, a strong-willed leader of the Court with many friends in Bonn's ruling CDU circles, would have to fight a pitched battle inside the First Senate to reverse the recommendation of the Reporter (Scholtissek) and thereby avoid an anti-government decision.

The decision itself was the best indicator of the scope of the conflict inside the First Senate; indeed, after oral arguments were completed, the Court re-

[59]For a general discussion of the Federal Constitutional Court's personnel see Donald P. Kommers, "The Federal Constitutional Court in the West German Political System" in *Frontiers of Judicial Research*, ed. Joel B. Grossman and Joseph Tanenhaus (New York: John Wiley and Sons, 1969), pp. 91–106.

[60]These observations are based on my interviews with government officials and with most of the judges of the Federal Constitutional Court. The interactions between the judges are described more fully in my forthcoming book, *The West German Federal Constitutional Court.*

quired nearly eight months of deliberation before handing down—predictably —a four-to-four decision.[61] The text of the ruling had the distinction of incorporating the first official dissenting opinion in the Court's history. Because of the statutory rule that no violation of the Basic Law can be found in the event of a tie vote, the complaint of *Der Spiegel* had to be dismissed; thus by the narrowest of margins the government won the day.

All eight judges agreed that the treason statutes themselves were not on their face unconstitutional. The four judges in favor of *Der Spiegel*, however, were of the opinion that the so-called "mosaic theory" could not constitutionally be applied to the press, nor could it be made the basis of an indictment or warrants for the arrest and seizure of a publication's editors and property. According to this theory of treason, a state secret may be divulged simply by organizing scattered facts already known to the public into a unified, coherent picture of the nation's military strategy. On the other hand, the four judges in favor of the government did not reach this issue, preferring to ignore it as irrelevant on the facts of the case. The two sides did come to grips with certain procedural questions, however. The dissenting judges severely reproached the judges of the Bundesgerichtshof for failing to apply constitutional standards in granting the warrants and orders requested by the attorney general. All these proceedings violated the Basic Law, they said, because not once did the Bundesgerichtshof seek to measure the state's interest in security against the requirements of a free press. The four judges who ruled in favor of the government simply denied the regime's arbitrariness against *Der Spiegel* and asserted that the judges of the Bundesgerichtshof had sufficient reason to believe that treason had been committed. In fact, they tended to treat the matter as if it were an ordinary criminal case, virtually ignoring the competing demands of a free press under Article 5 of the Basic Law.

Ironically, the government failed to achieve its objective—trial and conviction—in the conservative Bundesgerichtshof, yet it went on to win the constitutional argument in the somewhat more liberal Federal Constitutional Court. The publication of the dissenting opinion was itself a remarkable victory for the dissenters. The official publication of dissents, or even the raw vote in a case, is unknown to German jurisprudence, due to a profound belief among Germans that any such revelation of dissenting views, or votes, would weaken judicial authority and respect for the law. But not even the appearance of unanimity could be maintained here, for the polarization of views inside the court was simply too great.

The Constitutional Court ordinarily does not write an opinion in cases where the judges divide evenly. Given the public importance of the *Spiegel* affair, however, it was politically impossible for the Court not to assert itself in the face of the serious constitutional question with which it was dealing. Acquiescence in this case would have been construed as weakness. The dissenting opinion was a manifestation of judicial independence and, as Judge Hans Rupp, a member of the Second Senate, recently observed, "the equality

[61]See Decision of 5 August 1966, 20 BVerfGE 162–230 (1967).

of votes [in the *Spiegel* case] came as a profound but healthy shock. . . . [For] the government noticed with horror that it had had only a very narrow escape in the Constitutional Court."[62] Thus, much like the American Supreme Court in *Marbury* v. *Madison*, the German Court gave the government a victory, but simultaneously warned the regime of the limits of its power.[63]

THE IMPACT OF THE SPIEGEL AFFAIR

The regime's original intention was to use the courts as the best political means of defeating and discrediting *Der Spiegel*. But the law of treason proved a cumbersome weapon in this particular case. Resort to political trials in a constitutional democracy is, at best, a risk; where courts are independent of executive control there is no absolute assurance that the holders of power will gain the political advantage they anticipate. Before a constitutional regime decides to transfer its political quarrels into courts of law it must be sure of two things: that its authority is sufficient to command public support, and that its credibility will remain intact. In the *Spiegel* controversy the latter was substantially undermined by the circumstances of the affair and by the revelation of Strauss's role in it. A public opinion poll later showed that thirty-six percent of all Germans believed that Strauss himself ordered the arrest of *Der Spiegel*'s editors. It is no surprise, therefore, that the affair backfired on Strauss, and eventually led to his resignation as minister of defense.

Whether a treason charge—or trial—involving such a prominent personality as Rudolf Augstein can be turned into political profit depends also on the ability of a government to maintain its unity. At the time of the *Spiegel* affair West Germany was ruled by a relatively weak and unstable government coalition. The law of treason was a clumsy instrument to use in this case because of Augstein's access to the Free Democratic Party, and because defense policy was one important area in which there was considerable disagreement between the FDP and the CDU-CSU. The greatest error, from a strategic point of view, was to keep the minority partner of the coalition in the dark about the original plans to move against *Der Spiegel*. And when the FDP joined the SPD in condemning the action, the result was—for a short time—the collapse of the coalition and a loss of support for the government.

But perhaps the major consequence of the *Spiegel* affair was its influence on the development of free speech and press in Germany. Bonn's leaders have not been too concerned with free expression as a means of sharpening aware-

---

[62]Hans G. Rupp, "The Federal Constitutional Court in Germany: Scope of Its Jurisdiction and Procedure," *Notre Dame Lawyer* 44 (April 1969): 553.

[63]1 Cr. 137 (1803). It is not wholly spurious to suggest that the Federal Constitutional Court was approximately at a point in 1966 that the Supreme Court of the United States had reached in 1803. Both tribunals were themselves still largely "on trial" at these widely separated times; both had functioned in newly created political systems little more than sixteen years old; both were distrusted by executive and legislative power holders; and both felt an urgent need to establish their independence while prudently avoiding head-on confrontations with the regime's rulers.

ness of alternative policies on such critical issues as war and peace. This is one measure of the condition of free speech in the Federal Republic. Freedom in West Germany today, much like freedom in nineteenth-century America, is perceived largely in personal and economic terms; that is, the typical German finds his freedom rooted in his right to privacy, economic security, and the unhindered pursuit of personal pleasure.[64]

Neither Parliament nor the judiciary had drawn a very satisfactory line between permissible and impermissible speech in West Germany. By the same token neither branch of government appears to have given much thought to the requisites of popular participation in the processes of democracy. The critical question in the *Spiegel* case was whether West German citizens, in order to form a rational political judgment about defense policy, were entitled as a matter of course to know the contents of the articles published by the magazine. Some West German officials behaved as if military policy were the legitimate preserve and concern only of the special elite commissioned by the state to deal with these matters. Given the prevalence of such attitudes in West Germany, it is easy to see why the government sought to bring *Der Spiegel* before the bar of political justice.

When the politicians in Bonn decided to seek judicial confirmation of their charges against *Der Spiegel,* however, the conflict had to be waged under rules and regulations different from those which govern ordinary political battles. The game was now to be played on the limited field of the legal order with its more precise boundaries. These boundaries were the constitutional principles of the Basic Law, the rules of courts, and the Code of Criminal Procedure. Any democratic government seeking to transfer a political conflict to a court of law whose independence is protected by a written constitution must risk carrying on the fight within narrowly drawn rules of procedure. The hacksaw may be sufficient in politics, but the surgeon's scalpel is frequently a prerequisite in courtroom operations. Courts do not ordinarily deal in generalities; the particularization of both fact and issue is the essence of the judicial process.

This was partly the source of the government's undoing. The politicians, of course, miscalculated by thinking that the courts, in this case the Bundesgerichtshof, would simply ratify the charge of treason made by the government. One reason the government had to wait three years before filing formal charges against *Der Spiegel* was the lack of evidence to sustain its allegations. The government's suspicions and generalized complaints could not be processed through the judiciary's delicate machinery. At the same time the Bundesgerichtshof could hardly ignore the political context in which it was operating. After all, the government's suit was also a political demand that the five judges of the Third Penal Division were not altogether willing to reject. In view of the circumstances of this case, however, in purely political terms the judges themselves could not afford simply to rubber-stamp the actions of the government. The court itelf was in the political spotlight, in part because of the background of some of its judges, particularly the president of the Third

---

[64]See Kommers, "*The Federal Constitutional Court,*" p. 117.

Division. And it was being closely watched by many groups, including the SPD and the FDP.

Subjected to these cross pressures, the court might well have calculated that the best way out in this instance was not to decide. This was, in fact, the first time the Bundesgerichtshof had ever dismissed formal charges by the government without a trial. In doing so, however, the court gave neither *Der Spiegel* nor the government a clear victory. But in not allowing the government to prevail, a critical boundary of action was materially denied to government trespass. German disregard for certain degrees of freedom of the press may never be the same. The dissenting opinion by the Federal Constitutional Court added several exclamation points.

Professor Horst Ehmke, currently State Secretary in the Ministry of Justice, informed the author that the attorney general's office is proceeding with a good deal more caution than before in pressing treason cases before the Bundesgerichtshof, although there seems to have been little lessening of the intensity with which the internal security laws generally are being enforced. It is his opinion also that the political hazard involved in such cases has forced the attorney general to train his guns on the real conspirators in the society, namely the hired agents of foreign powers seeking to subvert the established order.[65]

It is of course too early to assess the effect of the *Spiegel* decision on a more pervasive atmosphere of free speech in Germany. There is no certainty that it will actually expand the boundaries of free expression in view of the current political context. Recent disclosures of spy networks in West Germany, coupled with the Soviet invasion of Czechoslovakia, may actually revive the cold war and stiffen once again the resolve of the Federal Republic to resort to the legal order to punish those whose activities or speeches fall outside the limits of dissent.

It is difficult to assess the long-range impact of the affair upon West Germany's political system. But one is strongly tempted to conclude that the political situation in Germany had fairly well reverted to what it was before. The sociocultural, political, and institutional factors which contributed to the affair have not changed significantly.

One thing that seems to confirm these impressions has been an all-too-happy ending for the innumerable persons involved in the *Spiegel* affair. Not one of them suffered any permanent impairment of his career as a result of his indiscretion or mistakes. Not one of them showed any remorse for what he had done, or gave a second thought to the propriety of his remaining in the government. The fact that nearly all of them, including those dismissed at the height and in the heat of the affair, have since been promoted to higher positions in the federal government, is in the best tradition of political satire. If this were not enough, the grand coalition itself restored Franz-Josef Strauss to power in Bonn, as minister of finance, and brought him into association with the man he accused of treason. For Conrad Ahlers became the head of the

[65]Ehmke interview, 11 July 1968.

Federal Press Office and chief spokesman of the West German government. It is a truly bizarre spectacle to watch Ahlers treat the critics of Bonn's current defense policies with almost the same contempt with which he, as *Der Spiegel*'s military affairs editor, was treated by the Adenauer government's press agent. Meanwhile *Der Spiegel* itself, more prosperous than ever, continues its usual assaults on Strauss and on West Germany's foreign and defense policies.

All in all, the *Spiegel* affair, as a case study in judicial politics and political trials, shows risks involved—in the long and short runs—in the government's resort to the courts. These risks are particularly evident in a constitutional democracy such as West Germany.

GEORGE H. GADBOIS, JR.

2

KESHAV SINGH

contemptuous judges and contumacious legislators

Prior to 1964, Keshav Singh was an unknown, small-time Indian politician from Gorakhpur district, a depressed pocket in the northeastern corner of the state of Uttar Pradesh. He had been secretary of the local unit of the Socialist Party, an organization of much noise but little electoral success. He was in no sense a figure to be reckoned with in Uttar Pradesh state politics, and most certainly his name was unfamiliar outside that state. Yet national—in some measure even international—notoriety came to him in 1964 when his imprisonment set off an unprecedented battle between Indian judges and politicians.[1]

The Keshav Singh incident triggered an attempt by legislators to arrest high court judges, the convening of the largest bench of high court judges in Indian history, intervention by the prime minister and president of India, a thirteen-day hearing before the Supreme Court of India in which no less than 129 lawyers appeared representing 38 parties, and a landmark decision which brought cries from legislators throughout India that they had been emasculated by the judiciary.

At no time, however, was Singh tried in a court for any alleged wrongdoing, although he did spend seven days in jail—six days in March of 1964, and the seventh a year later. His conviction came at the hands of the legislators of Uttar Pradesh, the sentencing judge being the state's chief minister.

Events leading to Singh's incarceration began in 1963 when he and two other Socialist Party colleagues published, and distributed in the lobby of the Uttar Pradesh Legislative Assembly, a little pamphlet entitled *Exposure of Black*

---

[1]See, for example, the accounts of the Keshav Singh incident in *Time*, 23 October 1964, pp. 54, 56 and *The Economist*, 17 October 1964.

Deeds of Narsingh Narain Pandey. Pandey represented a Gorakhpur constituency in the legislative assembly. Elected in 1962 on a Socialist Party ticket, he subsequently became affiliated with the United Socialist Party, a new grouping made up of most of the Socialist Party and Praja Socialist Party members of the assembly. Still later, Pandey defected to the ruling Congress Party.

The pamphlet is not available now, but evidently it contained charges that Pandey was a crook, and that he was engaged in various forms of corruption. Precisely what inspired Singh and his associates to do this is not known, nor has anyone investigated the accuracy of the allegations. For this was hardly the first time someone inside or outside an Indian legislature had called a politician names. Ironically, Pandey himself is credited with inaugurating a spate of corruption and nepotism charges against several Congress Party ministers in 1963.[2]

At the time, the pamphlet seemed to raise only another routine breach-of-privilege question. Pandey's reaction followed the established pattern: he claimed he was an honest man and termed the charges false and defamatory. There are ordinary laws in India governing libel and slander, but legislators have an easier way of handling such problems. They can do what Pandey did —claim that the pamphlet represented not simply a breach of his privileges as an assembly member, but that it served to heap ridicule and contempt on *all* members of the assembly.

As is usually the result in such cases, Pandey's colleagues agreed with his estimate of the gravity of the evil represented by the pamphlet. The outcome was an assembly resolution summoning the authors of the pamphlet to appear before the legislators to receive a "reprimand."[3]

On 4 February 1964, the date fixed for the reprimand, neither Singh nor his colleagues appeared. Two weeks later, a second date having been established, Singh's two collaborators presented themselves, apologized, and submitted to a brief and quite innocuous scolding.

Although Singh did not appear, he did write to the Speaker saying that he could not afford the railway fare from Gorakhpur to Lucknow, the state capital. (This is a distance of some 150 miles, the fare for which would be the rupee equivalent of less than one dollar.) The Speaker of the House, exhibiting commendable patience, then fixed a third date (3 March), but the date came and passed and all the Speaker had for his efforts was another letter from Singh about his difficult financial plight.

His patience by this time exhausted, the Speaker sent not the railway fare but the marshal of the assembly armed with a warrant that Singh "be taken into custody on March 18, 1964 or earlier and produced before me at Lucknow forthwith."[4]

[2] *Link* (New Delhi) 6, no. 31 (15 March 1964): 19.
[3] *National Herald* (Lucknow), 19 December 1963.
[4] Quoted in Charu C. Chowdhuri, "Power of Committal of Indian Legislatures," Part I, *Law Quarterly* (Journal of the West Bengal State Unit of the Indian Law Institute) II, no. 1 (March 1965): 57. Of the nearly two dozen articles and books prepared by Indian scholars concerning the Keshav Singh incident, this article by Chowdhuri, published in three parts, is the most useful.

Upon learning of his imminent arrest, Singh sent off another letter to the Speaker, this one couched in rather firm language. He protested the reprimand sentence, claiming that each charge he had made against Pandey was correct, that he had "no hesitation in calling a corrupt person corrupt," and that "the dictatorial order [arrest warrant] strikes at the root of democracy."[5]

The marshal located and arrested Singh in Gorakhpur on 13 March. But transporting him to Lucknow and into the assembly hall presented some difficulties. Singh began by stretching out on the railway station platform. The following day, still refusing to cooperate, he had to be carried into the assembly hall by the marshal and four guards.[6] He was deposited before the Speaker, being placed "in the bar—a wooden rectangular cage—guarded by two guards and the Marshal."[7]

The Speaker addressed several questions to him, but Singh, "stiff and stone-eyed,"[8] refused to acknowledge his inquisitor's presence, and underscored his disdain by turning his back to the Speaker. The *Hindustan Times* correspondent wrote that "all his defence was stencilled in red letters in Hindi over his unbleached country-made cotton shirt. From a distance they looked like slogans and sermons on socialism and the duty of an individual to rise against 'the atrocities of majority rule.' "[9]

Undeterred, the Speaker administered the oft-postponed admonition:

> Being a citizen of independent Bharat [India], it is expected of you and of
> everyone to exercise self-restraint and prudence in describing the proceedings
> of the house with a view to preserving its privileges. In the name of the
> house and under its orders, I reprimand you for contempt of the house
> and for breach of privilege against Mr. Narsingh Narain Pandey.[10]

Having administered this harmless rebuke which, even though it had to be aimed at the back of Singh's head, presumably served to restore some of the assembly's wounded pride, the Speaker asked the chief minister—Mrs. Sucheta Kripalani—what she thought of Singh's most recent letter. Some members of the assembly claimed it amounted to another act of contempt of the house.

Chief Minister Kripalani, noting the manner in which Singh had been "flouting the orders of the House,"[11] said that the best way to handle such an irreverent Indian would be to put him behind bars. She thereupon introduced a resolution, overwhelmingly endorsed by voice vote, that Singh "be sentenced to imprisonment for seven days for having written a letter worded in language which constitutes contempt of the House, and [for] his misbehaviour in view of the House."[12]

[5]*Times of India* (New Delhi), 15 March 1964.
[6]*National Herald* (Lucknow), 15 March 1964.
[7]Ibid.
[8]*Hindustan Times* (New Delhi), 15 March 1964.
[9]Ibid.
[10]*National Herald* (Lucknow), 15 March 1964.
[11]Quoted in Chowdhuri, "Power of Committal," Part I, p. 58.
[12]Quoted in ibid.

At this juncture Singh was given one last opportunity to avoid imprisonment. The Speaker explained that if he would simply apologize "with folded hands" he might be forgiven for all the grief he had caused, and the jail sentence might be suspended.[13] Singh said nothing, and proceeded to lie prostrate again on the floor. The marshal, still assisted by the guards, then carried Singh from the chamber and delivered him to the Lucknow District Jail.

The jailing of a constituent by an Indian legislature is rare, but not unprecedented. There were at least three earlier instances of such action being taken. These occurred in Rajasthan in 1956, and in Madhya Pradesh in 1960 and 1962. All were similar in that the offensive behavior involved shouting slogans and throwing leaflets from the visitor's gallery, and leaping onto the floor of the house. Such disruptive activities resulted in the imprisonment of the individuals responsible for as long as fifteen days.[14]

In addition, there have been many instances since 1950 in which Indian legislatures have punished citizens for contempt by summoning them to appear before the legislatures to explain their conduct, administering an admonition, and extracting apologies. Indeed, so common are such cases that the secretariat of the lower house of the Indian National Parliament publishes the semiannual *Privileges Digest,* a periodical devoted to summaries of such cases.

What made the case of Keshav Singh a cause célèbre was the next step he took. During the sixth day (19 March) of his confinement, obviously incensed at having to suffer this punishment at the hands of politicians he did not respect, Singh did the only thing he could have done—he applied to the Lucknow Bench of the Allahabad (Uttar Pradesh) High Court for a writ of *habeas corpus,* claiming that he had been deprived of his personal liberty without any authority of law. He named as respondents the Speaker of the House, the entire house membership, the chief minister, and the jail superintendent. Singh thus questioned the power of legislators to jail critics—something Indians jailed earlier by legislators had not dared to do.[15]

HISTORICAL AND CULTURAL BACKGROUND

In order to grasp the contextual significance of the "constitutional crisis" which followed Singh's petition to the judges, brief mention must be made of

[13]*Hindustan Times* (New Delhi), 15 March 1964.

[14]Chowdhuri, "Power of Committal," Part II, *Law Quarterly* II, no. 3 (September 1965): 277.

[15]There was, however, a quite similar incident more than a decade earlier. In 1952, the acting editor of *Blitz,* a sensational leftist weekly, was charged with contempt by the Uttar Pradesh Legislative Assembly for "casting reflections" on the deputy Speaker. He also refused to go to Lucknow, was arrested in Bombay under a warrant issued by the Speaker, and was brought to Lucknow and kept in "Speaker's custody." But he was not placed in jail. In a *habeas corpus* proceeding, the Supreme Court released him on the technical ground that he had not been produced before a magistrate within the constitutionally prescribed twenty-four hour period after his arrest. Whether the legislature had the power to arrest a person did not arise in this case. *Reddy* v. *Nafisul Hasan, All India Reporter* 1954 Supreme Court 636.

some features of the Indian political and legal cultures. Most relevant to a proper appraisal of the ensuing rounds of the Singh incident is the fact that the higher judiciary is held in great esteem by Indians. And the major reason why this incident attracted such an enormous amount of attention is because this judiciary, for more than a century a symbol of resolute independence and compassionate justice, was imperiled by the legislators of Uttar Pradesh.

Judicial institutions were introduced early in the colonial period in India. Though initially staffed entirely by Englishmen, neither the higher courts nor the judges were perceived by Indians as integral parts of the colonial machinery. Especially after the mid-nineteenth century the high courts were considerably differentiated from other governmental structures, and this structural differentiation was accompanied by a remarkable degree of functional autonomy.

Moreover, the courts were Indianized earlier and more rapidly than the bureaucracy. This contributed to the appearance of a judiciary that was more an indigenous than an alien institution, and it added an emotional ingredient to the public esteem which judges and courts came to enjoy. The key to this prestige is the widely held view that the judges are men of uncommon integrity and honesty, and that one can receive a fairer, more impartial hearing from them than from any other agency or authority in the political and social system.

The review powers of the courts were not extensive during the period of British rule, but the courts were incredibly diligent in protecting what few liberties the Indian subjects had. For example, during World War II the colonial rulers armed themselves with a variety of sedition, preventive detention, and special criminal court measures, and proceeded to jail tens of thousands of Indians. At this time the courts were literally the only forum to which these Indians could turn for redress.

In a series of remarkable and usually unanimous decisions, the federal court, composed of an Englishman, a Hindu, and a Muslim, found fault with several of these weapons of suppression. One decision alone ordered the executive to release 11,700 jailed Indian nationalists, including Gandhi and other prominent leaders, on the ground that the executive had exceeded the authority with which it had endowed itself.[16]

It came as no surprise when those who had the responsibility of determining the institutional mix of the post-colonial political system sought to build upon this legacy. The framers of the Indian Constitution increased the jurisdiction of the high courts, created a Supreme Court patterned on the American model, and explicitly endowed these courts with the power of judicial review.

But a strong and prestigious judiciary was only one among several ends sought by the constitution makers. Leading political figures were committed

---

[16]*Keshav Talpade* v. *The King-Emperor*, 1943 *Federal Court Reports* 49. Cf. the author's "The Federal Court of India: 1937–1950," *Journal of the Indian Law Institute* VI (April–September 1964): 253–315.

also to the parliamentary form of government and to a bill of rights. There arose the difficult problem of reconciling a strong judiciary modeled on the American experience with a parliamentary system fashioned according to the British prototype. It became a question, then, of who would have the last word—judges or politicians.

The issue came to a head in the debate over the proposed inclusion of a due process clause in the bill of rights. The first draft of the constitution included such a clause but it was later deleted, chiefly because the framers, who were serving simultaneously as the provisional Parliament, concluded that it would give the judges too much power to sit in judgment over legislators.[17]

When the Constitution became operative in 1950, Indians flocked to the courts to test the validity of virtually every major piece of legislation. The Constitution makes access to the courts extremely easy for those who claim that their individual rights (called Fundamental Rights in India) have been infringed. In fact, an aggrieved Indian may, if he wishes, go directly to the Supreme Court in New Delhi without climbing the long ladder of appeals. Both the Supreme Court and the sixteen state high courts are empowered to issue writs (*habeas corpus, mandamus,* prohibition, *quo warranto,* and *certiorari*) to compel the government to act in a particular way, or to restrain it from acting injuriously to individual liberties deemed to be of superior importance.

The courts have taken their role as the guarantors of individual rights very seriously, and tens of thousands of writs have been issued, to all levels of government, over the past two decades. The *Supreme Court Reports* disclose that there were more than two thousand cases of encounters between the government and individuals during the period 1950–1967 which were adjudicated by the Supreme Court. The government emerged the winner in less than sixty percent of these cases.[18] Few, if any, other governments enjoy so little success in encounters with their citizens. And these data reveal something about the Indian Supreme Court—obviously it does not cower before the legislators and the executive branch.

Also relevant to a proper appraisal of the Keshav Singh incident is the enormous gulf which separates Indian judges from politicians. The typical high court or Supreme Court justice has never been an active political party

[17]The late Felix Frankfurter played a part in the dropping of due process. Shortly after the draft constitution was prepared, the Constituent Assembly's Constitutional Adviser, Sir Benegal Narsing Rau, met with Frankfurter in Washington, D.C. According to Rau's account, "A Visit to U.S.A., Canada, Eire and Great Britain," *India's Constitution in the Making,* ed. B. Shiva Rao (Madras: Orient Longmans, 1960), p. 303, Frankfurter told him that "the power of judicial review implied in the due process clause . . . is not only undemocratic (because it gives a few judges the power of vetoing legislation enacted by the representatives of the nation) but also throws an unfair burden upon the judiciary." Upon his return to India, Rau urged that the due process clause be taken out, and it was.

[18]George H. Gadbois, Jr., "The Supreme Court of India: a Preliminary Report of an Empirical Study" (Paper read before the Annual Meeting of the American Political Science Association, New York, 5 September 1969), p. 6.

member. In marked contrast to the American tradition, no one prominent in public affairs has ever been appointed to the Indian Supreme Court.[19] This detachment from politics is a major source of their prestige and legitimacy and is nurtured by the refusal of most judges to appear at social functions attended by political figures. Such behavior strengthens the popular image of judges as impartial legal wizards whose decisions are unaffected by political or partisan considerations.

Few Indian politicians or bureaucrats enjoy such public adulation. Indian participation in legislative bodies during the colonial period was too limited for any hoary traditions to evolve. The bureaucracy, though strong and relatively effective, was by the time of independence popularly considered a symbol of alien rule. Contemporary India's legislators are viewed as ordinary mortals—individuals of uncertain principles—men more interested in enhancing their own positions than in promoting the public interest. Newspapers, which do very little to flatter Indian lawmakers, regularly report legislative sessions marked by varieties of turmoil: boycotts, walkouts, paperweights hurled at the Speaker, free-for-alls on the floor, members being dragged out of the assembly by the marshal, and other disruptive occurrences.[20] The Uttar Pradesh Legislative Assembly is especially well-known for such antics. Yet these are the same legislators who in the Keshav Singh case enthusiastically wrapped themselves in traditions of the Mother of Parliaments.

KESHAV SINGH STRIKES BACK

Keshav Singh's *habeas corpus* petition was taken up by the two-judge Lucknow Bench of the Uttar Pradesh (Allahabad) High Court at two o'clock in the afternoon of 19 March. (It is not uncommon for such petitions to be taken up the day they are filed.) Present was the assistant government advocate, who immediately requested an hour's postponement so that he could receive high-level instructions concerning defense strategy. The court agreed, but when the hour passed the attorney had not returned. No explanation was given for this failure to reappear, but there is every reason to believe, in view of later developments, that the respondents simply chose not to recognize any court jurisdiction. The judges then admitted Singh's petition, directed that notices be issued to the respondents, stipulated that an early date be set for the hearing, and ordered Singh released on bail.

The next day these developments were discussed in the assembly by excited

[19]Cf. the author's "Indian Supreme Court Judges: A Portrait," *Law and Society Review* III, nos. 2 and 3 (November 1968–February 1969): 317–36.

[20]While the Supreme Court was hearing the oral arguments in the Keshav Singh case, the newspapers reported that a Mr. Dhote, a Democratic Front member of the Maharashtra Legislative Assembly, had been arrested (by virtue of an order issued by the Speaker) for assaulting and physically injuring both the Speaker and the marshal of the house. Preceding his attack on these men, he had hurled a paperweight at the operator of the house microphone system. *Times of India* (New Delhi), 13 August 1964.

legislators who were enraged by the fact that the judges had even listened to Singh's petition, much less released him. And on the twenty-first, by a 129–19 vote,[21] the following unprecedented resolution was passed:

> This House is of the definite view that Sri G. D. Sahgal, Sri N. U. Beg [the two judges], Sri Keshav Singh and Sri S. Solomon [Singh's attorney] have committed contempt of this House. Therefore it is ordered that Sri Keshav Singh should immediately be taken into custody and kept confined in the District Jail, Lucknow for the remaining term of his imprisonment, and Sarvasri N. U. Beg, G. D. Sahgal and S. Solomon should be brought in custody before the House. After Sri Keshav Singh has completed his term of imprisonment, he should be brought before the House for having again committed contempt of the House on March 19, 1964.

The legislators believed most emphatically that they possessed the power not only to punish for their contempt but also to imprison individuals whenever they wished; that these powers were absolute; and that their exercise was not subject to one whit of judicial review. So enraged were they by what they considered to be singularly presumptuous judicial behavior that the judges were to be brought *in custody* into the assembly hall.

Judges Sahgal and Beg learned of their impending arrest over the radio. Understandably anxious to avoid arrest, they rushed off to Allahabad, headquarters of the state high court, and petitioned their colleagues for writs of their own. They claimed that the assembly's resolution was unconstitutional because it violated a provision prohibiting criticism of judges in state legislatures. Moreover, they argued that the resolution amounted to a contempt of court. They named as respondents the Speaker, all the state legislators, the marshal, and the entire state government.

These petitions were filed on 23 March and were acted upon immediately by the full bench of the high court, composed of twenty-eight judges. Never before had so many judges sat *en banc* to hear a petition or decide a case. But never before had the judicial role and prerogative been so gravely jeopardized. The full bench unanimously came to the aid of their brothers and issued an order serving to prevent the implementation of the resolution and the execution of the arrest warrants. A similar order was issued staying the execution of the arrest warrants for Singh and his attorney.

At this juncture there was a virtual standoff: the politicians refusing to appear in a courtroom, claiming that the judges were guilty of contempt of the legislature; and the judges refusing to enter the legislative assembly hall, claiming that the legislators were guilty of contempt of court.

Reports circulated that the high court chief justice and the chief minister had met, but there was no indication that they found any solution to the dilemma.[23] Evidence that Mrs. Kripalani and other key figures in the state gov-

---

[21]Almost all of the dissenters were members of the Socialist Party who, following the vote, stomped out of the assembly shouting "long live the revolution." *Times of India* (New Delhi), 22 March 1964.

[22]Quoted in Chowdhuri, "Power of Committal," Part I, p. 60.

[23]*Hindustan Times* (New Delhi), 23 March 1964.

ernment were seeking to ease the tension came on 25 March, when another resolution was introduced in the Uttar Pradesh Assembly and declared passed by voice vote. It stated that the earlier resolution had been misunderstood, that the legislators never really meant to determine the guilt of the judges, Singh, or his attorney without first giving them an opportunity to explain their position before the house. Hence these men were told to appear before the privileges committee on 6 April "to make their submission, if any."[24]

Although this resolution hardly represented any major concession, it provoked wild scenes in the legislature. Some fifty lawmakers, unwilling to give an inch to the judges, began shouting, thumping on tables, and raising such a ruckus that further business could not be conducted and the assembly had to be adjourned for the day. The *Times of India* correspondent reported that the "tumult and shouting in the House was deafening," and that one particularly agitated legislator vowed to "shed his blood" to resist the resolution.[25]

Although the warrants for their arrest were withdrawn, Justices Beg and Sahgal were no more anxious to comply with the second resolution than the first. They again scurried off to Allahabad and secured from their colleagues another order staying the implementation of this resolution.[26]

All of these events were being reported on the front pages of the national newspapers and were being discussed in other state legislatures and in Parliament in New Delhi. Anguished legal pundits proclaimed that the judge-legislator battle had created "a complicated situation unparalleled in the legal history of India or any other country."[27] In a country such as India it is difficult to assess public opinion on issues such as this one, but there is every reason to believe that informed public opinion supported the judges. Newspaper editorials invariably supported the right of the judiciary to protect the liberties of individuals.

There being no likelihood that an acceptable solution could be worked out in Lucknow or Allahabad, Chief Minister Kripalani took the initiative and requested the intervention of the central government. Without seeking the approval of the legislative assembly, she asked Prime Minister Lal Bahadur Shastri to invoke the advisory jurisdiction of the Supreme Court. This request was approved, and on 26 March the President of India, Dr. Sarvapelli Radhakrishnan, announced that he had asked the Supreme Court to examine the situation and provide him with an advisory opinion.[28] When the Supreme Court announced that it would offer an opinion, the crisis was temporarily de-fused, and both sides agreed to maintain the status quo.[29]

[24]Chowdhuri, "Power of Committal," Part I, p. 62.
[25]26 March 1964.
[26]*National Herald* (Lucknow), 28 March 1964.
[27]*Times of India* (New Delhi), 23 March 1964.
[28]This marked the fifth time since 1950 that the president had invoked the Supreme Court's advisory jurisdiction. Technically, advisory opinions are different from decisions arising out of formal litigation, and they are not officially binding on any parties. In practice, however, advisory opinions have never been rejected by the executive, and they have virtually the same weight as regular opinions. The Court is not obliged to express an opinion, but it has never turned down a request from the president.
[29]Chowdhuri, "Power of Committal," Part I, p. 64.

THE SUPREME COURT VERDICT

The Supreme Court took up the case on 27 July and proceeded to listen to nearly three weeks of formal argument. The Court acknowledged the fact that its opinion would have implications for all state legislatures and high courts by inviting representatives of these institutions and any other interested parties to participate in the hearings. Widespread interest in the dispute was demonstrated when a total of 38 parties appeared, representing most of the high courts and legislative assemblies. Altogether 129 lawyers participated—a group which included the cream of India's bar.

Principal spokesman for the legislators was H. M. Seervai, Advocate General of Maharashtra State. He began by saying that though he was standing before the bar of the Supreme Court, this should not be construed as any indication that the legislatures were submitting to the jurisdiction of the Supreme Court, or that the legislatures would accept whatever opinion the Court offered. But he did present some twenty-two hours of arguments on behalf of the legislatures.

The main thrust of Seervai's case was that Indian legislatures, based on English precedent, had an unfettered power to jail individuals for contempt, and that the exercise of this power was beyond the scrutiny of any court. Legislatures are the sole and exclusive judge both as to what constitutes their contempt and what type of punishment is to be imposed, Seervai contended. When a legislature issues a general or "unspeaking" warrant—a warrant not stating the facts constituting the contempt—the courts must regard the warrant as absolutely sacrosanct.

Seervai's entire argument rested upon his interpretation of one part of one article of the Indian Constitution. This was article 194 which, after providing for freedom of speech in the legislatures and attributing immunity to the official publication of legislative proceedings, declares that

> In other respects, the powers, privileges and immunities of a House of the Legislature of a State, and of the members and the committees of a House of such Legislature shall be such as may from time to time be defined by the Legislature by law, and, until so defined, shall be those of the House of Commons of Parliament of the United Kingdom, and of its members and committees, at the commencement of this Constitution.[30]

Since no Indian legislature had yet codified its privileges and immunities, and since the House of Commons has the power to punish for contempt, the Indian legislatures possessed the same powers, privileges and immunities as the Mother of Parliaments, according to Seervai. And, he continued, when the latter issued general warrants, United Kingdom courts treated such warrants as exclusive and unreviewable. Indian courts, therefore, were obliged to behave with no less circumspection when general contempt warrants were issued.

[30]Republic of India, *Constitution*, Article 194 (3).

Seervai did agree that the Indian judiciary had been conceded the general power of authoritatively interpreting the Constitution, but he said the legislatures alone determined the scope of their privileges and immunities.

The judges' case was argued principally by M. C. Setalvad, recently retired Attorney General of India, a man considered by many to be the country's most distinguished lawyer. He began by affirming that the courts, not the legislatures, had the task of interpreting the Constitution, and that the courts were as entitled to interpret authoritatively article 194 (3) as any other part. Since article 194 was but one of several hundred provisions in the Constitution, he stressed that it must be read within the context of a Constitution which guarantees individual rights and explicitly confers review powers and a writ jurisdiction on the courts. He argued that since India is not the United Kingdom, the totality of legislative privileges once claimed by the House of Commons from hostile lords and kings over the centuries could hardly be imported, *in toto,* into contemporary India. Conceding that English courts do treat a general warrant as conclusive, he called this a convention evolved from the period when the Parliament was the highest court of justice and when the House of Commons came to be regarded as a superior court of record. Since the Indian courts are specifically empowered to deal with claims made by citizens who allege violations of their freedoms, Setalvad concluded that when an application for *habeas corpus* is made, even a general warrant issued by a legislature cannot claim conclusiveness.

Seven weeks after the hearings were completed, the Supreme Court announced its opinion.[31] By a vote of six to one the Court rejected, or at any rate was understood by the legislators to have rejected, their major arguments. The Court held that whatever might be the system in the United Kingdom, India was a constitutional democracy, and the Constitution was ultimately interpreted exclusively by the Supreme Court. So article 194, and every other provision, means what the Court says it means. The Mother of Parliaments may be sovereign, but Indian legislatures must rid themselves of the delusion that they share the same status.

The majority held that Keshav Singh, who believed that his fundamental right to personal liberty was infringed by the Uttar Pradesh Legislative Assembly, was justified in petitioning the high court for a writ of *habeas corpus;* and that the judges, in entertaining the application, were most certainly not committing contempt of the legislature. With regard to the action taken by the assembly against the two judges, the majority was emphatic in pointing out that the Constitution declares unequivocally that no discussion—much less a contempt proceeding—can take place in any state legislature concerning the conduct of any judge in the discharge of his duties.

In reply to the arguments of Seervai, the majority agreed that when the House of Commons issues a general warrant in contempt cases, courts in the United Kingdom do not examine the reasons which led the House to take

---

[31] Announced on 30 September 1964 and cited as *Special Reference No. 1 of 1964, 1965 Supreme Court Reports* 413.

such action. But this was the situation, they said, because the House of Commons was once a judicial as well as a legislative body, hence the phrase "High Court of Parliament." Indian legislatures, on the other hand, had evolved under entirely different circumstances, and had never functioned as courts. Hence any claim that the Indian legislatures have powers, privileges and immunities identical to the House of Commons is absurd. Or, in the majority's words, "legal fiction can hardly introduce historical facts from one country to another."[32]

But perhaps the heart of the majority opinion was that the Indian Constitution elevated the Fundamental Rights to a special, judicially protected position, and that legislatures simply cannot claim powers which conflict with the rights of citizens. Here the Court reiterated with added emphasis a point it had made dozens of times since 1950: that Indians have a constitutional right to approach the judiciary whenever they believe one of their freedoms has been contravened. These protected freedoms, said the majority, take second place to nothing found elsewhere in the Constitution. Thus legislative privileges may be exercised only up to the point where they affect adversely the liberty of the individual. Legislatures may determine when their contempt has been committed, but general warrants issued in contempt cases will not be treated as conclusive by Indian courts, for to do so would be to dilute the Fundamental Rights.

Having said all this with almost papal firmness, the Court, for reasons not explained too clearly, then went on to limit the application of this judgment to instances of alleged contempt "committed by a citizen who is not a Member of the House outside the four walls of the House."[33] Keshav Singh had committed at least four distinct acts of alleged contempt: one, publishing the pamphlet calling Pandey a crook; two, writing a strongly worded letter to the Speaker after learning of his impending arrest; three, behaving irreverently in the assembly hall; and four, petitioning for a writ of *habeas corpus*. All but the third of these were committed outside the assembly. But it was obviously the third offense—his antics inside the legislative chamber—that precipitated his incarceration. In any event, the Supreme Court did not touch upon the matter of most concern to Keshav Singh: whether the legislature had acted legally, or had sufficient reason, to put him behind bars.

In addition, the opinion fell far short of providing an answer to the obviously central questions of what powers legislatures do have in contempt cases, and what the courts are supposed to do when a citizen jailed by legislators on a general warrant seeks a writ of *habeas corpus*. The majority clearly said that Indian courts would not consider general warrants as conclusive, but it left open the question of whether or not courts could determine if the legislature had good reason to jail a citizen.

What the majority seems to have implied—and one must read between the lines to piece together this implication—is that Indian legislatures need some

[32]*1965 Supreme Court Reports* 413, 491.
[33]Ibid., 413, 501.

kind of authority to protect themselves from obstruction and insult; that they may even need the power to impose jail sentences; but that when they seek to imprison someone they should issue only "speaking" warrants—warrants which spell out the reasons the legislature believes justify confinement. Since all parties to this dispute agreed that English courts have long enjoyed the authority to examine speaking warrants, presumably the Indian courts would have the same authority.

The majority concluded with the following gratuitous-sounding words of advice to the legislators:

> Wise Judges never forget that the best way to sustain the dignity and status
> of their office is to deserve respect from the public at large by the quality of their
> judgments, the fearlessness, fairness and objectivity of their approach, and by the
> restraint, dignity and decorum which they observe in their judicial conduct.
> We venture to think that what is true of the Judicature is equally true of
> the Legislatures.[34]

There was no ambiguity in the trenchant dissenting opinion of Justice A. K. Sarkar. Of article 194 (3) he said, "I cannot imagine more plain language than this."[35] In his view that provision clearly confers the privileges of the House of Commons on Indian legislators. Since English courts treat general warrants issued by the House of Commons as conclusive, Indian courts must do the same, and an Indian jailed for contempt has no right to approach the courts. But in this case neither the judges nor Singh and his attorney committed contempt on 19 March, he said, for none of these parties was informed by the legislature that Singh was jailed pursuant to a general warrant.

Nor was there anything ambiguous about the reactions of the legislators to the Supreme Court's opinion—not only in Lucknow but also in New Delhi and throughout the country. They were furious. A few hours after the announcement of the opinion, Parliament was in session and the matter was being discussed in a heated atmosphere. The Law Minister of India deplored the judgment, which he said "will have the effect of causing a deep erosion into the privileges as we have known them."[36] The Speaker of the Lower House of Parliament, Sardar Hukum Singh, said the Supreme Court had reduced legislatures to the status of inferior courts, and demanded an amendment to the Constitution which would serve to restore legislative privileges to their proper place—above the Fundamental Rights and beyond the scrutiny of the judiciary.[37] In Uttar Pradesh criticism of the opinion was equally strong, with many legislators taking the position that the opinion was not binding upon them. One of the few voices of moderation at the time was that of Prime Minister Shastri, who urged "the utmost caution in dealing with this delicate matter."[38]

The initial outburst of denunciations was followed by salvos of criticism

[34]Ibid.
[35]*1965 Supreme Court Reports* 413, 511.
[36]*Times of India* (New Delhi), 2 October 1964.
[37]Ibid.
[38]Ibid.

launched at various intervals over the next few months by disgruntled legislators.[39] The central government, however, seemed to have decided that the most appropriate course was to do nothing at all. This was evident in the Union Law Minister's statement on 28 November, nearly two months after the Supreme Court's opinion: "The Union Government does not intend to take any decision in the matter without proper and mature consideration."[40]

CONCLUSION

During the battle between judges and legislators, although Keshav Singh was back in Gorakhpur, he was only temporarily free, for in March the Lucknow Bench had merely released him on bail pending the final hearing. Virtually unnoticed, his *habeas corpus* petition was finally taken up by a two-judge Criminal Bench of the Allahabad High Court on 10 March 1965. Although the respondents included the Speaker, the chief minister, and the entire house, none of these personally appeared in court.

Singh's major contention was unchanged: that he was illegally detained because the legislative assembly had no power to jail those it finds guilty of its contempt. Yet this Allahabad Bench, with only passing references to the Supreme Court's opinion, dismissed Singh's petition and sent him back to jail to serve the remaining one day of his imprisonment. In effect, the high court judges endorsed Sarkar's dissenting opinion, for they held that if the House of Commons had the power to commit for contempt, the legislative assembly, by virtue of article 194 (3), enjoyed the same power. Finding that the House of Commons had such power, the court said judicial scrutiny must go no further, for "we cannot go into the correctness, propriety or legality of the commitment. The Legislative Assembly is the master of its own procedure and is the sole judge of the question whether its contempt has been committed or not."[41]

Of course, this was precisely the position the lawmakers had been arguing all along. The battle won, the legislators of Uttar Pradesh decided not to attempt to punish the judges, and were content with getting in the last word.

---

[39]Not all reactions to the Court's decision were hostile. Newspaper editorials applauded the decision, and lawyer's groups invariably praised the Court's wisdom. Perhaps the most significant vote of confidence came from an unusually odd assortment of prominent figures who participated in a symposium entitled "Privileges of Legislatures," arranged by the Bar Association of India, of which M. C. Setalvad happened to be president. Speakers at this gathering covered the political spectrum from left to right, including such individuals as Hiren Mookerjee, leader of the Communist Party in Parliament; V. K. Krishna Menon, erstwhile Defense Minister and nemesis of the United States; N. C. Chatterjee, leading independent member of Parliament; and P. N. Sapru, a prominent Congressman. Though their political differences were many, all shared the view that the majority opinion was a good one, and that the Court had done no more than reaffirm the liberties of Indian citizens. See further, "Symposium on the Privileges of Indian Legislatures, 1964," *Indian Advocate* IV (July 1965): 66–118.

[40]*Hindustan Times* (New Delhi), 29 November 1964.

[41]*Keshav Singh v. Speaker, Legislative Assembly, U.P. and Others*, in *All India Reporter* 1965 Allahabad 349, 355.

The latter is found in the report of the assembly's committee of privileges, announced in July of 1965. Though the committee reiterated that all the judges of the high court, as well as Keshav Singh and his attorney, were guilty of contempt of the House, the committee decided that

> in view of the importance of the harmonious functioning of the two important organs of the State, i.e., the Legislature and the Judiciary, and the recent judicial pronouncements, the Committee feels that the ends of justice would be met and the dignity of the House vindicated if the House express its displeasure.[42]

Thus ended the saga of Keshav Singh, and there the matter stands today. If the Supreme Court majority meant that general warrants would not be considered inviolable by courts, this was accepted neither by the legislators nor by the Allahabad High Court.

Perhaps the ambiguity of the Supreme Court's opinion was intentional. The Keshav Singh incident had united legislators throughout India as few other issues have ever succeeded in doing, and the Court may have decided that a stronger, unequivocal stand on behalf of individual freedom might have precipitated a more vehement attack on the judiciary than could be withstood. Moreover, the Supreme Court was obviously faced with a virtually impossible task: that of reconciling institutions, practices, and individual liberties which were patently irreconcilable. Even in more tranquil situations, with the collective wrath of India's legislators no longer hovering over the judges, it would be no simple matter to reconcile a judicially protected bill of rights with the exclusive power of legislatures to jail critics.

The Keshav Singh incident is neither a milestone in the evolution of Indian democracy, nor a millstone around its neck. Perhaps its main significance derives from a point too easily obscured by reports of the many problems India has experienced since independence—that real or apparent deviations from constitutional norms are less characteristic of the Indian political system than of most developing countries, and that constitutional law issues are discussed with fervor in tea rooms, public forums, and in the nation's press. These are most healthy signals in a country which lacks virtually all the preconditions usually considered essential if liberal democracy is to work successfully.

---

[42]Quoted in Chowdhuri, "Power of Committal," Part III, *Law Quarterly* III, no. 3 (September 1966): 191.

THEODORE L. BECKER*

3

IGINUHIT NG TADHANA

the decreed-by-fate case

Ernesto Maceda was a bright and hard-driving young man. He was an attorney and had been city councilor of Manila. However, in March of 1962, he held a high executive position with the largest motion picture company in the Philippines. At about this time a big moment arrived in Maceda's life: he was to be married. The festivities included a morning ceremony and an afternoon reception. Both were sumptuous affairs, especially the latter. After all, the bride's father happened to own that largest motion picture company. Thus, at the reception, celebrities abounded. Among them was a youngish, vigorous, and well-known senator, Ferdinand Marcos, then President of the Senate. But Marcos was more than just another invited guest. He was the groom's "ninong"— the sponsor, who is a combination of witness and godfather.

Still, all was not innocuous cocktail party chatter that day for Marcos and Maceda. Sometime during the post-nuptial partying they began to talk politics. In the course of their discussion, Maceda proposed a different kind of marriage: one of politics and motion pictures. As a Marcos intimate, Maceda knew of the senator's aspirations toward the presidency of the Philippines. Moreover, since Maceda had always been a political animal, and was now involved in the motion picture industry, it is not surprising that he would think of the political propaganda potential in a cinematic drama about the glamorous life of Marcos. Films about top political candidates were certainly not uncommon in Philippine political life. Nevertheless Marcos was unimpressed; the suggestion failed to move him.

*The author wishes to express his gratitude to the Faculty Research Committee of the University of Hawaii and to William Lebra of the Social Science Research Institute for his support of the necessary field research.

Two years later Marcos, still President of the Senate, began his drive toward the presidency by deserting one major party (the Liberal Party) and capturing the presidential nomination of the other (the Nationalist Party). This occurred in December 1964 and was quite a political tour de force. Shortly after nomination, Marcos approached Maceda and asked him to serve as a chief aide-de-camp in the campaign.[1] Maceda, quick to agree, was equally quick to revive his plan for a motion picture based on Marcos's life. Maceda plumped for a commercially attractive, dramatic presentation; Marcos's public relations advisors liked the general idea but argued that the movie had to be a documentary. This disagreement lasted for some time and, according to Maceda, "Marcos kept the project's possibility open only out of respect for our friendship."

As the campaign wore on—and on—and on, trouble began to loom ahead for Marcos. After a popularity peak in December, his private polls revealed a steady dimming of his luster. His opponent, President Diosdado Macapagal, seemed to be gaining strength. Though no president of the Philippines had ever been reelected, Macapagal's campaign tactics appeared to be collecting dividends. Meanwhile, Maceda had finally managed to divert some of the Marcos war chest into financing the early stages of the movie, which was to be called "Iginuhit ng Tadhana," or "Decreed by Fate." Maceda set up a "front" company to handle the filming and distribution; for good luck he named it 777 Film Productions. The basic idea of the movie was to glorify several stages of the challenger's life: Marcos the student; Marcos the war hero; Marcos the statesman. He was to be painted in vivid tones: Man of Destiny—Winner—*Paladin Extraordinaire*.

Nontheless, "Iginuhit" was in slow motion. There were numerous delays. Some were caused by other Marcos advisors who still resisted the idea of making the film; others were strictly accidental. Among the calamities, the star named to play young Marcos suffered a nervous breakdown, and the movie lagged months behind schedule. However, sometime in July, Marcos's attitude toward the production began to change, though it is difficult to pinpoint exactly what brought this about. Perhaps it was the fact that M. J. Gonzales, one of the Marcos top public relations men, stressed that Marcos was still an underdog. This was in large measure due to the increased tempo of Macapagal's campaign, which was increasingly throwing strong light on some of the allegedly shadier aspects of Marcos's past.

The Macapagal advertisements spoke of the various "documented sins of Marcos" which included landgrabbing, forgery, false war claims, and the Nalundasan Murder Case. The latter referred to the fact that Marcos had once been convicted of assassinating his father's chief political opponent, though the decision was later reversed by the Supreme Court on a question of proper evidence. To press this issue home, the Macapagal advertisements trumpeted the disclosure that Nalundasan's son still believed Marcos was the murderer.

---

[1] A typical presidential campaign in the Philippines is quite long, compared with its American counterpart. It lasts nearly a year, and to win the election, staffing and planning must start early.

It seems likely that this onslaught gave Marcos the impetus to put the completion of "Iginuhit" on a crash program. Since Macapagal's most telling attacks were of a personal nature, some medium was necessary to project the Marcos image in more flattering tones. A movie effectively showing him as an obedient son, dedicated patriot, and devoted husband could be a strong countermeasure.

Meanwhile, though the president's own pollsters showed his stock steadily rising since December, they also showed him still *trailing* Marcos by about four percentage points in mid-July. (Marcos led with forty-four percent of the predicted vote; Macapagal had forty, and a third party candidate accounted for the remainder.) At a meeting that same month in Malacanang (the presidential mansion), some of Macapagal's advisors rattled off a list of all that was wrong in his campaign. "Iginuhit" was mentioned, though only casually. It was not to become visible to the Macapagal forces until the following month.

By the third week of August, the primary raison d'être of 777 Film Productions ceased—"Iginuhit ng Tadhana" was ready for screening. Maceda, the proud father, was more than ever convinced that it would turn the tide irreversibly in Marcos's favor. As one columnist who subsequently reviewed it said:

> Louder than a jingle, more photogenic than a poster, the finished product—
> though it may not give Ingmar Bergman or Amalia Fuentes any trouble—is frankly
> aimed at the election polls and will probably collect many a fan at the
> November box office . . . Is Tadhana . . . really worth a tear? The answer is
> yes, in buckets.

Yet Marcos, according to Maceda, still entertained doubts about the movie's value. Undaunted, Maceda filed application with the Philippine Board of Censors for an exhibition permit, and word of this reached Malacanang. Macapagal heard, but did nothing.

At this point, the campaign situation was unclear to both candidates. Because each found indications that the election was losable, and neither was convinced of certain victory, both developed a willingness to make the kinds of delicate strategic choices they had avoided earlier in the campaign. Narrow margins sometimes nurture panic.

THE CENSORS' CENSURE

The Philippine Board of Censors is an arm of the national executive branch. It would be odd, therefore, if it were not heavily staffed by supporters of the chief executive. However friendly the individual members may have been with Macapagal in 1965, as a board, its jurisdiction and area of discretion are nonetheless limited. The board can refuse to issue a permit only if it finds a film to be "immoral," "indecent," "contrary to law and/or good customs," or "injurious to the prestige of the Republic of the Philippines or its people." Because there are so many movies for the board to screen, subcommittees do much of the actual viewing, and issue or deny permits. So "Iginuhit" was slated for a subcommittee.

José "Joe" Guevara, a popular columnist for Manila's biggest and most prestigious newspaper, the *Manila Times,* was the chairman of the Board of Censors. At that precise moment, however, he was out of town, in Taipei. Mrs. Rosalina Castro, the acting chairman, scheduled a showing of the movie before a subcommittee of the board for the evening of 24 August. A general rule limited attendance to the subcommittee membership plus a guest or two per member. Nonetheless, when Mrs. Castro arrived, Senator Marcos, his wife, and many of his campaign coterie were gathered for the viewing. Marcos had not seen "Iginuhit" before; supposedly he had requested that his party be admitted and an exception had been made. As Mrs. Castro said later, "After all, he *was* the President of the Senate, and it was a movie about *his* life."

The subcommittee, its guests, and the Marcos entourage all sat through the three-hour-plus Tagalog melodrama. Shortly thereafter, displaying an admirable objectivity in view of their probable political proclivities, the subcommittee found nothing objectionable or immoral about the film. However, there was some doubt as to the accuracy of the events it described. Nevertheless, according to the law, the permit was granted. Maceda was elated. Marcos was pleased. The movie began to run in the provinces and as Maceda had hoped, the peasantry was moved to tears. Word of this reaction was received back in Manila and relayed to Malacanang, to the ears of Macapagal, and a gloom settled over his campaign managers.

It is at this point that events and motivations become very obscure and difficult to piece together. A good guess seems to be that President Macapagal, contrary to some advice but pursuant to other, believed he should stop the exhibition of "Iginuhit." Work was already in progress on a movie concerning Macapagal's life, but this seemed too little, too late. Counsel suggesting a more direct approach against "Iginuhit" prevailed.

The incumbent's advisors probably reasoned that fewer votes would be lost by banning the movie than by allowing it to continue swaying voters in critical provinces. José Guevara estimated (in a personal interview with the author) that the Liberal Party's highest echelon feared they would lose 500,000 votes in rural areas due to "Iginuhit." Besides this, President Macapagal apparently was seriously disturbed by certain portions of a previously published book about Marcos's life entitled *For Every Tear a Victory.* Since many of the same points were made in the movie, he felt it should be banned because of similar distortions and biases. Furthermore, Macapagal was certain that Marcos, his book, and the movie were, to say the least, immoral. Thus, for political and moral reasons, wheels were set in motion against difficult odds, for the movie had already been approved by the Board of Censors.

Yet, there was precedent on the basis of which the Board of Censors could recall motion pictures for *en banc* (full board) viewing after a subcommittee had previously granted approval. This had been done on *several* occasions, each time following a public outcry. Consequently, a tsunami of telegrams, letters, and telephone calls inundated the Board of Censors. The message was clear and the tone was pious: the film was immoral, and should be banned.

Since the board was directly responsible to the president, additional pressures were applied to certain members. For example, two of Macapagal's key ministers did some rapid dialing to Chairman Guevara. First, he received a call from the Secretary of National Defense, Macario Peralta, inviting him to breakfast. Guevara declined. Next, it seems that the Secretary of Justice Salvador Marino telephoned; breakfast was again the topic. This time Guevara agreed and was told to be at Peralta's house. Once there he was informed that his friend (Macapagal) was in trouble. The unusually lengthy meal—some three hours long—ended with Guevara yielding to his host's request. He agreed to call for a showing before the full board. Subsequently a notice informed the producer of "Iginuhit" on 1 September 1965 that "it has been decided . . . to have another screening." This was scheduled *for the same evening* the note was sent. The reason for the rush was that the Manila opening was scheduled for the next day, as a press preview, in the plush suburb of Makati. It was to be an ultra-high society event.

At this point planners in the Marcos camp began to consider the possibility, even the *desirability,* of getting "Iginuhit" banned. The act of censorship itself could benefit their cause; further advantage might be gained from the political impact of a protracted and highly publicized legal action culminating in a court victory.

Maceda, however, later denied that his next move was motivated by a desire to force a test case; he showed up the evening of 1 September, in obedience to the notice, but without a print of "Iginuhit." Apologetic and diffident, he told the subcommittee members that there was no print available, that all were in the provinces. This was only technically true, for one could have been obtained without much difficulty. But no screening could be held without a copy.

Immediately thereafter a meeting of the board was convened in its offices in downtown Manila. About half the board was present, as well as two representatives from the administration; Chairman Guevara, however, was conspicuously absent. It should be mentioned that although Guevara was a Macapagal appointee, he was also a personal friend of Ferdinand Marcos. Indeed, he had been the ninong at Marcos's wedding—and therefore was even a prominent character in the movie.

Despite the low attendance and the absence of the chairman, the meeting went on. But what it lacked in numbers, it possessed in spirit. After vigorous debate, some members wanted the film censored outright; others questioned its legality. The result was a compromise of sorts. The board's resolution read:

Upon motion of Member Castro . . . the board resolved to suspend the public
exhibition of the picture entitled "Iginuhit ng Tadhana," for the reason that the
producers failed to submit their picture for preview *en banc* before the
public exhibition. Your strict compliance is hereby enjoined.

This lit the fuse. The explosion came the next day after a copy of the resolution was forwarded to 777 Film Productions. After receiving it, Maceda ingeniously persuaded the messenger to get lost for a time and to redeliver the resolution anew, immediately prior to the press preview at the fancy Rizal Theater at 2 P.M.

The press was at the Rizal in force. Waiting in the lobby were members of the Marcos reception party, all fashionably dressed. Reporters and political leaders were ushered to their seats to await the dimming of the lights and the raising of the curtain. At a few minutes past two o'clock, Maceda went up to the stage with the "just delivered" resolution in his hand. The crowd fell silent, and Maceda conveyed the "bad" news. A wave of indignation rolled through the crowd. The scene was set perfectly for Marcos himself, in response to the swelling din, to take the stage and announce: "I know you are aware the administration made a mistake. Mistakes of this nature should be corrected on November 9."

Earlier that very morning, Guevara had announced his resignation as chairman of the Board of Censors—but it was too late to hit the morning papers. The evening papers in Manila, however, pounced on the story, and the press began what became a unanimous and steady tirade against Macapagal for what many believed was incredibly heavy-handed action. "A dark lettered day in censors' history" cried one prominent columnist; "a valiant effort at one-upmanship that blew up like a loaded cigar," said another. "Like Hitler" one politico was quoted as saying; "tyrannical," another said. It was quite possible at that moment to see this turn of events as a fatal blow to Macapagal.

Not surprisingly, then, a gala party was held in the elegant Sulo Restaurant on the evening of the second of September, quite near the Rizal Theater, scene of that afternoon's political spectacle. "We have won," Marcos was heard to say to Guevara, and he had cause to be sanguine.

That evening another meeting took place between various Marcos advisors; the legal strategy was being mapped out. It had become clear that legal action held great promise for the Marcos forces and that there was little to lose in bringing suit. Outright defiance of the board's orders might give further substance to Macapagal's campaign strategy of portraying Marcos as a ruthless man, a man not averse to defying the law. To obey the injunction not to show the film anymore would be to lose the highly beneficial propaganda effects that had become apparent during the exhibitions in the provinces. Thus, attacking the injunction in court was the most inviting tactic.

A court victory would embarrass, perhaps even humiliate, Macapagal. Risks for Marcos were almost nonexistent. Even if the Supreme Court decided in favor of the board, there were circumstances which could still be used to Marcos's advantage.

THE BRAMBLE BUSH

Although the laws of the Philippines are a potpourri of ingredients from many cultures over many centuries, the present judicial system, like the country's political system, is fundamentally American in character. This is not to say that actual practices within the legal system itself do not vary in many significant ways from those within the American system. They do. It is simply to say that the formal prescriptive arrangements within which the participants must operate are extremely similar to American forms originally introduced during the American colonial period from 1899 to 1946.

First of all, there are three levels to the judicial system. These are roughly equivalent to the American: a lower, original jurisdiction trial court (The Court of First Instance); an intermediate appellate court (The Court of Appeals); and finally, a highest court of last resort (The Supreme Court). The staffing is much the same, too, although the Supreme Court of the Philippines consists of ten associate justices and a Chief Justice. Each justice is appointed by the president and must be confirmed by the Senate. The term of office is virtually permanent until the age of seventy, when retirement becomes mandatory. Furthermore, the Supreme Court's procedures are strikingly similar to those of its American counterpart, from the conduct of the justices and lawyers during oral argument to the conduct of discussion in the closed deliberations among the justices following argument. There is one difference between Philippine and American judicial rules, however, which has some significance in the "Iginuhit" case.

According to the Philippine Constitution, a majority of the entire court (six votes) is necessary to resolve constitutional issues. On the other hand, there is a similarity between the judicial processes of the Philippines and the United States that played, perhaps, a critical role in this case. This was the extreme independence of the Supreme Court from *direct* executive or legislative attempts to influence its decisions. In fact, it could be said that the Philippine Supreme Court displays even more independence than its American prototype.

If independence of a supreme court is measured by the number of times it decides in opposition to a chief executive upon important political matters, then the Philippine Supreme Court has independence and it has that quality in abundance. During Macapagal's tenure of office, the Court thwarted presidential desires on several extremely important political issues. For example, there was the case of *Gonzales* v. *Hechanova* (1963).

Early in his term, President Macapagal ordered the importation of rice for the alleged purpose of feeding the army. However, the rice was released to an executive agency, the Rice and Corn Administration (RCA), and eventually was sold to the public at low prices. Legal exception was taken to this procedure and eventually the Supreme Court rejected the Macapagal maneuver. In effect, the Court said that the government was subsidizing the people and that this was beyond the scope of its legitimate power.

Another instance of judicial independence was the case of *Garcia* v. *Executive Secretary* (1962), in which Macapagal tried to remove Garcia, an appointee of his predecessor. Macapagal's choice for the National Science Development Board was a man named Salcedo, whom he appointed after firing Garcia. The Court reversed this action as well. As a legal precedent, this case extended the provisions of the Civil Service Act to presidential appointees as well as to career civil servants.

In addition to the independence of the Court in general, and specifically vis-à-vis Macapagal, another factor proved to be of importance in the "Iginuhit" episode. The Chief Justice at the time was Cesar Bengzon, and the "Bengzon Court" was said to be a "civil liberties" tribunal. At least this was widely believed in legal circles, and it is likely to have played some role in the thinking of Marcos's legal advisors. As one prominent legal writer stated in a nationally circulated magazine, Chief Justice Bengzon's career was characterized by his "deep concern" in matters of civil liberties.

Finally, since the Philippine Supreme Court applies American precedents, the law in this case was clear enough. Movies would undoubtedly be brought within the protection of "freedom of speech" by the Court *if* the Court concluded there was administrative intent to interfere with the free expression of this political medium ("Iginuhit").

At the same time, though the strictly legal aspects of the case looked favorable for Marcos, there were some extralegal conditions that augured well for the Macapagal position. First, an unfilled vacancy on the Court at the time left ten justices available to decide the case. Second, three of the justices were abroad; this left seven to hear the case. Third, of the seven remaining justices, three were appointed by President Macapagal himself. Fourth, as was noted before, six justices were needed to affirm the unconstitutionality of any executive action. And finally, many people believed that the justices of a court— even the Supreme Court—would simply vote the party line. Thus, the use of the courts was not a sure thing for Marcos either.

Naturally, the outcome of the legal contest was of concern to the Macapagal camp. On one occasion, a cabinet member telephoned one of the Macapagal appointees on the Supreme Court to ask what the justice thought the other justices would do should the suit reach the Court. The justice replied that he believed the Court would strike down the ban. Meanwhile, the Marcos legal contingent, headed by Claudio Teehankee, Juan Ponce Enrile, José Barredo, and Maceda, developed the first phase of their legal attack. They decided to seek an injunction against the board. The defense of the board was undertaken by no less than the Solicitor-General of the Philippines himself, Arturo Alafriz.[2]

The government's major defense was to dispute the narrow construction of the board's jurisdiction as urged by the Marcos contingent. A subsidiary argument was that because 777 Film Productions had accepted a permit, and because the permit, *on its face,* set forth the condition that the picture could be recalled for another screening, 777 should be estopped from challenging that action. For at the foot of the "Permit Certificate" was the following announcement: "NOTE: This permit may be suspended or revoked any time without prior notice by the board." A third point made by the defense was that 777 had not exhausted its administrative remedy. In other words, according to statute, any appeal from a board ruling first had to be made to the appellate committee composed of the undersecretaries of defense, education,

---

[2]The Solicitor-General is the equivalent of the United States Attorney General. The United States Solicitor General is the second-ranking legal official in the national executive branch. In the Philippines, the Solicitor-General is the first-ranked.

and justice. The secretary of defense, it is well to recall, was Peralta and the secretary of justice was Marino—already familiar names in this case.

The hearing was scheduled for Monday morning at eight o'clock, 6 September. The *Manila Times* front page headline announced in bold print: "Marcos Movie in Court Today." And the legal drama moved from rehearsal to the stage. Ernesto Soriano, the presiding judge, listened intently to the argument on both sides. The debate was understandably heated, and a brilliant light of publicity was cast on the principal actors. Nonetheless, the proceeding was short, in keeping with the rather frenzied pace of events. Judge Soriano issued the following order almost immediately following the case summaries:

> Considering the prayer of petitioner that pending hearing on the merits, this Court issues a writ of preliminary injunction restraining, enjoining and/or prohibiting respondent board including its agents, representatives and all persons acting for and in its behalf, from suspending and/or interfering from the public exhibition of the said "Iginuhit ng Tadhana" motion picture film and from enforcing their Resolution No. 28–65—at the hearing of which counsel for both parties adduced extensive oral arguments and some documentary evidence—and finding from said arguments and evidence that the continuance of the acts complained of would work injustice on the petitioner, the said writ of preliminary injunction is hereby granted . . .

Thus the first round ended in decisive victory for Marcos, both in court and outside of court. Manila newspapers, radio, and television were glutted with news of the event, for some court cases in the Philippines, as in other parts of the world, function like all dramas. They are mass entertainment, and they impose order on seemingly absurd events. At any rate, the government had no recourse but to appeal. The setback had already cost the loss of the censorship, as well as another defeat in court for Macapagal.

The question then became: appeal to whom? The Supreme Court was already perceived as hostile. After all, one justice had previously told a Macapagal advisor that the Court would most probably react unfavorably to the board's action on "Iginuhit." Besides, another Macapagal appointee to the Court had remarked at a private party to some members of the Macapagal inner circle that they had made a terrible political blunder. He implied strongly that there was nothing he could do to extricate them. Only the Court of Appeals remained in the path of certain judicially inflicted defeat. Fortunately, there seemed to be an available contention that the Court of Appeals had jurisdiction to hear the appeal.

In the Philippines, the Court of Appeals can entertain appeals only when there is a question of fact and law. It has no jurisdiction when the question is of law alone. Still, as in American jurisprudence, what is a question of law and what is a question of fact are not easily answered. The line of demarcation between questions of law and fact is hardly precise, for all court decisions are at least partially based on each court's view of the facts. Nevertheless, after lengthy discussion, the three justices of the Court of Appeals unanimously decided to hear the case on its merits. Thus the Macapagal legal holding action had produced at least some payoff—even if nothing more than a delay of the inevitable. Of course, as in the United States, all the "legal" questions were argued again before the tribunal: namely, estoppel, exhaustion of remedy, and the like. But the real questions involved were simply and purely: did the board actually abuse its discretion in this case? And was the abuse of such a degree and character that an immediate judicial remedy was necessary?

It so happened that the three judges on this panel disagreed with their lower court colleague, Justice Soriano, and reversed his decision, thereby enjoining him from enjoining the board from enjoining the distributors. In the interim, more than a week had elapsed. The Marcos people had been dealt their initial defeat in the courts, but the Supreme Court was still the ultimate arena. There was absolutely nothing for Marcos to lose in resorting to it. Moreover, since there was still substantial feeling in Marcos circles that the film itself packed a strong political wallop, appeal had to be made in haste, for the middle of September was upon them. The trial of the polls was less than two months distant. Final trial by legal ordeal had to be at once.

And so it was. The Supreme Court rapidly certified, heard, and decided the appeal in favor of the Marcos position. With seven justices sitting, the vote was unanimous. 777 had a seven-to-nothing decision. The case was over, and another Supreme Court defeat had been pinned on Macapagal.

20-20 RETROSPECT

Depth interviews conducted by the author in early 1967 with the seven members of the Philippine Supreme Court who participated in this case revealed that each justice had followed the presidential campaign with deep interest. There are, of course, vast differences in their views concerning the degree to which a judge should be isolated from problems his court ultimately might have to resolve. Still, it was impossible for any man concerned about the political life of his nation to remain oblivious to the censorship of "Iginuhit." Only a hermit could have evaded *some* exposure to the celebrated movie ban; moreover, no one could have avoided the political implications in this case made clear by almost every reporter, radio newsman, and political analyst in the Manila area. The seven justices admitted that, indeed, they had followed the progress of the "facts" before these "facts"—that is, the two legal versions of them—appeared before them in legal briefs. Even justices of a supreme court are not, after all is said and done, political celibates. They are, for better or for worse, alert to the world about them. In this case, it seems fair to say that certain predispositions had been formed concerning certain key facts of the case.

For example, it became quite clear during the interviews that each judge believed, even before the case reached him, that the board was motivated primarily by political considerations. This is not to say that the Court knew about, or even cared about, the "rumors" that Macapagal's top advisors had directly tried to influence the board. Indeed, they probably did not. But the situation still seemed to speak for itself. It would not be unfair to suggest that a foundation had been laid, at the outset, for the Court's taking *"judicial notice"* of the fact that political interest was the principal motivation of the board. If this was true it helps to account for various actions of the Court—including its final decision.

In the first place, the case was certified, heard, and decided in an extremely short period of time. The Court of Appeals handed down its decision on 14 September, and the Supreme Court handed down its decision only *four* days later. In order for this to happen, several rules were relaxed—and though this was not exactly unprecedented, the rapidity of the relaxation was rather unusual. Each judge rationalized the haste with which the case was pushed through by explaining that the election was not too far off and that a failure to hear the case immediately would put it in danger of becoming moot.

It was later acknowledged that each justice believed (on the basis of what he had heard or what he believed about Philippine politics in general) that the movie *itself* would tend to influence citizens to vote for Marcos. It is a short step from this belief to the one about the "political significance" of the case. Once "political significance" is believed to exist, there is hardly any gap between that belief and the one about political interest and motivation on the part of the board. Thus, it is pure legalism to couch the rationale for quick disposition in terms of "mootness," and pure euphemism to couch it in terms of the proximity of elections. In other words, the Court believed Marcos's statement of the facts even before they heard Marcos's lawyers, and they decided the case accordingly.

Another reason the Court gave for its speed in coming to decision was the fact that Chief Justice Bengzon was scheduled to leave the country very shortly, and the Court was already undermanned. The justices produced this rationale quickly when quizzed about the speedup of the hearing. However, one cannot help but wonder why the Chief Justice's trip could not have been cancelled pending the hearing of such an important case. Again, a rationale seems to be more of a rationalization. And again, upon piercing the veil of reason, the acceleration of procedures is a strong indication that the decision was largely resolved in the individual minds of the several justices of the Court before it was heard. Furthermore, it is likely that each justice suspected his colleagues held opinions on this case similar to his own.

Such an unspoken consensus would account for another slight alteration of Court rules that occurred—the "holding" of an informal "conference" in the anteroom to the courtroom before the actual argument was to begin. At this "meeting" each judge noted that in his view there was "no jurisdiction" for the Court of Appeals to hear the case. Thus the conclusion was foregone, as "no jurisdiction" was the major point of contention of the Marcos case. Indeed, to accede to this view—that there was no question of fact for the Court of Appeals to decide—each Justice had to believe firmly that he already knew what the facts were, what had *really* happened. Each had to assume in advance the political motivations of the board. Such a conclusion is inevitable, since there were actually *many* disputed "facts" that were germane to the case itself. For example:

> I. Since there was sufficient precedent for the board to recall movies to which it had already granted permits, upon recognizing the existence of a substantial public protest, various questions of facts were raised; for example, was all of this protest
>   A. of the same kind?
>   B. of the same degree?
>   C. sincere?
> II. If the Board did have legal ground to recall the movie,
>   A. did it operate in good faith in recalling it as it did?
>   B. did 777 act in good faith in refusing to bring a print to the scheduled reshowing?

Of course, all of these factual issues rest upon certain legal (as opposed to factual) questions. First, does the granting of authority (by the legislature) to issue permits imply a grant of authority to recall them at all? Second, if it does not do so in general, does it authorize recall for reconsideration once a public protest has been lodged against a particular film? The crucial issue here is that although the Supreme Court may have believed the board had no authority to recall permits, this point had not been decided as a matter of law by any past Supreme Court decision. It would seem that this issue had to be settled by the Court before it could determine that there was no question of fact to be heard at the Court of Appeals level. Yet the Supreme Court did not do this; all it did was to say that there was no question of fact. It did not consider the very question of law that was a prerequisite for any consideration of facts. The Court only rendered what is known as a "Minute Resolution," which is simply a decision ("There was no question of fact") unsupported by legal reasoning.

Apparently, the Court saw a political injustice being perpetrated which was, in its view, clearly unconstitutional. For various reasons the justices felt they should and could remedy the situation. They sensed their role to provide a bastion for individual rights against arbitrary governmental action, and this case triggered a very strong mechanism in them. When such intensely held views are involved, scholars of modern jurisprudence and social science suggest that procedures and rules (even laws) will be circumvented, particularly if they are somewhat vague or flexible.[3] This case demonstrates clearly that there can be contradictory or confusing component parts to the complex role structure of a supreme court justice. The roles of supreme court justice and politically concerned citizen are not easily reconciled.

Speculation over the justices' motives becomes all the more intriguing when it is also recognized that several members of the Court were not only staunch adherents to the Liberal Party, but personal friends of Macapagal's as well. For

---

[3]See, among many others, Karl Llewellyn, *The Common Law Tradition* (Boston: Little, Brown, 1961).

instance, before his appointment to the Court, Justice Zaldivar had been executive secretary to President Macapagal. Additionally, had Zaldivar and Justice José Bengzon (a cousin of the Chief Justice and a Macapagal appointee) refrained from voting because of "conflict of interest" grounds, the Court would have lacked the minimum number of members to rule on a constitutional issue, and the Court of Appeals decision would have been affirmed automatically. Yet Zaldivar and Bengzon participated in the case. They not only heard the case but also decided against clear Macapagal interests. Their reasons are not easily identified. However, institutional pressures and roles can and do constrain strong individual political proclivities of a judge (serving on a court of last resort) in a democratic-judicial review system. In the words of one of the Philippine justices a year and a half later:

> I would have lost the respect of my friends and colleagues. They know I was a Macapagal man. It would appear I was trying to frustrate the work of the Court. It was a test of how we would act subsequently. To have held for Macapagal would have made us appear ridiculous.

To be fair to the skeptics, it should also be noted that both Justice Zaldivar and Justice Bengzon were, at the time, recent appointees who were both still unconfirmed by the Senate. It could be argued, then, that political expediency, rather than a strongly held concept of the importance of judicial role, was the key to their action. Marcos, who undoubtedly remembered the "Iginuhit" decision, ultimately became the president whose appointment led to their confirmation.

IGINUHIT'S IMPACT

When "Iginuhit ng Tadhana" is discussed by inside-dopesters in the Philippines it is commonplace to remark that "it cost Macapagal the election." Yet, though many agree that the "Iginuhit" incident had an impact, there is wide disagreement about which aspect of it was most critical. A few believe the movie itself was a very influential factor in the election. Many contend that the censorship furor was the decisive factor; some believe the Supreme Court ruling itself contributed heavily to Macapagal's defeat. Of course, there are those who believe it was a combination of the three that did Macapagal in.

As mentioned before, there is some impressionistic evidence that the movie did have a pro-Marcos effect on the peasantry, and that this was responsible for some of the panic in August at Malacanang. However, only Maceda, of the major participants who were interviewed, believed that the movie itself—uncensored—would have been crucial in the election. The others felt that, lacking the board's ban and the concomitant Supreme Court decision, "Iginuhit" would not have had nearly the vote-getting power that it gained, and that it probably would not have become decisive.

Several observers agreed that the entire "Iginuhit" caper had substantial, if not critical, impact, but there was also wide variation in the reasons given to support this view. The theory most frequently advanced concerns a reversal in the public images of both Macapagal and Marcos.

In the first place, up to the time of censorship, Marcos had a reputation for being cunning and ruthless. In contrast Macapagal, a Ph.D. in economics, was regarded as a scholarly and well-intentioned public servant. However, after the banning and the publicity which swirled about the trials, a switch in images seems to have occurred. Marcos was seen as the persecuted victim, while Macapagal had become an oppressor in the eyes of the public.

The Macapagal image was dealt a few other telling blows. On the one hand, Macapagal remained quite silent as the censorship hearings and subsequent litigation progressed. In the face of the widespread view that the board was acting under his orders, or under those of his close subordinates, his reluctance to speak was interpreted widely as a desire to avoid responsibilities. These evasions developed into a credibility gap. In addition, the defeat in Court helped to reinforce the view that President Macapagal was an inefficient administrator. Efficient administrators seldom make such blatant blunders, and when they do, they disguise them with greater aplomb than Macapagal displayed during this incident.

In addition to the damage done to the Macapagal image, the Supreme Court decision itself gave the film two other selling points. First, and most obviously, the picture became a sensation—everyone wanted to see it. No longer simply a motion picture, it had become an event. Even several of the Supreme Court justices who said they would not have seen it otherwise, fell victim to their curiosity. In the second place, the decision may well have ratified the content of the film. Signs were seen in some sections of the country billing "Iginuhit" as "The Movie the Supreme Court has Ordered Shown to You!" It is not difficult to grasp why so many Filipinos directly or indirectly involved in politics believe this extravaganza played a vital part in the presidential election of 1965.

Still, despite such overwhelming accord among most observers, there is some evidence that this case (the movie, the censorship, and the trials) was not of much consequence at all. As was noted previously, Macapagal had been told privately in July by some of his pollsters that he was trailing Marcos by four to six percent of the predicted vote. Of course, the electoral polling process in the Philippines in 1965 was a relatively young business, not as highly developed as it is in the United States. Yet there was a very high level of competence among the most sophisticated Philippine pollsters. Thus, in midsummer (long before the ban), Macapagal's chief pollster estimated that the president would lose the election within a few percentage points. Private charts showed a brief surge in Macapagal strength in mid-October, when he took a brief lead. This upswing occurred after the final decision in "Iginuhit" and could hardly be attributed to his defeat by the Court.

It is possible, then, that all the members of the Supreme Court, the many prominent attorneys, newspapermen, and governmental and academic officials who were interviewed in 1967 could have been wrong about the extent of impact. For there was and is a tremendous gap in the Philippines between the establishment and the masses. The establishment deals in civics class types of abstractions and theories, rather than coming to grips with the grim realities of a political system that seems to be, in the main, unresponsive to serious social and economic demands. It fits neatly packaged, classical theories about democratic government to believe that a substantial number of voters would be affected by the "Iginuhit" ban and the succession of trials. But the Macapagal surge in October indicates that it probably did not happen that way. In other words, it is highly dubious that the "Iginuhit" controversy influenced the election at all. But this does not mean that "Iginuhit" had *no* effect.

Most significantly, the case reaffirmed the faith of those supporters of the established order who were committed to the belief that independent courts are essential to a viable political system. These persons could take pride in their appellate court system, which is as independent as a judiciary can be, and possibly surpasses the degree of independence exercised by comparable American courts. The "Iginuhit" decision was not only an indicator of that independence, but also may have contributed to the furtherance of judicial independence by demonstrating such an effective use of it. Exercise builds muscle.

Another positive result that may yet flow from the "Iginuhit" case is the future impact of the law implied in the decision—the political precedent that "Iginuhit" established. There is no question that this was a landmark decision in favor of freedom of political expression against an incumbent administration, despite the legal facade that the Court hid behind. That such a highly political, anti-administration decision was rendered in what is often considered "an underdeveloped nation" has more than limited significance. As one Philippine political scientist put it:

> From the strengthened brew of politics that was the consequence of the Iginuhit case can emerge the ultimate realization of the ideas of liberty, democracy and justice promised in the Philippine Constitution. Never underestimate the consequences of the law, even if for the moment it merely favors the establishment. Remember the Magna Carta of 1215? It favored and helped only the barons and other nobility of England when it was promulgated. But you know it later helped in the democratization of England, not only in a political sense, but also in a socioeconomic sense.

It is surely true that a legitimated statement of individual rights may have effects reaching far beyond those visible at one point in time. This could be the case with "Iginuhit," for the Philippines may yet become the most successful practicing democracy in Asia. Although this case probably had much less influence on the choice of the president in 1965 than many still believe, it speaks well for the growth of politics in the Philippines. The role of an independent judiciary in the politics of the Philippines will certainly not solve the major economic and social problems of that society—but it is a vivid demonstration that one Asian society is giving an *open* political system a fair try at it.

WILLIAM G. FLEMING

4

THE TRIALS OF CHIEF ENAHORO

courts and politics in great britain and nigeria

In the late evening of 19 September 1962 a large WK 1212 sports car stopped before the Idiroko frontier post on Nigeria's border with Dahomey. The occupants, not ordinary men, were not on ordinary business. One was Dr. Chike Obi, the leader of a small political party; the other was Chief Anthony Enahoro, deputy leader of the Action Group, the official Nigerian opposition party.

Enahoro had just that afternoon taken final leave of his leader, Chief Obafemi Awolowo, who was under house arrest in Lagos. The Action Group had been under heavy attack from the government for nearly six months, and Tony Enahoro had agreed to go to London to mount a campaign for international support. He had asked his old friend Dr. Obi to accompany him to the border and to return later with his driver to Lagos.

It must have been with some trepidation that Enahoro handed the immigration officer his passport. His mission was vital for the continued existence of his party; he himself had been released from restriction only since the middle of July. There was no telling what his political enemies—the current Nigerian administration—might do. In the office, as he filled out his travel documents, he became alarmed by suspicious-sounding conversation between various officials.

Quickly he left the building and walked to the Idiroko marketplace a short distance away. A general tumult followed soon afterward, with much shouting and police cars rushing about. Enahoro disappeared into the market crowd; as though he were an innocent bystander, he watched the frantic activity, knowing full well that he was the cause of all the commotion. Later that evening, avoiding patrols, he walked across the border to Dahomey and freedom.

Chief Enahoro made his way from Dahomey through Togo and Ghana and finally to Ireland. Intending to go to London to press forward with his mission, he learned that Nigerian authorities might be after him. Through a friend, he contacted a firm of solicitors, Slaughter and May, who made inquiries at the British Home Office. The friend was assured by a senior civil servant on several occasions that it would be safe for the chief to travel to the United Kingdom on papers other than a passport—Enahoro had lost his at Idiroko. The official emphasized the British tradition of political asylum.

These assurances notwithstanding, on 25 November 1962, two days after the deputy leader of the Action Group entered London and a matter of hours before a scheduled interview at the Home Office, he was arrested by detectives from Scotland Yard and charged under the Fugitive Offenders Act of 1881. A warrant had been issued by a London magistrate to give effect to the Nigerian government's application for extradition.[1]

The warrant which had been issued in Lagos the morning of the same day of his arrest in London charged Enahoro with treasonable felony, conspiracy to commit treason, and contravention of the firearms act. The affidavits of the Nigerian government were not immediately available, so the hearing was rescheduled for the twelfth of December by a magistrate in the Bow Street Court.

In the subsequent hearing depositions were made against Enahoro by four witnesses, two of whom were under detention in Lagos awaiting trial. The magistrate listened to a defense argument by the renowned barrister, Dingle Foot, an outstanding figure of the legal elite as well as a Labour member of Parliament. Foot held that there was no case for a strong presumption of guilt, that the deponents were being held in custody by the Nigerian government in order to intimidate them, and that the extradition request was all part of a process of general political persecution. The judge may have been surprised to have such an impressive representative of a political family plead in his court, but he found in favor of the government, and signed the extradition order.

By this time, however, political forces in Britain were already on the move. Newspapers headlined the story; various members of both the Labour and Conservative parties began showing interest in Enahoro's cause. In this way the chief found himself accomplishing the very mission that had brought him to London—but by a means neither of his choosing nor to his liking.[2]

Enahoro's predicament and its denouement offer an opportunity to compare the workings of courts in politics in two separate countries—Great Britain and Nigeria. By focusing on the political trials of Enahoro, one may investigate the functioning of the judiciary and its interplay with politicians in a long established and "developed" political system, and in a newly independent and "modernizing" system.

Since Nigeria, and particularly its legal-judicial framework, are the work of

[1]Anthony Enahoro, *Fugitive Offender: An Autobiography* (London: Cassell & Co., 1965), pp. 202–5.
[2]See the *Times* (London), 27 November 1962.

British imperialism, both systems share many common features in procedure and law that may be profitably compared and contrasted. Both are adversary systems based on the common law of England—although at the local level in Nigeria some attempt is made to apply African law and custom. Most Nigerian lawyers, particularly in the early 1960s, were trained in the United Kingdom. At that time, judicial robes, legal rhetoric, and court practices were the same for both countries.

However, there were also some important differences. Whereas Britain is an old stable polity, its judicial system a long-trusted and prestigious part of its gradual political evolution, Nigeria was created almost within the last generation—its judicial system, as many other parts of its polity, imposed from outside. Within Nigeria there was little widespread national loyalty, and few established norms of political behavior. An examination of its historical and political background will reveal the kinds of internal battles and ethnic divisions that could quite easily lead to a situation where the leaders of a major political party could be tried for treason.

THE HISTORICAL SETTING

The Federal Republic of Nigeria is the largest country in Africa. Its boundaries encompass some fifty-five million people—about fifteen percent of the continent's total population. The tragic civil war which ravaged the country for two-and-a-half years is but one bloody example of the tribal cleavages dividing the country.

In addition to the three main tribal groups—Hausa-Fulani in the north, Yoruba in the west, and Ibo in the east—there are 250 distinct languages in the country. The Hausa-Fulani are, for the most part, Muslim, and are organized in traditional states with emirs as kings. The urbanized Yoruba have a common language but are separated into many competing chiefdoms. The Ibo, a staunchly individualistic and achievement-oriented people, disperse their authority through various family and village leaders. The British ruled the traditional groups with varying degrees of success and with different consequences for each tribe. For example, while the power of the traditional northern emirs was often solidified by British administrative practices, the Ibo were quick to modernize themselves and to accept Western religious, educational, and business values.

By the time Nigeria received independence from Britain in 1960 only a slight change in the beliefs and attitudes of the people had occurred. Even the newly educated elite tended to identify with their traditional communal origins. Nigeria was, and is, a state without a concept of nationality; or rather, a state containing many small nations competing with each other within its boundaries. In the early 1960s political consensus was minimal. The potential for conflict subsequently became actualized in the terrible internecine war which very nearly decimated the Ibos (the former Biafrans).

British colonialism bequeathed to Nigeria all the formal apparatus of a modern state—a constitution, parliaments, judges, premiers, symbols. But there was little national loyalty or support for these throughout the whole country. A federal system, agreed to in principle in 1954, divided the state into three main regions, the borders of which corresponded to the main tribal cleavages. Each of the regions had a governor, a legislature, a cabinet, and a dominant political party. There was also a federal territory, similar to the District of Columbia, which surrounded the capital at Lagos.

The central federal government was a bicameral parliamentary system based on the British pattern. Even though Nigeria was constitutionally and politically independent from the United Kingdom, it still recognized Queen Elizabeth II as sovereign; the titular head of state was a governor-general. (Eventually Nigeria became a republic within the Commonwealth of Nations with an elected president as head of state.) During the period of this account, real political power was in the hands of the prime minister and his cabinet, who were chosen from the majority in the lower house of Parliament. This body, the House of Representatives, had 312 members popularly elected from single-member constituencies throughout the federation. This meant that the heavily populated Hausa-Fulani Northern Region was allotted over 160 seats. There was also a virtually powerless Senate.

The central government had exclusive control over such matters as foreign affairs, defense, and customs, but it shared power with the regions on questions of education, prisons, and economic development. There were also certain subjects reserved exclusively for the regions—among which were local government, traditional courts, agriculture, and land tenure.

Although the constitution provided for a dual system of courts, only a Supreme Court was in fact established by Parliament. In addition to original jurisdiction, appeals lay to this body from the Lagos and regional courts. Judges of all systems, except for the special Muslim courts in the North, were appointed for good behavior on the advice of an independent judicial service commission. This helped to guarantee the independence of the judiciary. Unfortunately the commission was abolished shortly before the Enahoro trials began.

Political leadership in Nigeria was divided among three competing parties, each of which drew almost exclusive support from the dominant tribe in each of the three regions. In the East the National Council of Nigeria and the Cameroons (later the National Council of Nigerian Citizens), led by Dr. Nnamdi Azikiwe, was one of the first radical and anti-regional parties in the country. The NCNC came to be identified with the articulation of Ibo interests. However, Azikiwe, who is often recognized as the father of Nigerian nationalism, resigned from politics to become the first governor-general and later president of the country.

Under the leadership of Chief Obafemi Awolowo, a party representing Yoruba interests was organized in the Western Region. This party, the Action Group, advocated communal development and regional autonomy. Later its leadership also espoused Fabian socialism and championed the interests of cultural minorities in other regions.

The conservative and backward areas of the Hausa-Fulani emirates were slow to develop modern nationalist sentiments. Eventually the traditionalistic leadership in the Northern Region converted a group known as the Northern People's Congress into a full-fledged political party. The NPC was dominated by conservative leaders closely tied to the customary authority of the emirs. Because it controlled the most populous region of the federation it played an important part in forming the first coalition government after independence; its leader, Sir Abubakar Tafawa Balewa, became the first prime minister.

This complicated federal system bequeathed to Nigeria by Britain was one which obviously demanded consummate ability and good will to operate. However, there is little doubt that the rules of the political game were not agreed upon by the elites, nor did the new institutions gain popular support. What was on paper was not in the hearts and minds of the people.[3]

THE POLITICAL BACKGROUND

In the two years from independence until the beginning of the trials of the leaders of the Action Group, the politics of Nigeria were characterized by increasing upheaval and conflict. This is not unusual in the development of any new nation. Indeed, the early history of the United States, with its Whisky Rebellion, alien and sedition acts, and the alleged treason and trial of Aaron Burr (a former vice-president), indicates a similar pattern.

The Nigerian federal regime was constructed by the British primarily as a compromise agreement among the elites of the three major parties, and the first federal administration formed under colonial rule was made up of the leaders of the NCNC, the AG and the NPC. However, during the 1959 elections immediately preceding independence, the Action Group, promoting Chief Awolowo's ideas of communal autonomy, had campaigned for new regions to be cut out of both the East and the North. Its demands for new boundaries which would have transferred some half million Yorubas from the Northern to the Western Region particularly irked the NPC leadership. The AG's activities in all regions during the campaign forced the aristocratic NPC leaders to get out and mingle with the masses. The Sarduna of Sokoto is reported to have said that he would never forgive Awolowo for this.

In the election, with 300 seats at stake, the NPC won 134, the NCNC and allies took 89, and the AG 73. Both the latter parties made impressive gains in regions other than their own. However, the general enmity that had developed, particularly between the Action Group and the Northern People's Congress, led to the formation of an NCNC-NPC coalition designed to lead the country to independence in 1960. Azikiwe became president of the Senate and Abubakar Tafawa Balewa became prime minister. Awolowo, Enahoro, and all the other leaders of the AG were completely excluded from power. As the

[3]For historical accounts see James S. Coleman, *Nigeria: Background to Nationalism* (Berkeley and Los Angeles: University of California Press, 1958) and Michael Crowder, *The Story of Nigeria* (London: Faber and Faber, 1966).

official opposition in the Federal House of Representatives, they began immediately to consolidate their control of the Western Region and to stimulate the development of the party throughout the rest of the federation.

After 1960 the power of the federal government, under the control of the NCNC-NPC coalition, tended to increase. These centripetal tendencies greatly increased the fears of Action Group leaders, who continued to support the regional concept, and who began to develop strategies to defend the party against future exigencies. The coalition government pushed for a referendum to carve a new Midwestern Region out of the West. Its majority in the House rejected an AG resolution for similar referenda in the East and North. The NCNC followers also called for an extension of the federal territory of Lagos into the Western Region, and one government spokesman even asserted that a regional administration could be suspended by federal authorities.[4]

The harassment of the Action Group was also pressed forward in the legal arena. The central government undertook an investigation of the National Bank of Nigeria, a major source of support for the AG which had received over two million dollars of investment funds from the Western Region Marketing Board. A judicial inquiry, under an expatriate English judge, disclosed that the National Bank had made unsecured loans to the AG, that a fictitious business had been organized for this purpose, that this front company had received over fifteen million dollars from the marketing board, and that there were various other instances of misappropriation and maladministration of public funds to the advantage of the Action Group.

In addition to these battles with its political enemies, a split developed in the leadership of the AG. Awolowo's increasing "socialism" and his drive to make the party an effective opposition at the national level led to a disgruntled Western Regional leadership. In an attempt to snuff out the incipient rebellion, the executive committee of the Action Group directed Chief Akintola, Western Regional premier and leader of the regionalist faction, to resign. He refused, but was eventually removed by the governor of the Western Region upon receipt of a letter from a majority of members indicating that they no longer supported him. When the Western House of Assembly met in May 1962 to vote for Awolowo's new choice for premier, NCNC members and AG factionalists staged a riot on the floor of the House.

This disruption was precisely the excuse the federal government needed. Prime Minister Sir Abubakar Tafawa Balewa called a special session of Parliament and moved to declare a state of emergency in the Western Region. Naturally this was vigorously opposed by the Action Group leaders in the House. Chief Awolowo pointed out that the disturbances were not widespread but had been confined to the regional legislature, and that during earlier riots in both the Eastern and Northern Regions the government had not seen fit to take such drastic action. Chief Enahoro, the deputy leader, emphasized the danger of setting such a precedent. Nevertheless the motion passed, a state of

---

[4]For an analysis of Nigerian politics see especially Richard L. Sklar, "Contradictions in the Nigerian Political System," *Journal of Modern African Studies* III, no. 2 (August 1965): 101–213.

emergency was declared in the Western Region, the civil government was suspended, and authority was vested in a federal administrator.

Immediately Awolowo, Enahoro and several other Action Group leaders were served with "restricted movement" orders. Enahoro was released from restriction, but in September 1962, at the approximate time he began his journey out of the country, the police discovered an "arms plot" involving several AG members. Awolowo was placed under house arrest and in November, when Enahoro had already reached London, he was charged with treasonable felony. In a nationwide broadcast the federal prime minister implicated all AG leaders in a plot to overthrow the government.[5]

THE BRITISH EXTRADITION TRIALS

The extradition request for Enahoro, made out in Nigeria, became the major concern of the British courts—and later of the politicians and public. The chief was to be returned to stand trial for treasonable felony along with Awolowo and other leaders of the AG. Under the Fugitive Offenders Act of 1881, any subject of the queen can be extradited for a criminal offense from the place where he is apprehended to the locality where the crime took place. This act was passed in the days of empire when all British colonies and dominions were under one sovereignty. It did not anticipate a situation involving independent nations loosely held together in a vestigial confederation—in other words, the modern Commonwealth. Nevertheless the 1881 act was in legal force and the Nigerian government had every right to apply it. It meant that Commonwealth citizens could not claim political asylum in the United Kingdom; before ordering extradition, the examining magistrate need only be satisfied that the evidence "raises a strong or probable presumption of guilt."[6]

It will be recalled that the magistrate in the Bow Street Court had listened to arguments and concluded that Enahoro should be returned to Nigeria for trial. Within the week, however, Dingle Foot had applied for a writ of *habeas corpus* to Lord Chief Justice Parker in the Queen's Bench Division Court. Foot again argued that the charges against the chief were trumped up and were, in fact, part of a larger plan on the part of the Nigerian government to destroy the Action Group as an effective opposition party. By this time the treason trial of Chief Awolowo, already under way in Lagos, had generated great public interest in the circumstances surrounding the Nigerian request for extradition. At one point Awolowo's chosen counsel, an expatriate member of the Nigerian bar, was turned away at the Lagos airport, and refused admission to Nigeria.

These disclosures seemed to interest Lord Parker. He specifically asked the barrister representing Nigeria if the government would allow Enahoro to choose his own lawyer. He was assured that it was necessary to obtain the

---

[5] J. P. Mackintosh, "Politics in Nigeria: The Action Group Crisis of 1962," *Political Studies* XI, no. 2 (June 1963): 126–55.

[6] The Fugitive Offenders Act 1881, *Halsbury's Statutes of England*, vol. 9, p. 896.

permission of the Chief Justice of Nigeria, but that any attorney with a right to appear in the federal courts would not be refused entry. Upon receiving this guaranty, the British chief justice decided to uphold the lower court's ruling and denied *habeas corpus*. Although he found little persuasiveness in the defense's contention that the Nigerian government was plotting to exterminate a political party, there appeared some evidence that treason may have been committed. Lord Parker stressed that his decision was based mainly on the promises regarding freedom of counsel. He was obviously convinced of the good faith of the Nigerian government.

A petition to appeal to the House of Lords was denied. But at the hearing before the appeals committee, the counsel for the Nigerian government admitted that even though the federal chief justice might give permission for a lawyer to appear in a case, he might still be barred from entry into the country by authorities applying the Immigration Act. Thus all the earlier assurances were of little value.

Meanwhile, Chief Enahoro remained in Brixton Prison while his friends on the outside prepared to take the case out of the courts and into politics. The 1881 act gave the home secretary almost complete discretion in ordering a fugitive's return. Unlike the courts, he could take into consideration the political nature of a case. In the previous year, for example, he had prevented the deportation of two Cypriotes whom the British courts considered to be "probably" guilty of murder charges awaiting them in Cyprus.

In early February, over two hundred Nigerian students in London petitioned Henry Brooke, the Conservative home secretary, asking him to exercise his discretion and grant asylum to Chief Enahoro. A delegation, consisting of both Tories and Labourites, met with the minister of state and the Parliamentary undersecretary of state of Commonwealth relations to discuss the Nigerian question and how it related to the Enahoro case. The Nigerian students lobbied the House of Commons in favor of the chief. The all-party delegation, including former ministers and influential back-benchers, next went to Brooke to request that asylum be granted. Meanwhile, the newspapers had picked up the story and were featuring it as a leading item from day to day.

The bitter political battle which followed crossed party lines, convulsed the House of Commons, and consumed debate time on seven occasions for the next two-and-one-half months. At one time the attorney general was arraigned before the benchers of his own Inn of Court (Inner Temple); the British High Commissioner (ambassador) in Nigeria threatened to resign; a serious split developed on the Conservative front bench between the home secretary, the attorney general, and the Commonwealth relations secretary; and NPC leaders in Lagos threatened to take Nigeria out of the Commonwealth.

The issues which aroused such antagonisms were not complex. Enahoro's supporters believed it unjust for him to be extradited to Nigeria, there to face possible persecution and elimination, under the terms of an outmoded Fugitive Offenders Act. To their minds, it was hardly fair for a Commonwealth citizen to be accorded rights *less* favorable than an alien who most certainly would have been granted political asylum. It is true that some left-wing members of the Labour Party were already deeply embroiled in the Nigerian fracas. (Previously, Dingle Foot himself had been expelled from the former colony.) These people could see no justice in British authorities applying the act as though Nigeria were still in fact part of the queen's dominions, when Nigeria herself treated British lawyers, who were legal members of the *Nigerian* bar, as if they were foreigners.

On the other side, MacMillan's Tory government decided that Enahoro must be sent back in order to keep peace with Nigeria. It is not clear whether or not this decision could have been avoided if the authorities had handled the case differently. As debates and trials wore on, more and more public attention focused on the Enahoro affair, and on the Awolowo proceedings in Lagos. The Nigerian leaders prosecuting the treason cases became furious at this "interference"—for the British Parliament was debating the very issues of the treason trials while they were *sub judice.*

Enahoro's legal representatives attempted to obtain another writ of *habeas corpus* under a section of the Fugitive Offenders Act which permitted a defendant to be discharged if he were not conveyed out of the country within one month of his initial committal. By this time, however, the Tory government was irrevocably committed to expelling him. The attorney general for the crown appeared before Lord Chief Justice Parker once again in the Queen's Bench Division Court. Parker denied *habeas corpus,* and withheld leave to appeal to the House of Lords.

The interplay of politics between judicial and legislative-executive mechanisms of conflict resolution was never more obvious. The primary reason prompting a new plea for release was that the Tory government promised, at the request of opposition leaders, not to extradite Enahoro before the entire matter had been fully considered by the House of Commons. There had already been a great deal of debate, but the government, unable to give assurances that the chief would not face the death penalty, had agreed not to return him to Nigeria until this possibility had been investigated. At one point, in an earlier debate, the home secretary said that he had an unqualified assurance from the Nigerian High Commission in London that the death penalty would not be imposed. However, the Labour opposition countered that if it were true that the Nigerian courts were not subject to political pressure, as the home secretary and Commonwealth secretary maintained, then how was it possible for a political agency to give assurances for what a court would do? In any event, the one-month time limit for detention under the act had elapsed and a petition for a release was in order. This was denied.

A new petition was made to the appeals committee on the basis of new evidence. However, the home secretary directed that the petition must be ready in three days (normally, the limit was fourteen days); it was obvious that the Tory government was becoming impatient and was under pressure from the British High Commissioner in Lagos. In this last trial the chief represented himself. Lords Simonds, Hodson, and Morris heard his plea in a crowded room in the Palace of Westminster. The room was filled with the press, members of Parliament, and other supporters. The chief asked for a delay to obtain his new evidence from Nigeria. Once again, this was rejected. He then proceeded to enter a defense which was much like the initial one. Their lordships listened politely to his quiet plea and then unanimously denied leave to appeal.

At the conclusion of this hearing, various M.P.s walked through the Palace of Westminster to the House of Commons and there entered a motion to engage in further debate concerning the Enahoro case. This was not to be the last such parliamentary deliberation, but it was the most vital, since the chief could not be sent out of the country until the House had debated the motion. During this sitting the home secretary revealed that he had spoken to the Nigerian Minister of Justice on the telephone that afternoon and that the latter had no intention of departing from the stated charges already made before the British courts; Enahoro would not face the death penalty. This tactic succeeded effortlessly—votes were taken and the chief lost again.

After Enahoro was returned to Nigeria, the government promptly announced its refusal to allow him the advocate of his choice—Dingle Foot. This generated further questions in the House of Commons, and the home secretary explained that he had understood all along that Foot and only Foot would not be allowed back onto Nigerian soil. He maintained, under accusations from the opposition, that he had not misled the House on this point. Still, there seems little cause to believe that he had done much to enlighten the assembly. Indeed, had Lord Parker known that the Nigerian authorities had communicated *this* information to the secretary, he probably would not have permitted the extradition.

So far as the British phase of the case is concerned, there can be little doubt that this was a political trial. The authorities, pursuing a foreign policy which would maintain the Commonwealth, found it necessary to repatriate a fugitive political offender to another Commonwealth country. The use of the courts in this process is instructive. The neutral position of the judges was probably unimpeachable. To what extent there was any "collusion" between judicial and executive authorities is difficult to assess. For instance, it is impossible to know if there was an implicit understanding between the judges and the government ministers (all members of the small British elite). But once the wishes of the home secretary had been published, the bench did very little to reinterpret the case, to consider new information, or to allow more time for the introduction of fresh advice.

ENAHORO: INTO THE NIGERIAN FIRE

It is difficult to determine the effect that the British trials and debates had on the concurrent and subsequent proceedings in Lagos. Some members of the elite in the capital city were outraged by the implied slur on the Nigerian judicial system.

By the time Chief Enahoro arrived in May 1963, the trial of Awolowo and his co-defendants had been in session for over six months. There had been many surprises. The original defense counsels had resigned from the case. One of the principal defendants, Dr. Maja, had turned state's evidence and become star witness for the prosecution. Allegations had been made concerning police brutality, torture, and intimidation to obtain affidavits and confessions. These were acknowledged by prosecution witnesses in court, and a certain police officer (ominously known only as Ceulman), a naturalized British subject of South African extraction, was singled out for his gross misconduct. The prosecution never bothered to produce this man or to refute the allegations.[7]

The government had decided to try the treason cases before courts consisting of single judges of the Federal High Court of Lagos. Justice G. S. Sowemimo presided over the Awolowo hearing, Justice S. O. Lambo over that of Enahoro. Both were newly appointed to the bench, inexperienced, and nominees of the government. Some months before, the Judicial Service Commission, which had controlled appointments to the bench, was abolished and its functions taken over by the executive.

Enahoro's trial was held in an environment of public agitation. When the plane carrying him landed at the airport, and he was transported by car into Lagos, crowds gathered along the way to cheer and voice their support for "Awo" and "Tony." The government made no attempt to suppress these demonstrations. The proceedings, which lasted over a month, were held in a courtroom filled with partisan spectators. As a precautionary measure, armed police surrounded the chief.

It is not necessary to analyze in detail the charges against Enahoro. He was accused, as were the other defendants in the separate Awolowo trial, of planning a coup d'etat against the federal government. Among other items, evidence was presented to indicate the existence of a "Tactical Committee" of the Action Group: a collection of arms and various other "suspicious" paraphernalia such as posters, flags, and torchlights. Enahoro was implicated both by witnesses and by circumstantial evidence. He was accused of having been personally in charge of the training and recruiting of potential coup members. His attorneys attempted to challenge the integrity and reliability of the witnesses, and to offer alternative plausible explanation of the circumstantial evidence.

That a "Tactical Committee" existed was never denied by either Enahoro or Awolowo—each gave such testimony in both trials. However, its purpose was to direct a general political campaign on behalf of the Action Group, not to organize an illegal seizure of the government. That Enahoro engaged in recruiting and training activities—including the use of facilities in Ghana—could not be repudiated; nor could the purchase of flags and posters. However, the evidence presented by witnesses concerning the military training and gathering of firearms seemed somewhat questionable. The small amount of equipment discovered was pitifully old and in exceptionally bad repair. It was, in fact, unusable.

[7]See especially L. K. Jakande, The Trial of Obafemi Awolowo (London: Secker & Warburg, 1966).

The witnesses themselves, who charged that they were members of the alleged plot, did not always stand up well under cross-examination. Indeed, a good part of the defense rested on showing how ludicrous the notion of such a plot was, given the low capability of the self-incriminated plotters (witnesses), and the absence of combat-ready equipment. Nevertheless, it could not be denied that Awolowo and Enahoro were engaged in activities that could threaten an insecure government.[8]

Although Enahoro's English barrister believed that enough doubt had been cast on the state's evidence (he even flew back to London before the verdict), Justice Lambo thought otherwise. He found the chief guilty and sentenced him to fifteen years' imprisonment. This was the most severe sentence meted out to any of the accused. It cannot be known what pressure, if any, the government brought to bear upon Lambo. However, it is generally believed that he was flown away from Lagos to the North within hours after delivering his verdict.

The defense counsel had shown some concern for maintaining the judge's objectivity by stating in the closing address: "I am not asking sympathy . . . but fair play . . . courts occupy a position of paramount importance in the modern constitution of Nigeria. They are the impartial judges between Government authorities and the subject. The preservation of respect for the law depends upon the impartial administration of the law by the courts." Surely these words would never have been addressed to a *British* judge, in a British court, by a British barrister. As has been pointed out, Justice Lambo was an inexperienced judge newly appointed by a political branch of the government. The counsel may have had good reason to worry.

CONCLUSIONS

In considering why the court was chosen as the primary device to curtail Enahoro's political activities, it must be stressed that in the tradition of the "developed" Western polity inherited from Great Britain, Enahoro's extradition and trial was the *only* "tactic" available to the government. The "political" element in the trial arose not so much by design of the elite, but more as a natural consequence of the long-accepted rules of the game—an individual's liberty was at stake, foreign policy was involved, and there was a lively and vigilant opposition. There was scarcely any other course open to the Tory government of the day but to legally defend its deportation order when challenged in the courts.

For the Nigerian trial of Enahoro, however, the answer to the question becomes much more difficult. If the chief was actually innocent of the charges, would it not have been easier to eliminate him in other ways? Why go through the procedure of a trial—particularly in Lagos, where there were literally

[8]See *The Queen v. Enahoro,* in *Record of Appeal from the High Court of Lagos to the Supreme Court of Nigeria* (1963).

thousands of Action Group supporters? On the other hand, if the defendant was guilty, there may have been no better way to expose him than a public hearing. In a developing political system, the law and the courts are as short on legitimacy as any other governmental institution. What better way to enhance their authority than letting them deal with traitors? However, in a system extremely lacking in such legitimacy, who is really a traitor? Perhaps the governmental elite in Nigeria actually used the courts as a scapegoat—a focus for the disaffected Action Group supporters. Thus the Awolowo and Enahoro trials might have served to "take the heat off" the government and at the same time eliminate the opposition. In a developing polity the courts may actually be used to further political goals of the entrenched elite and to mask that policy behind a facade of mythical judicial impartiality, magisterial ritual, and legal rhetoric.

The above characterizations fit nicely with Kirchheimer's definition of a political trial as one which swells "the area of political action by enlisting the services of the courts in behalf of political goals."[9] However, the British trial of Enahoro actually provides evidence for a second definition of as much validity. Thus a political trial may be one in which the issues raised in court transcend the established norms or law and activate a hitherto dormant but potential political opposition. Why, for example, were British politics convulsed by the judicial proceedings surrounding the extradition of an obscure accused Nigerian traitor, but never a sound was heard in the House over the extradition of James Earl Ray—an accused American assassin? Why did the courts become embroiled in politics in one instance and not the other? Certainly it must have been because the politicians were not activated, there were no transcending issues which caught the imagination or feelings of the elite—other than to support the deportation order. But had Ray been accused of murdering a less sympathetic figure—a Greek dictator or a southern American racist—what then would the honorable members have done?

What was the impact of the trial proceedings on the outcome of the trial itself? In the British case it seems fairly clear that Enahoro's defense counsel exhausted every legal remedy available to prevent his client from being extradited. However, had British law allowed the presentation of debates in the House of Commons as evidence, the magistrates might have been able to quash the deportation order. As things turned out, they could only consider the written evidence of the attorney general regarding the politics of the case. In the Nigerian trial it is difficult to speculate in this matter. Certainly the outcome appeared to be in the interest of the current leaders and there was enough evidence to provide some basis in fact for a guilty verdict. My personal evaluation is, however, that the proceedings produced more doubt than assurance on the guilt of the accused.

Finally, what were the long- and short-run effects on the political scene in both countries? The Enahoro extradition proceedings can be viewed as one of

<hr>

[9]Otto Kirchheimer, *Political Justice: The Use of Legal Procedure for Political Ends* (Princeton: Princeton University Press, 1961), p. 419.

the many incidents which led to the eventual defeat of the Conservative party in 1964. However, it also led to a general outcry against the Fugitive Offenders Act. That law was substantially amended as a result of the Enahoro affair.[10] As for Nigeria, the Awolowo and Enahoro trials led to a widening of existing political cleavages. Both men were in jail when the holocaust occurred; after the military coups of 1966 they were released. Today they are both high civilian officials working for the Lagos military government.

In closing it might be well to quote from the observations of a scholar of Nigerian politics:

> It is . . . less than realistic to expect men of eminence on the bench in a developing country to remain politically chaste for the sake of their judicial reputations. They can hardly fail to heed the call to political colours . . . Nigerian judges, like American judges, are in politics; inevitably the courts are used to achieve political ends. . . . The question, simply, is this: Will the government be so organized as to give the powerful forces of change their sway?[11]

bibliography

STUDIES

COLEMAN, JAMES S. *Nigeria: Background to Nationalism*. Berkeley and Los Angeles: University of California Press, 1958.

————, and ROSBERG, CARL, editors. *Political Parties and National Integration in Tropical Africa*. Berkeley: University of California Press, 1964.

CROWDER, MICHAEL. *The Story of Nigeria*. London: Faber and Faber, 1966.

DIAMOND, STANLEY. "The Trial of Awolowo." *Africa Today* X, no. 9 (November 1963): 22–28.

ENAHORO, ANTHONY. *Fugitive Offender: An Autobiography*. London: Cassell, 1965.

FEDERATION OF NIGERIA. "Comments of the Federal Government on the Report of Coker Commission of Inquiry into the Affairs of Certain Statutory Corporations in Western Nigeria." *Sessional Paper*, no. 4, 1962.

[10]See The Fugitive Offenders Act 1967, *Halsbury's Statutes of England*, vol. 47, p. 588.
[11]See Richard L. Sklar, "The Ordeal of Chief Awolowo: Nigerian Politics 1960–1965," in *Politics in Africa*, ed. G. M. Carter and A. F. Westin (New York: Harcourt, Brace & World, 1966), p. 162.

————. Report of "Coker Commission of Inquiry into the Affairs of Certain Statutory Corporations in Western Nigeria." 4 vols. Lagos, 1962.

JAKANDE, L. K. The Trial of Obafemi Awolowo. London: Secker & Warburg, 1966.

MACKINTOSH, J. P. "Politics in Nigeria: The Action Group Crisis of 1962." Political Studies XI, no. 2 (June 1963): 126–55.

NWABUEZE, B. O. Constitutional Law of the Nigerian Republic. London: Butterworth, 1964.

————. Machinery of Justice in Nigeria. London: Butterworth, 1964.

OTTENBERG, S. "Ibo Receptivity to Change." In Continuity and Change in African Cultures, edited by William R. Bascom and Melville J. Herskovits. Chicago: University of Chicago Press, 1959.

SCHILLER, A. A. "Law." Chapter 6 in The African World: A Survey Social Research, edited by R. Lystad. New York: Frederick Praeger, 1965.

SKLAR, RICHARD L. "Contradictions in the Nigerian Political System." Journal of Modern African Studies III, no. 2 (August 1965): 101–213.

————. "Nigeria." Chapter 16 in Political Parties and National Integration in Tropical Africa, edited by Coleman and Rosberg.

————. "The Ordeal of Chief Awolowo: Nigerian Politics 1960–1965." In Politics in Africa, edited by G. M. Carter and A. F. Westin. New York: Harcourt, Brace & World, 1966.

————, and C. S. WHITAKER, JR. "The Federal Republic of Nigeria." In National Unity and Regionalism in Eight African States, edited by Gwendolyn M. Carter. Ithaca, New York: Cornell University Press, 1966.

ZOLBERG, ARISTIDE. Creating Political Order: The Party States of West Africa. Chicago: Rand McNally, 1966.

DEBATES

HOUSE OF COMMONS DEBATES (Hansard): Vol. 673, no. 77, 14 March 1963; vol. 674, no. 86, 25 March 1963; vol. 675, nos. 95 and 96, 9 April 1963 and 10 April; vol. 676, no. 104, 1 May 1963; vol. 677, no. 114, 15 May 1963; vol. 678, no. 122, 27 May 1963; vol. 678, no. 125, 30 May 1963.

CASES

Doherty v. Balewa (1961) Nigerian Law Review 604.

Adgebenro v. Akintola (1962) Federal Supreme Court 187.

Adgebenro v. *Akintola* (1963) All E.R. 544.

The Queen and Maja and 30 others in re Omisade. Record of Appeal from the High Court of Lagos to the Federal Supreme Court. N.d.

The Queen v. *Enahoro. Record of Appeal from the High Court of Lagos to the Supreme Court of Nigeria* (1963).

STATUTES

The Fugitive Offenders Act 1881, *Halsbury's Statutes of England,* vol. 9, p. 896.

The Fugitive Offenders Act 1967, *Halsbury's Statutes of England,* vol. 47, p. 588.

two:

political trials

that become

political "trials"

WILLIAM B. HARVEY*

5

THE GHANA
TREASON TRIALS

a study in political irrationality

A long cavalcade of official cars moved southward from Upper Volta along a dusty road. Just ahead, in the small Ghanaian village of Kulungugu, a crowd waited, headed by the local district commissioner. No stop had been planned for the cavalcade in Kulungugu, but the district commissioner still hoped for an impromptu visit. The village dignitaries had assembled. Nearby stood a group of school children, excited by the unusual activity, ready for their role in the anticipated reception. At the last moment, the welcome signal was given and the cavalcade slowed to a stop.

From the lead car stepped Osagyefo Dr. Kwame Nkrumah, First President of the Republic of Ghana, self-styled unifier and liberator of Africa. Obsequious greetings and expressions of welcome reached the Great Man as the children surged toward him; there was sudden movement in the crowd—an object thrown toward the president—followed by the dull explosion of a grenade!

Ignoring the ensuing scramble of frightened and confused people, Dr. Nkrumah and his retinue retreated to their cars and sped toward the nearby town of Bawku, leaving behind the dead, the dying, and the injured. The grenade thrower, no doubt disappointed by his failure, slipped quickly out of the village and probably over the nearby border into the Republic of Togo and safety.

Dr. Nkrumah's superficial wounds were quickly treated in the hospital in Bawku; his active control of the government was uninterrupted. Nevertheless,

*The author was living and working in Ghana at the time of the treason trials. His essay is based on his own observations in court, study of the presiding judge's summary of the evidence introduced in the Adamafio trial, various newspaper accounts of the trials, and conversations with many of the participants.

his brush with death in that tiny northern Ghanaian village the afternoon of 1 August 1962 had both immediate and far-reaching consequences.

Immediate government response to the assassination attempt at Kulungugu was swift but relatively ineffective. Authorities declared an emergency in the Accra area, imposed a brief curfew, established roadblocks for perfunctory searches of persons and vehicles, and undertook fairly extensive house searches. More significantly, on 29 August three suspects were arrested and detained under the provisions of the Preventive Detention Act, which empowered the president to order the detention of persons for renewable periods of five years without specifying charges. However, official statements issued after the three suspects were in custody accused them of complicity in the Kulungugu episode. The identity of the three detainees revealed starkly the regime's insecurity: they were from the inner circle of the government, and members of the dominant Convention Peoples' Party (CPP).

By far the most important of the three detainees was Tawia Adamafio, Minister of Information and Broadcasting. In the unstable pecking order of Nkrumaist politics, Adamafio had been regarded for some time as the most influential member of the cabinet. He was a Ga from the Labadi district of Accra and had had an early association with one of the small opposition parties. In 1953, however, he joined the CPP. Fiercely ambitious, a shrewd organizer and manipulator, he advanced rapidly in the party secretariat in Accra. By 1956, when a Cocoa Marketing Board Scholarship took him to London to read law, he had become assistant general secretary of the party. In London his studies interfered little with his political activities; he propagandized for Nkrumah and organized many Ghanaian students into CPP affiliates. After his call to the bar in 1959, he returned to Ghana and continued his activist role. He served as secretary of the party until 1961, when he entered Parliament and became a member of the cabinet. As his power and influence waxed, his friends and supporters became more numerous in the party secretariat and around the presidential offices in Flagstaff House.

The second detainee was one of these Adamafio protégés, Hugh Horatio Cofie-Crabbe, who had succeeded Adamafio as executive secretary of the CPP. His role was limited to the party and, following in the shadow of the aggressively ambitious Adamafio, he had never been reckoned a significant power in his own right. The third, Ako Adjei, was minister for foreign affairs at the time of his detention. Adjei's association with Nkrumah had begun years earlier, during their student days at Lincoln University in Pennsylvania. He returned to the Gold Coast after being called to the English bar in 1947. Involved almost immediately in the old nationalist movement, the United Gold Coast Convention, he proposed that his friend Kwame Nkrumah be invited to return from London to become secretary of the UGCC. From this springboard, Nkrumah launched the Convention People's Party. Adjei joined the CPP in 1953, was elected to the Legislative Assembly in 1954, and thereafter held a series of ministerial posts. Conspicuous for neither vigor nor intelligence, Adjei seemed an unlikely conspirator.

The detentions, the declaration of emergency, and the various security measures did not halt the acts of terrorism begun at Kulungugu. In September other grenades exploded—in a CPP parade near Flagstaff House, at the residence of a cabinet minister, and in a Founder's Day procession in Accra. In November, another was pitched into a CPP gathering at Chorkor in Accra. On 8 January 1963, when the CPP staged a giant rally at the stadium in Accra to celebrate Nkrumah's 1949 call for Positive Action against the British, another grenade exploded in the throng shortly after the president had left the stadium. Nkrumah's response was entirely human. A wall was erected around Flagstaff House, the force of guards was increased, and Osagyefo the President rarely ventured from his retreat. The Lion of Africa was at bay.

Seven more persons were arrested in January and February and placed on trial during March and April of 1963. Charges ranged from treasonous participation in the terrorist bombings to failure to report information about them to the authorities. The trial was before a special criminal court authorized by a 1961 statute to try certain offenses against the security of the state. The court, which was regarded as a division of the high court, consisted of three justices of the Supreme Court, headed by Sir Arku Korsah, the chief justice. There was no jury. Under the 1961 statute such a court determined both the law and the facts. The opinion of a majority of the judges constituted the judgment of the court; disclosure of any dissenting opinion was barred. Furthermore, the judgment was final. Beyond it lay only the possibility of executive clemency.

THE FIRST TRIAL

The accused in the first treason trial were not represented by counsel. At the beginning of the trial the chief justice ruled that the state had no obligation to provide counsel when the charge involved an offense against the security of the state, even though the punishment on conviction was death. Representation would be permitted, however, if the defendants could procure counsel. Whatever efforts were made to enlist the aid of attorneys, the efforts failed—though it is not clear whether the failure came from the lawyers' fear of official reprisals or from the defendants' inability to pay. The accused thus were forced to handle their own defense, which they did with much spirit but appalling ineffectiveness.

The case developed against the first four defendants was reasonably solid. Teiko Tagoe, a tough little Hausaman, had been arrested with a grenade hidden in his baggy trousers. Another defendant disclosed to the police the location of a cache of grenades and other weapons. Seriously incriminating statements were made to the police by some defendants who had not received the caution customarily given in British criminal practice. Subsequently, after proper caution by the police, these statements were reaffirmed; in fact, they were substantially supported by the testimony of the accused in court.[1]

---

[1]We can only speculate on the reasons why the defendants described their activities so fully to the police and to the court. During the police interrogation, of course, they did not have the advice of counsel. At the trial they did try to impeach their earlier statements by

The details of the evidence can be omitted, but the grand design of treasonable activity sketched by the prosecution is important. Its version held that a conspiracy to overthrow the Nkrumah government by force had been hatched by Ghanaian exiles, who were known as the United Party in Exile. Obetsebi Lamptey, one of the leaders of the conspiracy, was said to have come from Lome, Republic of Togo, to Bawaleshie, a village near Accra, to distribute weapons and direct the activities of the "N.T. boys"[2] who had been recruited to follow the president and throw grenades when any opportunity arose. Obetsebi Lamptey was detained without charge prior to the trial but died in prison, reportedly of cancer. According to the prosecution, he was the person closest to high-level political leadership immediately associated with the conspiracy; the defendants themselves were low-level terrorists.

Testimony of two of the defendants forecast more damaging incriminations in a later trial. Malam Mama Tula and Joseph Adotei Addo testified that they were not only emissaries between Lamptey in his hideaway at Bawaleshie and the N.T. boys assembled in Accra; they also participated with him in planning and strategy sessions. Their testimony identified others who attended such meetings, provided Lamptey with operating funds, and supported the conspiracy. Among these were said to be Adamafio, Adjei and Cofie-Crabbe—but the witnesses went much further. Other Nkrumah associates mentioned were Krobo Edusei (minister of agriculture), Kweku Boateng (minister of the interior), and Kofi Asante (Aaron) Afori-Atta (minister of justice). Tula and Addo did not agree fully, however, on the identity of the visitors at Bawaleshie; they made identifications only to withdraw or qualify some of them later.

Whatever the credibility of the testimony of Tula and Addo about their own activities, it was difficult if not impossible to believe fully their statements about the activity of others. The motives for the defendants' promiscuous name-dropping were never clear, though it is tempting to speculate that they believed they assured their own longevity, whatever the judgment against them, by appearing as potential witnesses against a multitude of Nkrumah's foes—real or imagined—past, present, and future.

Events seem to have vindicated that belief. The seven defendants were convicted and sentenced: the first four, including Tula and Addo, to death. The death sentences were not carried out, however. All of the defendants remained in prison, some awaiting starring roles as witnesses for the prosecution in the second treason trial. The circumstances leading to that main event had been developing for more than a year, well before the first grenade was thrown.

---

contending that they had been induced by police threats and physical mistreatment, but these allegations were not accepted by the court. Perhaps not appreciating the possible independent effect of the absence of a caution on the admissibility in court of their initial pretrial statements, they may have seen no reason why they should not repeat, after cautions were given, what they had already told the police.

[2]Men from the Northern Territories, as the northern area of Ghana was known during the colonial period. After independence the area was divided into the Northern Region and the Upper Region.

THE LION APPREHENSIVE

By mid-1962, Nkrumah's increasing authoritarianism, epitomized by the hated Preventive Detention Act, had decimated the leadership of the opposition: many had fled the country, and most of those who remained had been imprisoned or frightened into silence. Despite the absence of an effective internal opposition, however, his popularity had declined seriously. How clearly Nkrumah perceived the softening of his political base is uncertain. He no longer moved freely about the country and therefore had little opportunity to form independent political judgments. Unwisely, he may have believed the outpourings of his own propaganda machine and the effusions of his sycophantic inner circle. There is reason to believe that some who had his ear stressed the growing influence of Adamafio and fed his fear of a rival. But even Nkrumah's isolation and flight from reality could not silence the exploding grenades at Kulungugu, Accra Stadium, and Flagstaff House. Obviously he had enemies who were prepared to act. They had access to arms and therefore he might have concluded that they had high-level contacts in his own government. Some known facts and some suspicions may have combined to convince Nkrumah that Adamafio must be brought under firm control in order to eliminate a serious risk to his power and even his life.

Even if this speculation on the psychology of the president is sound, there is still an enormous gap between that psychological set and a rational decision to bring Adamafio to trial for treason. In earlier years Nkrumah had been frustrated in efforts to deal with political opponents through the operation of the criminal law in the ordinary courts of the land. Prosecutions had been begun and lost for lack of evidence, and convictions had been reversed on appeal for what Nkrumah and his supporters regarded as "legal technicalities." Such experience should certainly have warned against launching another prosecution unless in the view of competent legal advisers the available evidence made an unusually strong case.

Nkrumah had such advisers. Geoffrey Bing, the English Queen's Counsel, who had served as attorney-general immediately after independence, was still available. Bing's self-image as the éminence grise of Ghanaian politics was outdated, but he was still a skillful legal jack-of-all-trades in Flagstaff House. He was an intelligent, well-trained, experienced lawyer. Also available was B. E. Kwaw-Swanzy, the attorney-general, another bright and knowledgeable attorney.

No definitive answer is possible concerning the roles such legal advisers may have played in the decision to prosecute Adamafio for treason. Both at the policy level and in the preparation for trial, however, Bing seems the much more likely participant, though he has denied any involvement.[3] In July 1967,

---

[3] In his memoirs of his years in Ghana, Bing asserts that he "had no connection with preparing the case against Adamafio." Indeed, he declares that after discussing the case with Austin Amissah, the director of public prosecutions, he concluded "that the evidence against both Ako Adjei and Adamafio was, even if it was all established in court, insufficient to

the new anti-Nkrumah government allowed me to interview Kwaw-Swanzy, who was being held in "protective custody." Kwaw-Swanzy denied any participation in the policy determination, declaring that he was merely advised of the decision to prosecute Adamafio. According to his account, he requested an opportunity to review the police files, and after each of three separate reviews refused to proceed on the ground that the evidence available would not sustain a conviction. After further police work and a fourth review, however, he decided that the available evidence did establish a prima facie case of treason. In spite of Kwaw-Swanzy's earlier reservations about the prosecution and his own reluctance to proceed, Nkrumah, he explained, was so convinced of the guilt of Adamafio and the other defendants in the planning of the attack at Kulungugu that he failed to appreciate the distinction between the contents of the police reports and the hard evidence, admissible in court, that would be required for conviction.[4]

Perhaps Nkrumah's deep-seated suspicion of Adamafio and his layman's view of the basis for a successful prosecution provide an adequate explanation of the decision to proceed. His fear, sharply focused and intensified by Kulungugu and the subsequent terrorism in Accra, was probably nurtured by Adamafio's political enemies. Even if he believed that Adamafio had no connection with these events, he probably would have found them a useful background for eliminating a political rival of the stature of Adamafio. Certainly the bell was tolling for Adamafio, whether through prosecution for specific criminal acts or otherwise. He was in detention, and the CPP propagandists were clamoring for him and his associates to be taken to Black Star Square and shot.

It is difficult to take seriously the CPP-inspired demands for Adamafio's summary execution. Nkrumah was vain, insecure, and harshly authoritarian, but not bloodthirsty. He had been quite willing to imprison his opponents but not to kill them. Also, he had always appreciated the niceties of legal formalities and their connection with legitimacy. If Adamafio were to be executed, a trial and conviction were essential.

Whether Nkrumah considered Adamafio a treasonous conspirator or merely a political threat to be isolated and neutralized, adequate control had surely been imposed by his detention. Under the Preventive Detention Act, Nkrumah had the legal power to hold Adamafio in prison indefinitely. Even if he saw further advantages in Adamafio's death, the decision to prosecute him for treason appears rational only on alternative premises: one, that Nkrumah believed him guilty and, perhaps against contrary advice from his legal advisers, that sufficient evidence of his guilt could be adduced in court; or two, that Nkrumah believed the judges were sufficiently intimidated to return the de-

---

secure a conviction," and that he told Nkrumah that he "thought the two former Ministers would both be acquitted." Bing, *Reap the Whirlwind* (London: MacGibbon & Kee, 1968), p. 410.

[4]Bing's account, based on reports he received when he returned to Ghana after the trial, is quite different. He was informed that Kwaw-Swanzy had left Nkrumah "with the impression that a conviction was certain." Ibid., p. 412.

sired conviction irrespective of the evidence presented. On either premise, however, a show trial before judges whose political reliability could not be guaranteed presented a risk, however slight, of an acquittal.

THE TRIAL OF THE NOTABLES

The Adamafio treason trial began in August 1963. The five defendants included Adamafio, Adjei, and Cofie-Crabbe, all of whom had long-standing and close ties with the CPP, and two men, R. B. Otchere and Joseph Yaw Manu, whose political association had been with the opposition United Party. Otchere, a member of Parliament representing a constituency in Ashanti, had been a refugee in the Ivory Coast for several months in 1961 and 1962. Following his arrest in January 1963, he allegedly attempted suicide while in police custody. At the time of his appearance in the treason trial, he was serving a sentence of three years' imprisonment for that offense. Yaw Manu, formerly a minor civil servant and storekeeper, also had fled to the Ivory Coast in 1961; while flying from Abidjan to Lome, Republic of Togo, on 7 November 1962, his plane landed at the Accra airport, and he was arrested immediately.

The legal structure, powers, and procedures of the court before which the trial was held were the same as in the earlier trial of the minor terrorists. Its membership differed somewhat, however. In both trials Sir Arku Korsah, the chief justice, presided. Korsah had had a long and distinguished career at the bar, in the old legislative council and executive council during the colonial period, and in the judiciary. Never a politician in the usual sense, Korsah was a shrewd navigator through the stormy waters of colonial and post-independence politics. He maintained good relations with Nkrumah and consequently became somewhat suspect in professional circles. Whatever his private views, he had avoided any connection with public criticism of the policies and the rapidly growing authoritarianism of the Nkrumah regime.

Justice William B. Van Lare also sat in the first treason trial. Second in seniority only to the chief justice, he reasonably could expect elevation to that office on Sir Arku's retirement—if he remained politically acceptable to the president. The third member, Justice Edward Akufo-Addo, was the anomaly on the bench. Prior to his appointment by Nkrumah to the Supreme Court in 1962, he had been the ablest and most successful Ghanaian practitioner at the bar. Elegant in dress and manner, married to the lovely Adeline Afori-Atta, daughter of the late Nana Sir Afori-Atta I[5] and niece of Dr. J. B. Danquah,[6]

[5]Paramount Chief of Akim Abuakwa. During long service as a member of the legislative council and later of the executive council, he cooperated with the colonial governors and other senior officials in a gradual broadening of African participation in government.

[6]A well-known lawyer, scholar, poet, and philosopher, he was described by a British commission of enquiry in 1948 as "the doyen" of Gold Coast politics. Defeated by Nkrumah in the presidential election of 1960, Danquah remained in the country as a courageous, frequently outspoken critic of the government. He died on 4 February 1965 in the condemned prisoners section of Nsawam Prison, where he had been sent under the provisions of the Preventive Detention Act.

Akufo-Addo's political alignment was clear. Though he had left active politics at about the time of Ghana's independence, he was still a prominent member of the aristocratic, intellectual group whose moderately nationalistic political organizations had been superseded and then brutally suppressed by the CPP and Nkrumah's government.

The presence of Korsah and Van Lare on the court was understandable; Akufo-Addo's was much more difficult to explain. The choice of judges to sit was made by the chief justice, undoubtedly after private consultation with Nkrumah. Korsah was generally regarded as willing to accommodate the regime. Van Lare's ambition to become chief justice well may have led the government to view him similarly. But how to explain Akufo-Addo? Did Nkrumah expect his judgment to be affected by personal hostility toward Adamafio or the other accused? It was rumored that Adamafio had once proposed the detention of Akufo-Addo. A perhaps apocryphal story circulated that when Adamafio first appeared in court and saw his judges, he despairingly told his lawyer that defense was futile.

There is no need to assume, however, that Nkrumah thought it necessary to "stack" the total court in favor of the prosecution. He may well have believed that any court, whatever its membership, would sustain the prosecution; he controlled the legal tools and had demonstrated the will to act ruthlessly against his political opponents. Moreover, a unanimous decision was not required for conviction. Akufo-Addo's presence on the court bolstered its prestige, contributed to the appearance of objectivity, and conceded nothing. His vote was not essential, and if outvoted, he was prohibited by law from disclosing his dissent.

Unlike the accused in the first trial, Adamafio and his codefendants were represented by counsel. Though the risk of political retaliation against attorneys probably had not lessened, many lawyers had had twinges of professional conscience over their failure to respond to the earlier need for defense counsel. That Adamafio and his codefendants were represented, however, is probably due primarily to the fact that they were financially able to pay. The defendants' counsel, retained by the defendants themselves and not provided by the state, were experienced men who enjoyed high standing at the bar. Clearly, a vigorous defense could be expected.

The prosecution was led by Attorney-General B. E. Kwaw-Swanzy, and Director of Public Prosecutions Austin Amissah. Both were able, intelligent lawyers. A CPP member, Kwaw-Swanzy had only recently left his practice to become Dr. Nkrumah's chief law officer. Amissah was a civil servant with no party ties. In ability, the prosecution could not be faulted. If the government had a case against the accused, it would be presented effectively.

The prosecution's theory and its evidence need not be examined in detail. The Lome-Abidjan conspiracy of United Party exiles to overthrow the Nkrumah government by force remained the central theme. While in police custody, both Otchere and Manu made damaging admissions of their own involvement in such a conspiracy. At the trial itself, both sought to impugn these by allegations of police mistreatment; they even denied having made some of the statements attributed to them. Otchere also contended that he made his statements while insane, and Manu presented an involved claim that he was actually a double agent with a primary loyalty to Nkrumah.

The only direct evidence against Adamafio, Adjei, and Cofie-Crabbe was their identification by Joseph Adotei Addo and Malam Mama Tula, two of the defendants convicted in the first trial, as persons who had visited Obetsebi Lamptey at Bawaleshie when plans were laid for the Kulungugu attempt on Nkrumah's life. Yet even this evidence was questionable, since Addo, after having made the identification, repudiated it. Tula remained firm in his identification of Adamafio but admitted that he had not been previously acquainted with Adjei and Cofie-Crabbe; he added to and removed from his Bawaleshie list the names of other leading CPP figures with a startling disregard for consistency. The prosecution also presented a maze of circumstantial evidence, most of it relating to Adamafio. Summed up, the state's case represented Adamafio as an inordinately ambitious, scheming, and grasping politician; it was utterly unpersuasive, however, on the question of involvement in a conspiracy leading to the assassination attempt at Kulungugu.

THE DECISION

The trial ended in November. The court handed down its judgment on 9 December 1963. Otchere and Manu were convicted of treason and sentenced to death. The principal defendants, Adamafio, Adjei, and Cofie-Crabbe, were acquitted on both the treason and conspiracy counts, and were ordered discharged! Instead of releasing them, however, the police immediately returned them to prison under the previously issued Preventive Detention Act orders. The full and unrestrained wrath of the government and the party then descended on the court.

At a press conference, the attorney-general, Kwaw-Swanzy, denounced the decision as "a travesty of justice." The CPP's *Evening News,* in its customary manner, shrilled:

The courts, ideally an instrument of Socialist education and discipline, not of class insolence and subversion, ye have made a den of thieves, robbers, assassins and corruption.
And the voices of the people say—Away with them! No more shall we entrust such vital machinery in the hands of the class enemy!

Dr. Nkrumah clearly indicated through the press his rejection of the judgment. He declared the chief justice especially culpable in failing to inform him in advance of the court's judgment so that adequate steps could be taken to control the anticipated wrath of the masses and to protect the prisoners. It seems improbable, however, that Korsah failed to inform Nkrumah. Indeed, it is likely that when he was told of the impending judgment, the president instructed Korsah to apply further pressure on the other two justices to modify their views and return convictions of all.

The president did not limit himself to verbal indignation, however. Two days after the acquittal, he abruptly dismissed Sir Arku Korsah from his office as chief justice. The dismissal, which was clearly within Nkrumah's constitutional powers, left Korsah on the Supreme Court, but on 13 December he resigned from the Judicial Service. Justice Van Lare also resigned a few days later. Justice Akufo-Addo, who was probably most responsible for the acquittals, sat tight. The president needed additional legal weapons to deal with him, and they were being prepared. Exercising powers granted to him by the Republican Constitution, Dr. Nkrumah ordered a plebiscite on a constitutional amendment that would vest in the president full discretionary power to dismiss any judge of the superior courts. In the plebiscite, held in January 1964, intimidation of the electorate and vote fraud were rampant, and the government made little effort to conceal either. Predictably, the amendment was approved, and Nkrumah immediately exercised his new power. Akufo-Addo and two other members of the Supreme Court were summarily dismissed.

The pursuit of Adamafio and his codefendants still was not concluded. While they waited in detention, legislation was rushed through Parliament to void the entire judgment, both the convictions and the acquittals. Companion legislation modified the structure and procedure of the special criminal court to provide for trial by jury before a single judge. In March of 1964 a new trial fulfilling these modified requirements placed the five defendants before Chief Justice Sarkodie-Ado, who had succeeded Korsah, and a "blue-ribbon" jury drawn from former students at the Kwame Nkrumah Ideological Institute at Winneba. The second trial, part of which was held *in camera*, produced the desired result. The five defendants were convicted of treason and sentenced to death. His ends achieved or possibly abandoned, Nkrumah commuted all the sentences to long imprisonment.

The significance of the Adamafio prosecution is not to be found in details of treasonous intrigue, for at least in the cases of Adamafio, Adjei, and Cofie-Crabbe, these were almost completely absent. A secondary but still meaningful aspect of the trial is its illustration of the mockery of justice that can be effected within the framework of the law. The principal interest lies, however, in the puzzle it presents: what was the motivation for a prosecution that only heaped scorn and derision on Nkrumaist justice? Although reliable, direct evidence is unattainable, inferences are available; these can throw light on the reasons prompting the prosecution, and provide significant insights into the nature of Nkrumah's rule in its twilight hours.

In its final years the cardinal feature of Nkrumah's government was not the systematic implementation of misguided or evil policies. In concept, his policies were often wise, imaginative, and benevolent. In practice, however, they were frequently unrelated to the actions of the government. Increasingly the conduct of officials, from the president on down, had no perceptible connection with any identifiable policy or plan, good or bad. The most characteristic aspect of latter-day Nkrumaism was its total lack of rationality, that is, the complete absence of coherent policy to which the daily conduct of officials could be related. Most decisions and actions appeared to be ad hoc, compounded of personal selfishness, vindictiveness, and overriding fear.

In this light the Adamafio treason trial can be understood, if not justified. Its consequences, not surprisingly, damaged the regime irreparably. The flimsiness of the actual evidence against prominent detainees was displayed publicly. When the court had the courage to resist the will of an authoritarian government, it raised a small rallying banner for others. Its decision and the government's response precipitated a profound constitutional crisis. The resolution of that crisis shattered irrevocably Nkrumah's claim that he respected an independent and responsible judiciary. The second trial demonstrated clearly the shoddy quality of his justice. Against these losses there were no compensating gains. Adamafio and the others were not executed, but remained in prison. That they were imprisoned as formally convicted traitors, not mere detainees, seemed to add little to the security of Nkrumah's government. This was demonstrated on 24 February 1966 when the army and police forces, in a coup met with public rejoicing, opted for a new beginning.

EPILOGUE: JULY 1969

The post-coup fates of the several participants in the second treason trial illustrate the relatively mild effects of political adversity in Ghana. The three justices who heard the case were rehabilitated. Korsah led certain international goodwill missions for the new regime before his death in 1967. Van Lare, before his death in 1969, had become Ghana's High Commissioner to Canada, and Akufo-Addo has returned to judicial office as chief justice of Ghana. One of his colleagues on the Court of Appeals is Austin Amissah, who served briefly as attorney-general after the coup before going on the bench.

The three principal defendants were released from prison shortly after the coup. Cofie-Crabbe is unemployed, but Adamafio and Adjei are practicing law in Accra. After being held for several months in "protective custody," Kwaw-Swanzy has also resumed his legal practice.

Nkrumah was on a journey to North Vietnam at the time of the coup and has not returned to Ghana. He is living in Conakry, Guinea. While he remains a figure of considerable ideological significance to many of the more militant African nationalists, he appears to have no significant support among the political activists of Ghana.

bibliography

AUSTIN, DENNIS. *Politics in Ghana, 1946–1960.* New York: Oxford University Press, 1964.

BING, GEOFFREY. *Reap the Whirlwind.* London: MacGibbon & Kee, 1968.

BRETTON, HENRY. *The Rise and Fall of Kwame Nkrumah.* New York: Praeger, 1966.

HARVEY, WILLIAM B. *Law and Social Change in Ghana.* Princeton: Princeton University Press, 1966.

NKRUMAH, KWAME. *Dark Days in Ghana.* Revised edition. New York: International, 1969.

FRANCISCO JOSÉ MORENO

6

THE CUBAN REVOLUTION *v.* BATISTA'S PILOTS

The period immediately following Fidel Castro's overthrow of Fulgencio Batista's regime on New Year's Day 1959 was followed by a series of revolutionary trials that attempted to weed out and punish supporters of the fallen dictatorship and enemies of the revolution. One of the most unusual of these political trials became a cause célèbre that called into question the general nature of law and justice in Castro's Cuba.

The triumph of the insurgent forces had been the final act of the most popular political upheaval Cuba had ever had. Since March 1952, when Batista took over the government through a military coup, antagonism toward him and his regime had been on the increase. The radical opposition, headed by students, young professionals, and a handful of labor leaders, had successfully precluded any electoral compromise between Batista and his less militant opponents. The refusal of the opposition to accept the electoral solutions offered by the regime tended to polarize and galvanize political positions. The more extremist and violent the opposition became, the more repressive and brutal the actions of the government.

The increase in violence had a marked effect on Cuban public opinion—it made martyrs and heroes out of the opposition forces and murderers out of Batista's supporters. This trend in opinion was determined by a series of factors. Batista, although popular among the soldiers, had always been disliked by the general population. His use of the military and overthrow of the constitutional system did not make him any more esteemed by his countrymen; he was hated most of all because his coup d'etat had prevented the very popular *Partido Ortodoxo* from an almost certain electoral victory. A strong tradition of idealizing struggles against the government also militated against the established order. In a cultural sense, the balance was tilted in favor of the rebels. In spite of the official propaganda machinery, a large majority of the island's population identified with, and supported in one way or another, the anti-Batista forces.

Fidel Castro was not the only leader in the struggle, but he soon became the best known. The only other charismatic figure, José Antonio Echeverría, was killed in 1957 after an unsuccessful attempt on Batista's life. The predominance of Castro's leadership was also assisted by the fact that those fighting in the cities, where most of the action took place, were forced to seek anonymity in order to stay alive. There is little question, though, that Fidel Castro's main leadership asset was his charismatic personality, and, of course, the Cubans' inclination toward this type of leadership.

During the late 1940s, Fidel Castro had been a student leader at the University of Havana. In 1951 he became a candidate for congress in the *Partido Ortodoxo*. From the day Batista took over, Castro became an ardent opponent of the new government. On 26 July 1953 he led an attack on the Moncada Barracks, an army installation in Oriente, the easternmost province of Cuba. The main objective of this action was to force the hand of other opposition groups that were then better organized and better supplied than his own. This attempt failed and Castro was put in jail. The long sentence was suspended by Batista in one of his many efforts to create a favorable electoral atmosphere in the country, and by the end of 1956 Castro was in the Sierra Maestra mountains. New Year's Day 1959 saw the coming to power of the revolutionary forces.

THE REVOLUTIONARY COURTS

Within two weeks after the downfall of the dictatorship, revolutionary courts were trying and executing military and civilian personnel of the Batista regime. These courts were usually made up of officers from the rebel forces. Although some efforts were made to insure that the judges had some legal training, this was not always the case. The main qualification to serve as judge in one of these courts was loyalty to the revolution, as demonstrated by active participation in the fight against Batista. These courts operated under the criminal code of the rebel army drawn up by Fidel Castro on 21 February 1958, at his headquarters in the Sierra Maestra.

Several articles of the 1940 Constitution were modified by the laws enacted by the new government. The death penalty was restored for repressive acts and espionage in wartime, and the penalties made retroactive to the period of the Batista regime. This made it possible to try individuals accused of having committed certain criminal acts under the prior government according to the criminal code of the 26th of July revolutionary army.

The summary judgments rendered by the revolutionary courts had, at least, two important effects. By establishing a system of punishment, Castro was able to restrain otherwise unruly elements. During the first few weeks of his rule, he was far from having effective control over all revolutionary groups. In the preceding three years bands of armed fighters had sprung up in many parts of the country. They had led a fairly independent existence and were only now beginning to be integrated into the new revolutionary institutions. These groups would have been prone to seek vengeance for themselves had not the Castro government provided the means for dealing with their enemies.

The second effect of summary trials was a negative international reaction. An important segment of the world press condemned the new judicial procedures as unfair and unjust. In the wake of these criticisms, and after having gained a much greater degree of control over the independent groups, the new government quickly began to formalize the functions of the revolutionary courts. Trials were no longer televised, regular press coverage was reduced, and the proceedings were reorganized to allow for a more proper defense. The membership of the court, however, was not altered.

THE ACCUSED

On 13 February 1959, in accordance with the new procedures, a revolutionary tribunal met in Santiago, capital of Oriente province, to hear the government's case against forty-five members of the Batista air force.

At the trial, nineteen pilots, ten gunners, and sixteen mechanics were charged with genocide, murder, and a series of other crimes, all stemming from some six hundred air attacks on various populated civilian areas in Oriente province during the last month of the Castro revolution. These attacks, which involved the use of approximately six thousand bombs and five million machine gun bullets, resulted in at least eight deaths and sixteen injuries, along with considerable property damage. The government asked the death penalty for all of the accused with the exception of five mechanics for whom a ten-year sentence was sought. Prior to the trial, Fidel Castro had called these men "the worst criminals of the Batista regime."

The revolutionary tribunal was presided over by Felix Lugerio Pena, an army major. The other two judges on the court were Adalberto Paruas, an army officer, and Antonio Michell Yabor, another army officer who was also a pilot. Apparently no special care had been taken by the government in the selection of the judges. To the general Cuban public they were unknown, and remained so after the trial. The prosecuting attorney, Antonio Cejas Sánchez, apparently had not been chosen for any special, official reason either. The accused had a battery of seven defense attorneys headed by Captain Arístides Dacosta, who had defended Major Jesús Sosa Blanco, the first war criminal to be tried by the new government.

The government's case against the accused was based on the eyewitness accounts of peasants from the bombarded areas and on the flight reports signed by pilots and gunners. The prosecution introduced over one hundred of these "confidential flight reports," ten of which had been signed by accused pilots. At the start of the trial, two pilots, Mario Bermúdez Esquivel and Roberto Lanz Rodríguez, admitted that they had indeed signed the reports that were entered as evidence against them. The defense contended, however, that the reports were deliberately falsified out of fear of reprisal from superior officers. That the pilots had dropped their ordnance on unpopulated areas was given as the reason for the very small number of deaths and injuries caused by air attacks. The prosecution rejected the contention of falsified reports, and offered in evidence the daily military operation accounts of Batista's intelligence department, which coincided completely with the pilots' official reports.

Several of the airmen on trial claimed they had not taken part in the raids, but the prosecution noted that those members of the Batista military forces who had refused to obey orders had either been put in jail or driven into exile. Moreover, army vouchers were introduced as evidence indicating that the accused had been paid for the air raids.

On 2 March 1959, after three weeks of testimony by some eighty witnesses, the revolutionary tribunal handed down its decision: all the accused were acquitted. The court discussed several grounds for acquittal after first pointing out that Castro's forces were located in many of the attacked villages and were, therefore, legitimate military targets. The government's charge of genocide was dismissed because no case could be made that there was an attempt to destroy racial, religious, or national groups. The murder charge was not sustained because, according to the court, the prosecution failed to prove premeditation. Most importantly, the men could not be found guilty beyond the shadow of a doubt because it was not possible to prove which of those on trial had actually produced the death and destruction for which they were tried.

The reaction of the Castro government was one of anger and frustration. Apparently Fidel Castro was caught by surprise. Since there seems to be no evidence that the trial had been fixed beforehand by the selection of the court members or by delivering specific instructions to them, we must assume that Castro had expected the court, as a matter of course, to follow his expressed belief in the guilt of the airmen as the basis for its decision.

There is little question that a difference of opinion existed between Castro and the judges concerning the role of the court. Castro saw the court as an arm of the revolution. The judges, all with impeccable revolutionary credentials, were concerned with preserving the integrity of judicial conceptions and mechanisms. However, this disagreement between what could appear to be a political and a juridical interpretation of the court's function may have been more imaginary than real. To understand the discrepancy between Castro's wishes and the court's action, the political situation in Cuba at the time must be taken into account.

THE REVOLUTIONARY OUTLOOK

In March 1959 the Cuban revolutionary regime was quite young. Fidel Castro was still in the process of consolidating his power and had not committed himself to a given political philosophy. He was still paying lip service to the 1940 Constitution and to the basic principles of liberal democracy. Under these circumstances, most of his followers, including those in official positions, were not sure which path to follow. The charismatic nature of his leadership, emphasizing emotional response to the leader rather than loyalty to any given set of ideas, allowed for this situation. The important thing was to support Castro. The philosophical basis upon which to rest that support was of only secondary importance.

Despite appearances, there seemed to be no deep-seated moral or philosophical disagreement between Castro and the members of the court. The judges in question never registered any official protest to Castro's criticisms. Furthermore, they were willing to serve in subsequent trials. The judges, therefore, seem to have taken a bit too seriously the revolutionary rhetoric of the first weeks of the revolutionary government. They obviously must have thought that the prosecution had failed to prove its case. Their decision was based on their "technical" opinion as judges, but, above everything else, it was made possible by the lack of clear directive from the revolutionary leaders. They felt free to voice their "technical" opinion because they had not been instructed clearly to the contrary. Castro's remarks on the subject, amid a series of unrelated actions that could have been considered support for a liberal democratic line, were not as definite as we now, in retrospect, make them out to be.

The day after the decision of the court was announced, Castro made a public statement indicating his displeasure with the outcome and declaring that a reversal of the decision would be sought:

> The revolutionary tribunal has made a big mistake by acquitting these criminal pilots. Such an action renders Batista a good service; and it is a way of encouraging other pilots to work for Trujillo and other enemies of the Revolution. These pilots would then be in a position to bombard anew the civil population of Cuba.
>
> It would be an act of extreme ingenuousness, for a people and for a revolution, to set free precisely those who were the most cowardly assassins in the service of the dictatorship. The revolutionary tribunals do not need any proofs other than the cities and towns that were devastated and the dozens of corpses of children and women that were produced by bullets and bombs. Or are we going to give a new opportunity to those miserable creatures to resume flying against Cuba and let them write once more their sinister history of mourning and tragedy from some base in the Dominican Republic or any other country where friends of tyranny have been given asylum? The Revolution was not made for that, and those of us who are leading it cannot permit such an error to be made.
>
> This is a matter pertaining to the security of the citizenry, and for this reason we are obliged to intervene in this problem, since we cannot remain silent after such a venture.
>
> The people of Santiago de Cuba should not become restless, because the sentence will be appealed, and a just tribunal shall try the case anew.

Castro's call for a "review" court was opposed by several groups within Cuba, especially the Havana, Santiago, and national bar associations. These groups felt that in exposing the men to what would really have to be a second trial, the government would be ignoring the principles of double jeopardy. They claimed that such a move was without precedent in Cuban judicial history. Although some incipient political opposition to the radicalization of the regime probably contributed to the reactions of the bar associations, their concern was couched primarily in "professional" terms. Castro's suggestion could be read as a clear challenge to the procedures and techniques upon which their profession was based.

On the other hand, the Cuban bar did not kick up as great a fuss as the American press made out. As a matter of fact, taking into consideration the clear violation of procedures on the part of Castro, the reaction of the bar was rather mild. And this, additionally, was a bar almost completely controlled by upper-middle class people who were adversely affected by the economic policies of the Castro government. Elsewhere in Latin America the situation was much the same: newspapers partial to the United States made the most out of the bar protests. Still, in the author's opinion, the majority of Latin Americans who were aware of the Castro action favored it. The disagreement seized upon by American and pro-American newspapers was far from a popular expression and represented a professional class attempt to ape the Anglo-Saxons.

THE REVIEW COURT CONVENES

Fidel Castro ignored the protests. He had chief defense counsel, Captain Arístides Dacosta, flown to Havana for private talks and sent Minister Augusto Martínez Sánchez to Santiago to set up the court for review. On television several days later, while warning of counterrevolutionary activities in Cuba, Castro accused reactionary elements of having played a part in securing the airmen's acquittal. He claimed that such an acquittal had been the result of political, rather than judicial, action. He reminded the country that revolutionary justice is based not on legal precepts but on the moral conviction of the people. He felt that since the accused were members of the Batista air force that had carried out bombing and destruction, they were criminals and should be punished.

The review court convened in Santiago on 7 March. It consisted of five members with army Major Manuel Piñeiro Losada presiding. Antonio Cejas Sánchez continued as prosecuting attorney and the team of defense lawyers was still headed by Captain Arístides Dacosta. It is difficult to know precisely on what basis the new presiding judge and his colleagues were chosen, or why the prosecutor and chief defense attorney were allowed to remain. However, at this point the details seem less important than the overall picture—it was now quite clear where the revolution, personified by Castro, stood.

The defense began by challenging the legality of the review court, but the court held that under Article 120 of the *Ley Procesal Penal* of the Republic in Arms, the state's attorney could ask for a review of the acquittal decision. Such a reading required a certain degree of interpretative laxity on the part of the court, since that article referred to cases in which technical violations could be used by the state, or the defense, to seek the annulment of the decision. To support their interpretation of this article the judges put together a logical argument that ran as follows: if the defense has the right to appeal, it is only fair for the prosecution to have the same right.

The review court found that there was enough evidence to try the accused of the said crimes and that genocide indeed had been committed, insofar as the attacks were made on Cubans who belonged to that part of the national group that refused to accept submission to the tyranny. In consequence, the decision of the lower court was annulled and forty-three accused individuals were found guilty of the crime of genocide. Twenty were given thirty-year sentences; nine were given twenty years; and two received two years. Two men were freed after having convinced the tribunal that they did not participate in the said crimes. They were able to prove to the court's satisfaction that they had had no part whatsoever in the air attacks and that they had been accused only by mistake.

The decision was obviously in accord with Castro's wishes. The only concession was in the nature of the sentences. The state had originally asked the death penalty for most of the men, but it was now content to accept the long prison terms imposed. The willingness to accept less than the death penalty, as well as Castro's attempt to justify the new decision, must both be viewed with reference to the existing political situation. Castro was still consolidating his power and had no apparent desire to antagonize more people than he had to. Some moderate elements in and out of the government, as well as certain arbiters of international opinion, had been upset by the retrial of the airmen. The relative moderation the government showed in not forcing the court to hand down death sentences may well have been in response to its desire to forestall further criticism.

On 23 March Castro once more answered the critics who condemned the war crimes trials as unlawful and unconstitutional. He explained the position of his government in demanding and carrying through the retrial of the forty-five men. His explanation is an eloquent statement of the *traditional* Latin-American (and Iberian) conception of law:

> We shall be respectful of the law, but of the revolutionary law; respectful of rights, but of revolutionary rights—not the old rights, but the new rights we are going to make. For the old law, no respect; for the new law, respect. Who has the right to modify the constitution? The majority. Who has the majority? The revolution.

In these words Castro made clear the dependence of law (*ley*) upon justice (*derecho*). The "new rights" would supersede the "old rights" because, according to him, the revolutionary majority was in a position to determine the just course of action.

The procedure and rationale used by Fidel Castro and his government in retrying the Cuban pilots have seldom been understood in this, their proper, context. There is no question that, to a large degree, humanitarian reasons prompted the condemnation of Castro's actions in the United States and other countries. Still, behind this disapproval was a non-Latin inability to comprehend the judicial conceptions to which Castro was referring. The main features of the Latin-American and Cuban conception of law must be understood if one is ever to comprehend the whole story behind this strange trial.

CUBAN LAW AND CUBAN JUSTICE

The equation of justice with law that allowed Fidel Castro to bypass completely, and even to countermand, the decision of one of his own revolutionary courts of justice is one of the most basic elements in the Latin-American interpretation of law, and one that is deeply rooted in Cuban culture. This equation has made the Latin-American peoples frequently liable to the charge of showing an unabashed disregard for the law. This tendency to supersede enacted legislation with abstract interpretations of justice produces an unwillingness to accept established legal devices as binding precedents and gives rise to a high degree of constitutional experimentation.

Throughout the years the Latin-American people, as well as their Iberian ancestors, have retained an understanding of law that can be easily identified. Any attempt to analyze the role of their judiciaries, either philosophically or behaviorally, must take this into account. For one thing, Spanish ideas concerning law have a definite Roman orientation. From 219 B.C. to A.D. 409 the Iberian peninsula was under the control of the Roman legions and under the domination of Roman culture. During those centuries Roman institutions and thought became deeply rooted in the customs of Iberia. The language of the Romans became, in modified versions, the language of the peninsula. And with the Latin language, Roman legal thinking became a part of the Iberian way of life.

Roman ideas and power did not, however, develop uniformly throughout Spain; Roman judicial principles influenced some areas more than others. Catalonia and the Basque country showed for many centuries a lesser degree of "Romanization" than Castile. But in spite of such regional distinctions, Roman institutions and ideas gained a permanent and expanding foothold over the people of the entire region.

Yet the Spanish acceptance of Roman law and its implicit philosophical commitments cannot be understood purely on the basis of historical determinism. For Spain, or any other country or people, to have taken over the Roman conceptions of law and justice, certain conditions must have existed in the country that made such a development possible.

Spain did not copy and adapt itself to a Roman legal system simply because the Romans were there, but because they wished to adopt and adapt some of the principles and conceptions. Specifically, the Spaniards seem to have been impressed with the Roman view that law is neither a systematization of communal customs nor an attempt to embody in legal precepts the local traditions. Law was for the Romans, above everything else, a moral interpretation of life—an effort to define those ethical goals that the political community should strive to attain. The works of Cicero, Seneca, and the later Roman lawyers offer numerous examples of this interpretation of the legal function.

Roman law became an attempt, based upon abstract ethical reasoning, to determine how people ought to behave. This conception of law was not necessarily a Roman invention. It is probably as old as human society. But whether new or old, it stimulated a search for theoretical perfection that soon became unconcerned with the ways in which people actually behaved.

Reason as the ability to discern right and wrong according to predetermined abstract moral principles was established as the main source of law. Reason as used by the Roman jurists and legal philosophers should not be confused with the ability to learn from experience. The Roman attempt to legislate on the basis of reason was an expression of idealistic thinking: they idealized the human reasoning ability. Idealism and universalism imbued the law with an essentially unrealistic character, and Roman legislation came to be identified with beautiful principles of conduct that were regularly more honored in the breach than in the observance.

From its very beginning written Spanish law was far more an expression of ideals to be attained than a reflection of social customs and traditions. It is not surprising, then, that the idealistic and universalistic legal heritage of the Romans easily took root in Spain. Whatever local customs and traditions there may have been in the peninsula that opposed this trend gave way to high-sounding ethical and spiritual principles as sources of law. As the *Etymologies*[1] of St. Isidore and the *Fuero Juzgo*[2] show, the strength of ancient local habits was undermined by a legal system that claimed moral superiority. Law could only be understood in terms of justice.

At this point it should be noted that the English term "law" cannot be adequately translated into Latin or Spanish. Romans and Spaniards developed two terms, neither one of which is the equivalent of "law." The Romans used the terms *Ius* and *Lex,* and the Spaniards the terms *Derecho* and *Ley. Ius* and *Derecho* are abstract terms both of which relate directly to the conception of justice. *Lex* and *Ley* are used to indicate written or enacted legislation. The relationship between the two conceptions is quite clear in the sense that both *Ius* and *Derecho* are more important ethically and clearly higher ranking juridically than *Lex* and *Ley.* All enacted legislation would have to be justified in terms of a conception of justice that legitimized, in the eyes of those concerned, every specific law. In fact, what the Romans and Spaniards did was to establish the direct priority of justice over law. Specific legislation could be either enacted or superseded on the basis of the abstract moral conceptions upheld by those legislating.

The Roman-Spanish conception of law was brought to Cuba at the beginning of the colonial days. As with many other Spanish institutions, it took deep

---

[1]One of the many works composed by St. Isidore of Seville. His influence as a thinker and philosopher of the Christian world extended well into the Middle Ages.
[2]The first Spanish compilation of laws of which there is recorded evidence.

root in the new colony and has not ceased to operate. A survey of legal textbooks and accepted principles of jurisprudence in the entire Latin-American area would corroborate this fact.

Of course, all systems of law, including that of the Anglo-Saxons, tend to equate, in one way or another, law and justice. What is characteristic of the Latin-American tradition is the establishment of a *direct* relationship between the conception of justice and the acceptance of the law. Latin-American legal thought and practice tend, therefore, to be relatively unconcerned with procedural guarantees. Such guarantees are often considered obstacles in the path of justice, and the idea that they may in themselves be a symbol or instrument of justice has never been accepted. Castro's appeal for a retrial was an effort, from his point of view, to establish a direct link between justice and law. The implementation of a moral interpretation was viewed by him, as it had been viewed in the past by Roman, Spanish, and Latin-American jurists and legal philosophers, as the proper function of the judiciary.

IDEALISM AND REALISM

The idea that justice—however defined—is the only acceptable foundation of legal institutions and processes is very much the result of idealistic and universalistic thinking. An ideal conception is, when reduced to its psychological components, a rejection of reality; its implementation is always an attempt to replace an existing reality with an intellectual abstraction. Idealism is a form of escapism—a way of avoiding or bypassing reality that is not to one's liking. Judicial idealism is an attempt to legislate an unwanted reality out of existence. By undertaking to change reality through the enactment of legal regulations, judicial idealism places upon the legal system a quasi-magical connotation. The wish to alter reality, when expressed through the formalistic ritual of the law, appeals to psychological and anthropological tendencies probably present in all societies and is especially strong in the Latin-American communities.

Of course idealism does not totally exclude *all* traces of pragmatism. After all, if idealism is to have substantial impact on legal or political behavior, it must be more than a mere exercise in unrealistic reasoning. Idealistic thinking is not simply abstract and speculative; it is also a way of performing some very practical functions. Idealism presents at least two different aspects. Whereas the content of the ideal formulas represents a denial of reality, the use made of such formulas may be indicative of a degree of realistic awareness. Although efforts to apply the ideal prescription would be by definition doomed to failure, the very formulation of such an ideal could be an activity which might successfully perform a given social function. In other words, there is another dimension to idealism apart from that of completely unrealistic substantive thinking.

From a more sociological point of view, the development and implementation of an abstract concept of justice, rather than the preservation of traditions as sources of law, is an indication of a low degree of social cohesiveness. Societies in which customs can be legally superseded by abstract ideas and intellectual speculation are societies in which the past is not looked upon as a repository of collective identification and security. Adherence to ideal formulas is an artificial way of seeking the unity and cohesiveness that traditional institutions can no longer, or never did, provide. When a society attempts to define ideal patterns of conduct, it is implicitly admitting to a potentially low degree of internal cohesiveness.

The case of Batista's pilots may be looked upon as an extreme example of the predominance of justice over law in Cuba, but it should not be interpreted as an aberration of that country's legal tradition. The Latin-American tendency to establish a direct link between the ideal concept of justice and the workings of the judiciary should help clarify the nature of the government's attitude toward and expectations concerning the case. Once Castro and his followers had equated their revolution with justice, they ascribed to the courts the function of punishing their enemies. In demanding a retrial they were simply implementing their conception of the court's role.

Castro's behavior was not, therefore, the result of any abstract, deterministic force. In trying to reestablish a direct link between justice and the court's decision, he was casting his ideas in a familiar cultural mold. Such a request was consistent with the goals of the revolution and with his kind of leadership. Furthermore, despite the protests already mentioned, Castro's action did not arouse any ill feeling toward him or the revolution among the Cuban people at large. At least there is no evidence that it did. The retrial of the airmen is perfectly understandable from a cultural-moral point of view. In political terms, Castro's way of handling the problem actually increased his popularity. He demonstrated his determination to seek justice in spite of institutional obstacles. Given the low esteem in which the institutions of the prior system were held by the Cuban people, his action earned more praise than condemnation.

The case in question, and the conception of law and the judiciary which it represents, should be of help in interpreting some of the most fundamental political characteristics of Latin-American societies. It should be evident that in these societies the judiciary is highly politicized and tends to come under the direct influences of the executive. This, of course, is the general rule. Executive pressure tends to increase in direct proportion to the political importance of the issues handled by the courts. The lower courts dealing mainly with nonpolitical matters enjoy the greatest degree of freedom from interference.

Latin-American tradition, as well as legal philosophy and practice, militate against a high degree of independence for the judiciary. Given a broad enough spectrum, all judiciary systems are politically partisan. Therefore Latin-American legal behavior, when compared to Anglo-Saxon counterparts, is more unique in form than in substance. Castro's blatant use of the court for political purposes, although perhaps shocking to some, was far from new. His idealized conception of the judicial system was in perfect accord with the cultural tradition from which he sprang. As is so often the case with reformers, he was following rather than leading.

three:
political
"trials"

JOHN E. TURNER*

7

ARTISTS IN ADVERSITY

the sinyavsky-daniel case

In 1959 and the early 1960s the literary works of two unknown Soviet writers —Abram Tertz and Nikolai Arzhak—were published in the West. Except for Tertz's critical essay, *On Socialist Realism,* the writings were satire and fantasy in the form of novels and short stories. Some Western commentators interpreted them as blistering indictments of the Soviet system. A number of seasoned critics, however, read other meaning from these works, appraising their merit according to the canons of literary criticism applicable to literature of fantasy. Some felt that the artistic quality of the stories was uneven, but there was general agreement that they were innovative and refreshing, a good step forward from the stereotyped themes and forms of the Stalin period.

In mid-September 1965, two Soviet citizens were secretly arrested and held in detention for three months before the authorities confirmed that the arrests had been made. When newspapers carried the announcement, the Soviet public learned that the defendants were being charged with "ideological sabotage." On 5 December about two hundred students and faculty members from the Gorky Institute of World Literature staged a demonstration in Moscow's Pushkin Square calling for an open trial of the two men.[1] The gathering was quickly dispersed by the police, and several of the agitators were detained,

*The author wishes to thank Mrs. Patricia Hayman-Chaffey for helping him with the research and in the preparation of the manuscript. He also acknowledges the suggestions given by his colleagues, Professors Robert T. Holt and Samuel Krislov, Department of Political Science, University of Minnesota. He is especially grateful to Professor Theofanis G. Stavrou, Department of History, University of Minnesota, who made some valuable comments and helped him with the materials from the *White Book.*

[1]*New York Times,* 12, 18 December 1965.

one of them being carted off to a mental asylum. According to reports, a number of students were expelled from the university.

This was the onset of a case that greatly agitated portions of the intellectual community in the USSR. As will be seen later, it helped to provoke other incidents, outbursts, and arrests, all of which had political overtones. To understand how the detention of two men generated such a reaction, it is necessary to consider briefly the uncertainty and ferment in the realm of Soviet literature since Stalin's death.

UNREST IN THE LITERARY WORLD

Soviet literature has burst into fresh blossom in the period since 1953. This has obviously been a matter of concern for the political authorities, who seem to prefer that Soviet writers remain within officially prescribed bounds. As a result, the cultural climate has not been consistently temperate, but has fluctuated between eras of moderate "thaw" and spells of less tolerant "freeze."[2] The zigzag pattern of literary development has been influenced by several factors.

One factor is the policy of "de-Stalinization." Immediately after Stalin's death, his successors proceeded to formulate policies that would attract popular support and dissociate their regime from the hardships and brutalities of the past. In pursuing this objective, they condemned the "cult of personality" and set about, at first in veiled fashion, to whittle down Stalin's reputation. Some writers perceived that the new rulers might tolerate a measure of artistic autonomy; they began to release frustrations which had been building up during the years when they had been forced to subordinate their artistic impulse to the injunction that they trumpet the virtues of the "cause." In literary essays they criticized the inferior quality of Soviet writing and denounced the forcing of art into a "single fixed mold." Breaking away from the standard pattern of stale characters, predictable plots, and prefabricated styles, these writers sought to depict Soviet life in a more balanced way. For their material, they turned to ordinary people (rather than heroes of production) in real-life situations, highlighting some of the conflicts and unrealized aspirations, and treating such material with human understanding. Like their predecessors in czarist times, the innovative novelists and poets were nurturing a social conscience, and attempting to articulate the tensions that existed in the social order.

New vistas for unorthodox writers were unintentionally opened up in 1956 when Khrushchev dismantled the Stalin myth at the Twentieth Party Congress.

---

[2]For detailed treatments of the ferment in the arts since 1953, see Harold Swayze, *Political Control of Literature in the USSR, 1946–1959* (Cambridge: Harvard University Press, 1962); Priscilla Johnson and Leopold Labedz, *Khrushchev and the Arts: The Politics of Soviet Culture, 1962–1964* (Cambridge, Mass.: The M.I.T. Press, 1965), especially pp. 1–89; the articles by Timothy McClure, George Gibian, and Sidney Monas in *Problems of Communism*, March–April 1967.

His disclosures touched the sensitive nerves of the artists, many of whom had compromised their own standards to do Stalin's bidding. Perhaps more significant in the long run, the unmasking of the dictator disenchanted large numbers of young people, some of whom turned to literature—especially poetry—as an outlet for expressing their skepticism and easing their intellectual discontent. The official renunciation of Stalinist methods, startling though it was at first, proved to be a boon for the writers. They could now interpret the new line as sanction for them to draw their subject matter from the antagonisms and frustrations of the Stalin era. Moreover, by officially eschewing Stalinist forms of coercion, the Soviet rulers denied themselves the use of some of the control mechanisms that had been employed to keep the literary world in subjection. Unconventional writers were now in a position to condemn strict censorship of their work as a "return to Stalinism," and to denounce irregular methods of punishment for artistic effort as violations of "socialist legality."

The emergence of "dissonant voices" in Soviet writing gave rise to a second factor that has had an impact upon literary developments, namely, the bitter controversies between the "revisionist" writers and the "conservatives" or "dogmatists"—struggles that have been punctuated by maneuvers for power within the literary bureaucracies. The revisionists, who have a few party members listed on their roster, are a heterogeneous group which attracted many young writers after 1956. These dissidents do not reject the Communist system as such, nor do they quarrel with the basic themes of its ideology. They plead instead for a loosening of party controls over literature, so that they can portray Soviet life more realistically, and in modes of their own choosing. On the opposite side, the conservatives—the backbone of the literary establishment—insist upon tight controls over artistic content and expression, largely in the Stalin-Zhdanov tradition.[3]

While these two groups feud over literary matters, their respective demands touch in a real sense upon the delicate question of what the political system should be like. Their disputes emerge into public view through their literary works, newspaper articles, and essays in professional journals. The conflicts can also be observed in the debates at writers' meetings and party gatherings, and in the competition for posts in the professional organizations and the editorial boards of literary journals. Writers in each camp have their political feelers pointed to the Kremlin, and when their assessment of official attitudes suggests a shift in literary policy one way or the other, they intensify the attack upon their opponents and attempt to remove them from positions of influence in the literary bureaucracies.

This leads us to the third factor influential in producing policies in the literary realm—the situation that exists at any given time within the ruling oligarchy itself. Sometimes the Communist leaders have been so preoccupied with other urgent problems that they have had little time to detect and to

[3]Immediately after World War II, Soviet leaders instituted a campaign for tightened controls, and for a time Andrei Zhdanov was in charge. Under his leadership, the shakeup was extended to the arts.

deal with unorthodox trends in belles lettres.[4] When this happens, the liberal writers tend to view the absence of official pronouncements as a sign of relaxed restraints. Similarly, struggles among politburo factions—as, for example, the Malenkov-Khrushchev imbroglio in 1954–1955—have generated intervals of political uncertainty during which dissenters have surfaced to air their opinions. It is likely, too, that when a group within the politburo is groping for wider support, it may adjust its policy, or even refrain from becoming identified with a policy, so as not to antagonize particular groups in the intellectual community.

Another factor that may influence the official attitude toward literature is "pressure" from outside the borders of the Soviet Union. This factor may be operative in at least two ways. First, an unfavorable turn in international events serves to discredit the *general program* of the dominant politburo faction, and this may prompt its leaders to soften or to harden their literary policy, in order to help weather the political storm. Second, how foreigners view the regime's treatment of its writers may be taken into account when the ruling clique seeks to improve its relations with particular groups or particular countries abroad. In recent years, as the Soviet authorities have sought to preserve the solidarity of the Communist bloc, they have been especially sensitive to the opinions of foreign Communists.

A good illustration of how external events and factional rivalries inside the politburo have an impact upon literary policy occurred when the "anti-party" group was bidding for power in 1956–1957. In the autumn of 1956, Khrushchev's regime became vulnerable to criticism because of an economic crisis at home, and attempted revolutions in Poland and Hungary (in which the native writers had played an important role). Khrushchev's struggle with his political enemies led to an abatement in the de-Stalinization program, and the conservative writers moved in to dominate the literary scene. Revisionists fell under severe attack for transgressing the literary commandments, and in the summer of 1957 the first secretary himself took the writers to task for their avant-garde works.[5]

Some writers, Khrushchev charged, were treating the criticism of Stalin as a "sweeping denial of the positive role" he had played in the country's development. He joined in the criticism of some recent works, including Vladimir Dudintsev's *Not by Bread Alone*, which, he pointed out, *was being used against the USSR by reactionary forces abroad.* He then presented the standard description of an artist's obligations in the Soviet system. Khrushchev's pronouncements marked an era of "freeze," during which Boris Pasternak was officially disgraced, not only because he had been awarded a Nobel Prize for

[4]In his speech to the Third Writers Congress in 1959, Khrushchev admitted that he was too busy to read literary works. See *Pravda*, 24 May 1959, translated in *Current Digest of the Soviet Press* 11, no. 21 (24 June 1959): 3.

[5]See N. S. Khrushchev, "For Close Ties between Literature and Art and the Life of the People," *Pravda*, 28 August 1957, translated in *Current Digest of the Soviet Press* 9, no. 35 (9 October 1957): 3–10.

Literature, but also because *Doctor Zhivago* had been published abroad and given an anti-Soviet interpretation by foreign critics.

From the time of the Pasternak episode until the end of 1962, the Kremlin leaders appeared to follow a course of guarded moderation on the literary front. At the Third Writers Congress in 1959, Khrushchev's views on literature had mellowed considerably from the dogmatic stand he had taken two years earlier.[6] On the assumption that revisionist views had suffered "total ideological defeat," he seemed willing to rely upon the judgment of editorial boards so long as they remained faithful to the general rules: "Therefore, comrades, don't burden the government with these matters. Decide them for yourselves in comradely fashion." It may be that a modus vivendi was being worked out according to which writers would have more freedom to experiment with new literary styles so long as they steered clear of politically colored materials.

With the hint that the political authorities might stand somewhat aside from the literary struggle, the liberals began to express themselves in a new wave of avant-garde writing. Many who could not get their work published through state-controlled outlets disseminated their stories and poems in the shadow of the underground, reading them to close friends or circulating handwritten or typed manuscripts within and among literary "circles." Some opted to write "for the drawer" in the hope that their work might be published at some future time when the censors wielded less power. Not content to gamble against such adverse odds, a few sent their manuscripts abroad to be published, usually under false names.

The unconventional writers who managed to get their compositions published through regular channels were infected by daring moods and a yearning for experimentation. They stressed the importance of artistic truth in literature, rejecting the "positive hero" as a relic of the grim past. Poets won the praise of critics and the applause of young people for their bold choice of themes and their portrayal of youth's inner conflicts. Noteworthy during this "thaw" were the spontaneous mass gatherings where poets recited their verse, often compositions that had been rejected by editors because of ideological impurity. In Moscow, a popular meeting place was at the Mayakovsky monument, where huge crowds—mostly young people—assembled to listen to poets like Yevgeny Yevtushenko and Andrei Voznesensky. Almost needless to say, the regime's agents also attended these meetings, but the poetry was not their main interest.

Although the Khrushchev period after 1958 was characterized by a moderate literary policy, the writers nevertheless experienced setbacks. A ripple appeared in the intellectual "calm" on 1 December 1962, when Khrushchev attended an art exhibit in Moscow and grew enraged at some of the unconventional paintings.[7] This incident was followed by a tightening of controls which lasted until the spring of 1963. The hardening of the official line may

[6]See N. S. Khrushchev, *Speech to the Writers Congress*, pp. 3–7, 29.
[7]For a reprinted version of Khrushchev's reaction, see Johnson and Labedz, *Khrushchev and the Arts*, pp. 101–5. A detailed treatment of the 1962–63 period is presented in this work.

be partially explained by external and domestic pressures on the Soviet leaders
—open differences with the Red Chinese, the Cuban crisis, and internal economic difficulties. The urgency of these problems may have convinced some
Kremlin leaders that the de-Stalinization strategy, which had been championed
again at the Party Congress in 1961, was being pushed too far, and that, in the
face of crisis, stiffened discipline was needed over discordant elements. In any
event, the regime summoned the artists to several conferences, and later
called a meeting of the Central Committee to discuss ideological questions.
What started out as a campaign against avant-garde canvases was soon broadened to include literature, and criticism was focused especially upon some of
the younger novelists and poets. Yevtushenko was called to account for having had his *Autobiography* published abroad without trying domestic outlets
first; Voznesensky was chastised for his "innovative" verse; and Alexander
Solzhenitsyn, whose *One Day in the Life of Ivan Denisovich* had originally
been published as a result of Khrushchev's intervention, was now assailed for
his novel, as well as for his more recent stories.

By 1963, however, it was evident that segments of the intellectual community were no longer content to "protest by silence," and the regime was
forced to reckon with more audacious strategies employed by the revisionists.
Although several young poets were called upon to confess their literary sins,
their recantations were ambiguous and half-hearted, and largely unsatisfactory
by conservative standards. Prominent intellectuals, including a few scientists
and representatives from the nonliterary arts, dispatched letters of protest to
the Communist leaders supporting artistic freedom and petitioning against a
return to Stalinist methods. These appeals were reinforced by the reaction of
foreign Communists, including some East Europeans, who expressed displeasure with the repression of the artists. The Soviet rulers were probably sensitive to this reaction, since they needed the support of Communist parties
abroad in their struggle with the Chinese.

Although by June 1963 the campaign against the writers had simmered
down, literary people were soon troubled by another "zag" in the zigzag pattern. This was the case of Joseph Brodsky, a young Leningrad poet who was
arrested and tried under the "anti-parasite" law. Several prominent writers
elected to testify in his behalf, and other creative artists protested to the
judicial authorities. The court, however, refused to recognize that writing
poetry was useful work, and it sent the defendant away for a five-year term of
"educative" labor on a collective farm. Reports of the trial provoked stinging
criticism in Western intellectual circles. Before two years of his sentence were
up, Brodsky was permitted to return to Leningrad.

By the end of the Khrushchev era in the fall of 1964, the main components
of the Soviet "literary problem" were becoming fairly distinct, and the
present-day rulers have had to wrestle with it:

First, despite sustained attacks by the conservatives and intermittent pressures applied by the politicians, the revisionist writers have refused to be
silenced, and Soviet literature has taken on new vitality. Two factors have
helped to nurture this development: One, the regime's denunciation of

Stalinism has provided the writers with new literary materials and has given them some protection against outrageous sanctions. Two, the regime's ambivalent policies toward literature have made the writers *uncertain* as to what the limits are—a situation that has encouraged some to play for optimal interpretations; the fact that Khrushchev occasionally overruled the literary bureaucrats and personally sanctioned publication of controversial works fostered hopes (however slight) that this might happen again.

Second, the freshness of themes and styles in the literary output, the vibrant life in the literary underground, and the spontaneous gatherings of poetry lovers have fired the courage of the writers, raising their expectations; equally important, these developments have facilitated better communication among intellectuals of all types.

Third, literary people have grown courageous enough to protest to the authorities when their colleagues have been accused of stepping out of bounds, and these protests have commanded the support of a surprising number of nonliterary intellectuals.

Fourth, the Soviet rulers have become alarmed by the ferment in the literary world. They are particularly disturbed by the fact that some writers have had their manuscripts published abroad where the materials can be used as "anti-Soviet" propaganda. However, the wavering policies governing literature, especially since 1958, suggest that the Communist leaders are not sure how to go about quieting dissident voices in a non-Stalinist setting.

Fifth, the members of the high command have grown increasingly uneasy about the reaction of foreigners to the treatment of Soviet writers, because the imperatives of their foreign policy now call for better relations with the West and for more imaginative ways of enlisting cooperation from Communist parties abroad. Adverse criticism of their literary policy by non-Russian Communists has distressed Soviet leaders, especially at a time when they are struggling to hold the Communist world together.

This, then, was the "literary problem" that Khrushchev passed on to his successors. For several months following his ouster, the new regime was preoccupied with other problems, and it issued no new injunctions to the artists. But the innovative writers were apprehensive; they were not sure that Khrushchev's relatively moderate policies after 1958 had been effective in producing a sustained, tolerant attitude in the Kremlin toward literature. Despite some concern and uncertainty, however, adventurous souls from the intellectual underground began, in the spring of 1965, to stick their heads into the open.

In mid-April 1965, for example, a group of dissident poets staged an unauthorized demonstration in the streets of Moscow, blocking traffic while they read their censorable poetry.[8] On another occasion, some students held a meeting at Moscow University at which a young speaker vigorously condemned Soviet leaders for their failure to punish those responsible for the

---

[8]These illustrations are taken from Timothy McClure, "The Politics of Soviet Culture, 1964–1967," *Problems of Communism*, March–April 1967, p. 33.

crimes of the Stalin era. Some other incidents of defiance by young people were not reported in the Soviet press or discovered by foreign journalists.

The Soviet regime and its agents were not accustomed to this type of behavior and were understandably disturbed by it. They moved into action during the summer of 1965, and the intellectual atmosphere grew more stifling. Not only did the conservative writers step up their attacks on the unorthodox writers, but also the enforcement authorities launched a campaign against segments of the broader intellectual community and closed in on some of the underground circles. The police rounded up nearly 100 intellectuals in the Ukraine, apprehended a group of Leningrad students for publishing an illegal journal, and made other arrests about which little is known.[9]

It was in this milieu that the case of the two men arrested in September 1965 took form.[10]

THE DEFENDANTS

One of the men was Abram Tertz—in real life, Andrei D. Sinyavsky, who had used "Tertz" as a pen name when his works were published abroad. A forty-year-old author and literary critic, Sinyavsky had attended Moscow University after the war, later obtained the degree of Candidate of Philological Sciences, and become a member of the senior research staff of the Gorky Institute of World Literature in Moscow. As a revisionist critic who was influenced by the revelations about the Stalin era, he defended works that had been attacked by the literary establishment, while his reviews of writing that had won acclaim from party ideologists and conventional essayists were often unflattering. Sinyavsky was a devotee of Pasternak, an analyst of his poetry, and a pallbearer at his funeral.

Inside the USSR Sinyavsky was best known for his work in literary criticism. However, nearly all of his fiction and a few essays—a total of nine manuscripts —were smuggled out of the country by a friend and published abroad under a pseudonym. The indictment listed three of these works as objectionable— two fantasies, *The Trial Begins* and *The Makepeace Experiment*, and one essay, *On Socialist Realism*. An unfinished manuscript, *An Essay in Self-Analysis*, was found in his home at the time of his arrest. As he pointed out at the trial, Sinyavsky had sent his creative works out of the country because he wanted

[9]See ibid., p. 38; George Luckyj, "Turmoil in the Ukraine," *Problems of Communism*, July– August 1968, especially pp. 17–18. See also the *Times* (London), 1 February 1966.

[10]In 1966, Max Hayward translated and edited a partial transcript of the Sinyavsky-Daniel trial which appeared as *On Trial: The Soviet State versus "Abram Tertz" and "Nikolai Arzhak"* (New York: Harper and Row, 1966). The author of this essay has relied heavily on this transcript for his presentation of the facts of the case and for his analysis of the trial procedures. Where quotations dealing with the trial appear without footnotes, they are taken from this work. Later, after most of the chapter was written, the author managed to secure a copy of the *White Book*, which is a collection of documents relevant to the case, including a transcript of the trial. The citation of this work is Alexander Ginzburg, ed., *Belaya kniga po delu A. Sinyavskogo i Yu. Danielya* [White Book on the Affairs of A. Sinyavsky and Yu. Daniel] (Frankfort, Germany: Posev-Verlag, 1967).

them preserved as literature, and he knew that their "artistic attitudes" made them unacceptable to Soviet publishers.

The other defendant was Nikolai Arzhak, or, stripped of camouflage, Yuli M. Daniel. Although the same age as Sinyavsky, he was little known in literary circles. His education had been interrupted by war service. After being demobilized as a result of wounds, he entered Kharkov University, then attended a training college. When he received his diploma, he secured a teaching position in Moscow. A few years later, he abandoned his teaching career to become a translator of poetry. He had once submitted a story for publication through regular channels, but it was never released to the book stalls.

Daniel had followed Sinyavsky's lead in sending some of his manuscripts abroad, where they were published under the alleged name of Arzhak. These writings—a novel fantasy, *This Is Moscow Speaking,* and three short stories, "Hands," "The Man from Minap," and "Atonement"—were listed in the indictment. At the hearing Daniel pointed out that he had sent his manuscripts out of the country because they were stained with politically sensitive themes and stood no chance of being published in the USSR.

Although the Soviet authorities delayed the announcement that Sinyavsky and Daniel had been apprehended, word of the arrests filtered through to the West, and on 9 October 1965, the imprisonment of the two writers was reported at a conference session of the European Community of Writers, which was meeting in Rome.[11] Prominent literary figures in the non-Communist world immediately rallied to the support of the defendants. Some tried to enlist the aid of Mikhail Sholokhov, a literary "conservative" and Nobel Prize winner; and some sent messages of protest to the chairman of the Council of Ministers, Alexei Kosygin, and to the secretary of the Writers Union.

Sinyavsky and Daniel were summoned to trial five months after their arrest. The indictment against them was based upon Section 1, Article 70 of the Criminal Code of the RSFSR, which defines as a crime:

Agitation or propaganda carried on for the purpose of subverting or weakening
Soviet authority or of committing particular, especially dangerous crimes
against the state, or circulating for the same purpose slanderous fabrications
which defame the Soviet state and social system, or circulating or preparing or
keeping, for the same purpose, literature of such content, . . .[12]

In specific terms, the indictment charged that the two authors had written anti-Soviet works which, under the guise of attacking the cult of personality, slandered the Soviet system and maligned its people. The defendants had had these objectionable writings smuggled out of the country so that they could be published abroad under the screen of pseudonyms. According to the complaint, the published works had been seized upon by hostile bourgeois groups

---

[11]For some of the Western reaction, see the *New York Times,* 23 October and 8 December 1965; *Times* (London), 13 November, 31 December 1965, and 31 January 1966.

[12]The translation is from Harold J. Berman and James W. Spindler, *Soviet Criminal Law and Procedure* (Cambridge: Harvard University Press, 1966), p. 180. RSFSR is the abbreviation for the Russian Socialist Federated Soviet Republic, which is the largest republic in the union.

which used them in propaganda campaigns against the Soviet Union—the indictment mentioned certain Russian émigré organizations and Radio Liberty in Munich.[13] The defendants were also accused of circulating their obnoxious literature among their acquaintances.

The Sinyavsky-Daniel case was distinctive because it was the first time that any Soviet writers had been brought to the dock for the *content* of their writings. In the past, to be sure, literary people had been denounced for anti-Soviet work, and most of them were punished (with varying degrees of severity). But these people were never brought into a public courtroom. The case was also unusual in that the two defendants did not confess during the trial.

THE CHOICE OF THE COURT AS A POLITICAL INSTRUMENT

Like their Czarist and Stalinist predecessors, the Communist rulers in 1965–1966 had reason to fear the Soviet writers. In the absence of channels for popular protest, the literary rebels were probably articulating some of the discontents felt by ordinary citizens. Even more serious, the avant-garde writers refused to give up, and now, along with other dissident intellectuals, they had the audacity to march in the streets and to send petitions of protest to leading political officials. The young writers, especially, were circumventing the regular control system by their outdoor poetry gatherings, by circulating their works in clandestine groups, and by even smuggling their manuscripts out of the country.

In dealing with recalcitrant writers, the regime faced a thorny problem. The Soviet rulers had to be concerned about the dissemination of unorthodox ideas which, in their view, challenged the existing power structure; given their code of operation, they could hardly be expected to endorse views that undermined the privileged role of the party, which was the basis of their legitimacy. But, as indicated earlier, in subscribing to a policy of de-Stalinization, the political authorities had robbed themselves of important methods of social control which had been used in the past to keep the writers in harness.

One course of action open to the regime was a return to mass suppression of the artists in the Stalin tradition—the midnight tap on the door, individuals quietly disappearing, inscrutable methods of confrontation, imprisonment or execution without trial. By generating an ethos of fear through the arbitrary use of force, the authorities would be able, at least for a time, to intimidate many of the dissenters, driving them to conformity or to refuge in "safe" activities, such as translating the classics.

But this Stalinist alternative entailed (and still does) certain risks for the Soviet rulers. For them to attempt to control the writers by resorting to brutal

---

[13]This radio station makes use of Russian émigrés to transmit propaganda broadcasts to the Soviet Union.

measures on a large scale would certainly alienate many people in the wider intellectual community—men of ideas, imagination, and scientific knowledge whose talents are needed to keep the society moving forward. Even if they did not protest openly, their opposition would be reflected in lowered morale and in their disinclination to exercise initiative in their work. In other words, with complex economic and social problems facing the country, the Communist leaders could not afford to precipitate a widening gulf between the intellectuals and the party. In addition, the regime had to face the prospect that terrorist methods applied to one group in society might be carried over to other groups because of the linkages among them. If the use of physically coercive measures spread, the impact would undoubtedly be felt in the non-intellectual areas of Soviet life. Fear of arbitrary arrest is not conducive to orderly living or to efficient performance on the job, both of which are essential in a maturing economy. A return to raw coercion would cast a pall over the entire society, dampening the spirit of the people and diminishing the vitality which had been evident in the USSR since 1953. Finally, the political leaders undoubtedly considered the possibility that widespread use of repressive methods might give rise to another dictator, thereby endangering their own position.

In contemplating such a program for handling literary dissenters, the Communist rulers could hardly overlook the probable reaction of foreigners, who have always been sensitive to Russia's treatment of her creative artists. Having staked so much on a de-Stalinized course, they would look foolish in the eyes of the world if they suddenly reversed field. Such an about-face would hamper the Soviet bid for the support of people in other countries and cripple the improving relations with the Western world. Especially important to the Soviet leaders at this time was the goodwill of Communist parties abroad, whose backing was needed in foreign policy matters, particularly in the engagement with Red China. The Soviet rulers, however, could no longer take the non-Russian parties for granted as they could in Stalin's day, particularly with respect to literary policy. The leaders of a foreign Communist party now had to be more concerned with their organization's standing among their own people, and they could not afford to be stamped as supporters of ruthless action against the writers. This fact would have been enough on its own to prompt the Russian authorities to be cautious.

If mass suppression of the artists was to be rejected as a hazardous undertaking, the regime still held the option of using Stalinist methods against some of the worst offenders on a selective basis. These people could be apprehended without fanfare, tried secretly or not tried at all, and sent off to a labor colony to have their outlooks broadened. In this way, some of the ringleaders in the literary underground might be removed from positions of influence. At the very least, by turning their wrath upon a few, the enforcement authorities might be able to intimidate many of the rest and thus deter them from engaging in unauthorized behavior. Furthermore, if the repressive measures were kept out of public view, it would be difficult for reports to be leaked out to other countries, and it would reduce the likelihood that wide-spread hostility would be provoked at home. According to scattered accounts this was the policy applied in 1965–66 to some dissidents who were whisked away without benefit of the legal procedures that people had come to expect. This strategy, of course, had to be implemented with great care, for it contained many of the risks inherent in a program of mass suppression.

The policy of "selective repression" would be difficult to apply against writers who had won national acclaim and enjoyed a popular following. For them to be punished by the judicial authorities in clear violation of legal norms would provoke the displeasure, not only of foreigners, but of the. Soviet intellectual community as well. By the same token, the regime would have to be careful how it handled dissident writers whose reputation among intellectuals abroad was actually greater than it was in the USSR. Repressive measures against them would certainly provoke a hostile reaction abroad, and this in turn would probably stir up opposition among intellectual circles in the Soviet Union.

The Sinyavsky-Daniel case had to be dealt with, but, as events developed, it had to be singled out for special treatment. After their identity had been established, the two authors were obvious candidates for some type of reprisal. They were undoubtedly an embarrassment to the political authorities because their writings—published through foreign outlets without Communist authorization—were being given an anti-Soviet twist by some Western critics, and some of their works had been used by Radio Liberty. A regime that tends to suffer from "social paranoia" could hardly overlook the behavior of Sinyavsky and Daniel. Although, admittedly, this is speculation, their actions provided ingredients that could conceivably be whipped together into a "provable" case and presented in believable form to ordinary citizens. Indeed, it might even be plausible to some foreigners.

Initially, the regime may have intended to try to scrape through by dealing with Sinyavsky and Daniel secretly, as it had apparently done with other cases on its agenda at the time. The two authors were apprehended in mid-September 1965, and news of the arrests did not appear on the Soviet radio or in the domestic press until the following January, after some Westerners had begun to exert pressure. Apparently some students were afraid that the defendants would be sent away in violation of regular procedures, as shown by their demonstration on December 5 in support of a public trial.

A speculative reason why the Soviet authorities decided to schedule a court-room drama, with at least the embroidery of "legality," is not hard to come by. The names of Abram Tertz and Nikolai Arzhak were well known in foreign literary circles, and some of their work had been warmly applauded. When the arrest of the authors became known, eminent literary figures in the West sent word to the Soviet authorities that the two artists should *never have been taken into custody.* In light of these protests, the Russian leaders may have perceived that they would seriously damage their image abroad if they sent these reputable defendants to prison without bothering to follow the legal procedures they continually praise. That the courtroom was being used—at least in part—to dramatize the fairness of Soviet proceedings is suggested by the first official press report of the trial, which devoted a considerable number of its opening lines to a discussion of how the defendants were being protected.[14]

Let us assume for the moment that the Soviet regime, once having decided upon a trial, wanted to sidestep foreign criticism and to manage the proceedings so as to derive optimal benefits with minimal costs. How could this best be done? News emanating from the courtroom would have to be restricted so that detailed reports of the proceedings would not be sent abroad. Dispatches to the local population would have to be colored so that ordinary citizens and dissident groups would not learn about the trial procedures or the defiant posture of the defendants. Through the reading of selected passages from their works, the courtroom could be a rostrum for exposing their "crimes," and through its reports of the trial the official press could be used to discredit the two writers, to alert the people to the dangers of anti-Soviet literature, and to arouse mass hostility against those who create it.

THE TRIAL

The Soviet court is officially regarded as a political and administrative instrument, and hence is more vulnerable to "nonjudicial" influences than are the court systems in many other countries. This vulnerability is most pronounced when the court is called upon to deal with "political crimes"—criminal acts that involve the security of the Soviet state. In such cases, the antennae of the court officials are sensitively attuned to the party line, and no defendant who has been brought to trial under Article 70 has ever been acquitted. In charges of this type, the pretrial investigation is especially important—for Sinyavsky and Daniel, this lasted for about five months—and the record is admissible in the trial itself.

Article 70 of the Criminal Code is a catchall which the regime has traditionally used to handle discordant elements by branding them as enemies of the state. It is so ambiguously drawn that virtually any act or any piece of literature disapproved by influential leaders can be designated as dangerous simply on the say-so of the authorities. Although the USSR does not like to have its writers publish their work abroad without first submitting the manuscripts to domestic publishing houses, this in itself is not a crime; in recent years, a number of Soviet writers—Yevtushenko is an example—have published their writings in foreign countries without being subjected to court discipline, although they have been censured in other ways.

Technically, two questions were involved in the Sinyavsky-Daniel case. First,

[14]*Izvestia*, 11 February 1966, translated in *Current Digest of the Soviet Press* 18, no. 6 (2 March 1966): 3–4.

were their literary works anti-Soviet or subversive in character? And second, if so, was this the *intent* of the authors? Although the question of intent is important in many legal systems, Soviet courts have tended to pay less attention to it. Historically, administrators and court officials have been inclined to judge a given act by its *consequences* rather than by the motivation of a defendant. Whether intended or not, an act that leads to a consequence which is deemed harmful to the state has been interpreted as deserving of punishment. In the political trials of the Stalin era, the enforcement authorities took cognizance of not only the actual consequences of an act, but also the probable or logical consequences.

Pretrial Publicity

Once the decision had been taken to summon Sinyavsky and Daniel to the courtroom, the Soviet press began to devote more attention to the case. Several weeks before the trial was scheduled to open, the two authors were viciously denounced in newspaper articles and in letters to the editor.[15]

The first and most prejudicial attack, which appeared in *Izvestia* on 13 January 1966, was prepared by Dmitri Yeremin, a writer in the conservative camp. The "turncoats," he charged, had "dipped their pens in the inkwell of venom" to write "dirty libels against their country." Quoting samples of their writing out of context, Yeremin accused the "scribblers" of defaming the Soviet people and of desecrating the names of Lenin and Chekhov. In sending their manuscripts abroad, they placed themselves "in the service of the most rabid enemies of Communism" and became a "tool for spreading psychological warfare against the Soviet Union." For these "hostile acts against the homeland," he concluded, the culprits should be shown no mercy. Yeremin's article immediately stimulated a number of letters to the editor, some of them written by artists, which branded the two authors as "traitors" who belonged in the dock.

On 22 January, Zoya Kedrina, an obscure critic and Sinyavsky's former colleague (who was to play a role at the trial), joined the campaign to discredit the accused. In an article in the *Literary Gazette,* she pointed out how bourgeois propagandists had used their "slander" as ammunition. Turning first to Daniel, she characterized *This Is Moscow Speaking* as sheer "fascism." She then centered her fire on Sinyavsky, disparaging his literary skill and charging him with plagiarism.

The pretrial coverage of the case in the newspapers in effect introduced the government's brief to Soviet readers; the major themes and out-of-context illustrations were repeated later in newspaper reports of the trial itself. Long before the court returned its verdict, ordinary citizens in the USSR had ample reason to believe that the defendants were guilty.

---

[15]For translations of these pretrial denunciations of Sinyavsky and Daniel, see *Current Digest of the Soviet Press* 18, no. 2 (2 February 1966): 11–12 and no. 3 (9 February 1966): 15–18.

Trial Procedures

The Sinyavsky-Daniel hearing opened at the Moscow Province Court on 10 February 1966 and ended four days later. Selected to preside over the affair was Lev N. Smirnov, Chairman of the Supreme Court of the RSFSR. The government's case was handled by Oleg P. Temushkin, Assistant Prosecutor-General of the USSR. Two "public accusers," one of whom was Zoya Kedrina, were chosen by the Writers Union to give expert literary testimony for the prosecution. Contrary to official claims, the trial was not an open, public hearing. Admission to the courtroom was by special permit, and Western observers, including even foreign Communists, were kept outside on the excuse that space was not available. This was probably an attempt to hold the proceedings secret except for official releases, the first of which emphasized the scrupulous regard for the defendants' legal rights.

During the long pretrial investigation, Sinyavsky and Daniel had denied that their works were anti-Soviet or that they intended them to be exploited for propaganda. But apparently Daniel was led to admit that he had been improvident in writing stories that were used by his country's enemies in the ideological struggle. At the outset of the trial, however, the defendants took the authorities off guard by pleading "not guilty" to all of the charges, a most unusual occurrence in Soviet court proceedings. During the course of the hearing, Daniel weakened the force of his plea by conceding that the writings contained indiscretions and by expressing regret that they had been published abroad. Later, while in prison, he wrote a letter to *Izvestia* retracting these statements. He pointed out that, for six months during the investigation and the trial, his interrogators sought to convince him that his and Sinyavsky's writings had been used *only* by Soviet enemies, and that, in the absence of objective information about the impact of their work, the assertions of the investigators and court officials had had an influence upon him.[16]

To avoid the criticism that had been leveled at the handling of the Brodsky case, the court paid more attention to the rights of the accused in the trial proceedings. Each of them had an opportunity to make a statement, although Sinyavsky was called ahead of schedule and did not have time to prepare. On the first day, during the questioning of Daniel, Judge Smirnov occasionally chastised the prosecutor for his pointed comments, and later in the hearing, when a question arose concerning the interpretation of some translations, the judge asked Sinyavsky whether he would like to have another translator called.

In other ways, however, the defendants were at a disadvantage. To begin with, the courtroom atmosphere was not conducive to a sober analysis of evidence. The members of the hand-picked audience were hostile to the defendants and frequently interrupted the proceedings with derisive laughter and jeering comments.

The defendants were also handicapped by the court's denial of most of their requests. Sinyavsky asked to be examined first, possibly because he had

[16]Ginzburg, ed., *White Book*, p. 395.

conceded less than his colleague, but the officials upheld the prosecutor's objection. The court also turned down the defense's petition to admit as evidence the written testimonials of three Soviet writers, including that of Konstantin G. Paustovsky, one of the older and distinguished liberal writers; the reason given was that the literary merits of the works were not at issue, although the public accusers from the writers' community were called upon to testify for the government.

Even more serious, the court refused to allow the defendants to call certain of their witnesses. When they requested that all of the foreign press clippings on Abram Tertz and Nikolai Arzhak be obtained from the Lenin Library, they were informed later that some of these materials were not available. A similar request had been turned down during the pretrial investigation. This meant, of course, that Sinyavsky and Daniel were unable to present all of their case. Assuming that evidence was important to the outcome, the newspaper clippings would have been useful to the defense, since the prosecutor and judge kept quoting only a limited number of interpretations by foreign critics, ignoring those that did not consider the writing to be anti-Soviet.

As is usual in Soviet trials, the judge did not perform in the role of disinterested arbiter, but conducted an extensive examination of Sinyavsky and Daniel from the bench. Judge Smirnov seemed concerned about whether their writing fitted into the prohibitions of Article 70. Frequently he quoted selected passages and then challenged the authors to admit that the statements were "slanderous" and not merely a "literary device."

The judge's approach to the case can be seen from some of his statements and rhetorical questions. He referred to one manuscript as containing unprintable language which need not be read in the courtroom, and at one point he made an insinuation about Sinyavsky's war record. Among the comments from the bench were the following:

> [After reading a passage from Daniel's writing:] "It is obvious that they would love to publish this abroad."
> [After reading a quotation from Sinyavsky's work:] "What is this if it is not a slander on the Russian people?"
> [To Sinyavsky:] "Radio Liberty . . . did three broadcasts on The Makepeace Experiment. Did they do it just for fun, or what?"
> [To Sinyavsky:] "Do you think that reactionary publishers would have printed your books so beautifully if there had been nothing anti-Soviet in them?"
> [To Sinyavsky:] "And your words in the text are blasphemous."

The risks involved in being a reluctant witness were made clear to Igor Golomshkok, an art critic. When summoned to the stand, he admitted that friends had given him Sinyavsky's works to read, but he refused to incriminate them by disclosing their names to the court. For this refusal, he was later tried, convicted, and given a six-months suspended sentence under Article 182 of the Criminal Code.[17]

[17]Times (London), 17 February 1966; New York Times, 4 May 1966. Several other creative artists refused to testify against Sinyavsky and Daniel at the trial.

The Government's Case

In efforts to show that the defendants' works were anti-Soviet, the prosecutor and judge read many passages from their books, and usually twisted such excerpts out of context. The words of fictional characters, they contended, were really the views of the authors themselves. The use of imaginary settings and bizarre situations as devices for character development was a technique that court officials were apparently unable or unwilling to comprehend. When the defendants sought to describe their writing as fantasy, the judge invariably informed them that the courtroom was no place for a literary debate. The court officials also tended to assume that the use of pseudonyms on works that had been smuggled to foreign publishers was in itself proof of the anti-Soviet nature of the manuscripts. As additional evidence of this, they cited some of the literary interpretations that had been placed upon them in the West. In considering *The Trial Begins,* for example, the judge placed considerable weight on the commentary by Boris Filippov, a Russian émigré, who saw the novel as an attack upon Soviet life.[18]

If the anti-Soviet charge was not demonstrated, the question of intent would not enter into the picture. The prosecutor and judge, however, attempted to show, but did not prove, that the accused knew that their works were being exploited by foreign propagandists but continued to send their manuscripts out of the country anyway. One of the public accusers implied in his questioning that the authors had done this for material gain.

In answering the charges hurled at them by the court officials, Sinyavsky and Daniel strongly objected to having quotations from their writings read out of context. It was erroneous, they argued, to equate the words of the characters in a story with the opinions of the author. They had used fantasy and other styles of expression merely as literary vehicles, and many of the "defamatory" passages were the statements of "negative" characters whom they as authors disliked. It is impossible, they insisted, to analyze literature with legal tools. The defendants denied that they harbored anti-Soviet views, affirming their devotion to the USSR and its people and citing some foreign critics who did not regard their writing as hostile to the Soviet system. Mere publication of a manuscript by a bourgeois publisher, Daniel contended, was not proof that the work was anti-Soviet. He had used a pen name because his livelihood as a translator depended upon good relations with domestic publishing houses. On the question of intent, the two men insisted that they did not know that their stories were being used abroad for propaganda purposes.

[18]Had the court brought in a complete file of reviews, it would have had to deal with different literary evaluations, among them one in *The Atlantic* for October 1960: "It would be a mistake to take this acidly funny and demurely unpleasant little book as evidence of Communist disaffection in Russia. The author is not attacking Communism in the classic sense, but merely the hysterical excesses of the last days of Stalin's regime. . . . The author was no doubt advised to send his work abroad. But the book is no vote of confidence in the West." During the trial, Sinyavsky quoted from a commentary on his essay *On Socialist Realism:* "American readers would be mistaken if they regarded Tertz as an enemy of Communist society."

Their defense was really a plea to clear away the barriers that were preventing writers from expressing themselves as true artists. "Our literature and press are silent about the things on which I write," Daniel pointed out. "But literature is entitled to deal with any period and any question. I feel that there should be no prohibited subjects in the life of society." Sinyavsky put it this way: "The viewpoint of the prosecution is that literature is a form of propaganda; and that there are only two kinds of propaganda—pro-Soviet or anti-Soviet. If literature is simply un-Soviet, it means that it is anti-Soviet. I cannot accept this. It is a poor business if writers are judged and categorized by such standards."

But their arguments and appeals appear to have made little impact—a situation that was apparently recognized by the defendants. At the conclusion of Daniel's final statement, in which he had exposed the fallacies in the prosecution's case, he anticipated the verdict with fatalistic composure: "I am ready to hear the sentence."

The Verdict

The verdict was not long in coming. In the case of Sinyavsky, the prosecutor had requested the maximum penalty as provided in the Criminal Code—deprivation of freedom for seven years and an additional five-year term of exile. For Daniel, he had asked for five years of imprisonment and three years of exile.

After considering the evidence, Judge Smirnov and the two lay assessors returned a verdict of "guilty" on all counts. Playing out the theme, perhaps, that literary "turncoats" in the USSR are treated with compassion, the court did not assess the degree of punishment requested by the prosecution. Sinyavsky was sentenced to seven years of imprisonment at hard labor, and Daniel to five years. Neither defendant was given an additional period of exile. The sentences were not subject to appeal.

IMPACT OF THE TRIAL

If one of the purposes of the trial was to persuade foreign intellectuals that Sinyavsky and Daniel had been given their day in open court, the effort of the judicial authorities fell short of the mark. Soon after the announcement of the sentences, Western intellectuals, speaking both as individuals and as members of professional organizations, lodged protests in newspapers and with high Soviet officials.[19] Representatives of International P.E.N. and the European Community of Writers journeyed to Moscow in an attempt to obtain clemency for the convicted men. The Swedish Academy dispatched a telegram to the titular head of the government urging him to grant the defendants clemency.

[19]For accounts of these protests, see the *New York Times,* 29 March, 17 and 19 April, 18 May, and 11 June 1966; *Times* (London), 22–23 February 1966.

The International Commission of Jurists termed the whole affair a "blundering travesty of justice."

Many Communist figures abroad were also annoyed by the trial and the verdict. The leader of the British Communists dissociated his organization from the case with this rebuke: "The atmosphere created by Soviet press comments before the trial, and the reports of the trial itself, have played into the hands of anti-Soviet elements in the West. . . . The handling of this affair has done a greater disservice to the Soviet Union than have the works of Sinyavsky and Daniel."[20] The Central Committee of the French Communist Party approved a lengthy resolution, which was presented by Louis Aragon, asserting that "experimental requirements of literature and art cannot be denied or shackled without gravely affecting the development of culture and the human spirit itself."[21] Disapproval of the Soviet action was also expressed by Communist officials in Italy, Belgium, Austria, and the Scandinavian countries. The Italian Communists reportedly scheduled a conference with Leonid Brezhnev, general secretary of the Communist Party, on the matter.[22]

Prominent intellectuals in at least two of the East European nations refused to endorse the Soviet treatment of the two writers.[23] The Polish chapter of P.E.N. requested the Union of Soviet Writers to use its influence to obtain clemency for them. After a lengthy discussion of the case, the Czechoslovak Writers Union dispatched three representatives to the USSR to get a full explanation.

If the harassment of Sinyavsky and Daniel was designed to frighten the revisionist writers into obedience and to intimidate nonliterary intellectuals, it had the opposite effect. Far from being cowed, the rebels were spurred to bolder action. Indeed, the regime's harsh measures and the defendants' fortitude turned the affair into a cause célèbre which unified the literary rebels and tightened their links with people in other fields who were alarmed by the turn of events. Though of varying outlooks, some more politically tinged than others, the dissenters were united in their opposition to the stifling of creativity and the neo-Stalinist methods of punishment. The open dissent that grew out of the Brodsky case was mild indeed, compared with the outbursts precipitated by the Sinyavsky-Daniel case.

The trial jarred intellectuals—scientists and academicians as well as writers and other creative artists—and this display of solidarity helped to produce a larger and broader community of dissent when other cases emerged in 1967 and 1968. In this short essay, reference can be made to only a sampling of the protests that were registered after the Sinyavsky-Daniel decision was handed down.[24] When interviewed by a foreign correspondent, Alexander Yesenin-

[20]*Daily Worker,* 15 February 1966.
[21]Reported in the *New York Times,* 16 March 1966.
[22]See the *Times* (London), 16 February 1966; *New York Times,* 17 February and 14 April 1966.
[23]*New York Times,* 16 March 1966.
[24]The examples used here are reported in ibid., 21 February, 16 and 21 March, and 14 and 19 November 1966.

Volpin, a member of the literary underground who had led the December rally in Pushkin Square, disputed the verdict on legal grounds. Forty writers from Leningrad and Moscow, including some prominent literary figures, sent petitions to the government. Twenty-five intellectuals—some atomic scientists among them—warned Brezhnev against the dangers of rehabilitating Stalin, pointing out that, in view of the international situation, the country could not afford to alienate fraternal parties in the West. To protest against the sentences and to warn against the possible resurgence of Stalinism, more than ninety-five leading writers signed letters addressed to newspapers, writers' organizations, and government organs. In letters to the Twenty-third Party Congress and high legislative bodies, sixty-three literary people argued that to condemn writers for their satirical work was a bad precedent; they offered themselves as "surety" if the defendants could be set free.

The opposition of certain dissidents went beyond the issuance of formal protests.[25] At Moscow University, some students walked out of a class when their professor admitted that he had been partly responsible for a letter condemning Sinyavsky and Daniel. When Judge Smirnov appeared before an assembly of the Writers Union to discuss the case, a group of dissidents reportedly heckled him with the criticism of the trial that had stirred the foreign Communists. More daring was the action of Alexander Ginzburg and some of his friends—all members of the literary underground—who compiled a set of documents on the case (the so-called *White Book*). This compilation was circulated among intellectuals and later sent to the West, where it was published.

One of the documents in the *White Book*—"A Letter to an Old Friend"— expresses some of the feeling that the case provoked.[26] Sinyavsky and Daniel, according to the unknown author, were not guilty under the provisions of the Criminal Code. Writings which portrayed Stalinist crimes truthfully could not be as "grotesque" as the evils revealed at the Twenty-second Party Congress, and hence their authors could hardly be accused of "slander." He decried the fact that the expertise of engineers is used in ditchdigging, but in complex literary matters the opinions of amateurs had been sufficient. The trial, he felt, had been a "show" for the benefit of the West and for the training of young judges who needed a demonstration of how such cases could be handled in a "democratic" way. "In the courage of Sinyavsky and Daniel," he pointed out, "in their nobility and their victory, there is a drop of our blood, our sufferings, our battle against humiliation and lies, against murderers and traitors of all sorts. . . . [They] have etched their names in gold letters for their fight in the cause of freedom of conscience, freedom of creativity and freedom of individuality."

Young people who shared these feelings and were conscious of support from intellectuals outside the country were not easily silenced, and their activities brought down the regime's wrath upon them. Several were detained on 5 March 1966 for holding an anti-Stalin rally in Red Square on the anniversary

---

[25]Ibid., 19 March and 27 June 1966.
[26]The quotations from this letter are taken from the translation in *Problems of Communism*, July–August 1968, pp. 39–42.

of the dictator's death. Later, when a clandestine literary magazine, *Phoenix 1966*, published a defense of Sinyavsky and Daniel, several of the editors were arrested. Protesting against these arrests, a group of about fifty students and young writers staged a demonstration in Pushkin Square on 22 January 1967, demanding the release of the editors, the abrogation of a recently issued decree governing street activities and public order, and the revision of Article 70, which had trapped Sinyavsky and Daniel. Plainclothesmen quickly moved in on the demonstrators, making several arrests. Four young writers, including Vladimir I. Bukovsky, were tried and sentenced under procedures resembling those in the Sinyavsky-Daniel case. This action precipitated another flurry of protests, and some of the relevant documents, including Bukovsky's defiant statement to the court, were made available to the West—despite threats from the secret police—by Pavel M. Litvinov, a physicist and grandson of former Foreign Minister Maxim M. Litvinov.[27]

Another trial linked with the Sinyavsky-Daniel affair was held in January 1968. This case involved four young defendants—Alexander Ginzburg, Yuri Galanskov, Alexei Dobrovolsky, and Vera Lashkova, all members of the literary underground—who had already been in prison for a year.[28] Booked under Article 70, they were accused of being connected with *Phoenix 1966* and of having compiled the *White Book* on the Sinyavsky-Daniel case. To make its case more serious, the prosecution tried to link the defendants with a subversive émigré organization in Germany. Although one of the defendants pleaded guilty, turning state's evidence, and another admitted partial guilt, Ginzburg and Galanskov vigorously asserted their innocence and questioned the trial procedures. The hearing was cut from the same cloth as the others: a hand-picked audience, restrictions on the defense, and biased press reports, but with an added prohibition against anyone taking notes. The defendants were given the sentences requested by the prosecutor. No sooner had the trial ended than Litvinov and Mrs. Daniel termed the proceedings a "mockery" and issued an appeal "To World Public Opinion," urging that it be disseminated by Western press and radio because an appeal through the Soviet press would be "hopeless."[29]

In the wave of trials that followed the Sinyavsky-Daniel case, the young defendants (with a few exceptions) valiantly stood up for their rights, and revealed an amazing knowledge of the law and its technicalities. On several occasions during his final plea, Bukovsky heaped scorn on the police for their investigative methods, and infuriated the court officials by his curt remarks to the judge: "Do not interfere with my statement," and "I object to your infringement of my right of defense." In his plea, Ginzburg, too, struck at the core of the prosecution's case as though he were a seasoned practitioner. The

[27]On this case, see the *New York Times*, 24 January, 31 August–2 September, and 27 December 1967.

[28]For accounts of this case, see ibid., 9–13 January 1968.

[29]A very useful collection of documents on these later cases, which include letters of protest and some of the defendants' final statements to the court, is found in *Problems of Communism*, July–August and September–October 1968. The author has drawn upon these documents for this section of the chapter.

courage exhibited by the accused in the courtroom was matched in the corridors by Litvinov and Mrs. Daniel, who continued to give the defendants support in unorthodox ways, until they themselves were imprisoned for protesting in Red Square against the Soviet action in Czechoslovakia.

As suggested earlier, the volume and solidarity of protest manifested in the Sinyavsky-Daniel case helped to encourage more dissidence and stronger demands by the time Ginzburg and Galanskov were sent to prison. It is important to recognize that these cases, beginning with the arrest of Sinyavsky and Daniel, evoked open protests and appeals which had not been witnessed since the establishment of the dictatorship. Scientists, professors, teachers, doctors, economists, mathematicians, and engineers joined with creative artists to denounce the proceedings and to plead for the defendants. Some, of course, were protected by their eminence, but many of lesser renown were not afraid to identify themselves on the petitions, even to the point of listing their home addresses. The protests were delivered over a broad spectrum: to individual Communist leaders, the politburo, high judicial authorities, leading officials in the Supreme Soviet, officers in the trial courts, newspaper editors, writers' organizations, and even the Consultative Conference of Communist Parties.

The substance of the protests was as politically significant as the fact that they were sent at all. The appellants were not interested in lacing their arguments with tired quotations from Lenin. Instead, they went to the heart of the matter with legal and pragmatic argument, and the need for political change was implicit in many of the demands. They contended that the charges against the defendants and the trial procedures were incompatible with sections of the Constitution, the Universal Declaration of Human Rights (to which the USSR is a party), the United Nations convention on forced labor, and the operating norms of foreign Communist parties. The defendants, they emphasized, were arrested and punished in clear violation of article 125 of the Soviet Constitution which guarantees freedom of speech, press, assembly, mass meetings, and street processions and demonstrations.

In making their protests, the dissidents publicized accounts of police interrogation, discrepancies in court testimony, and deliberate perversion of facts by the press, all of which, they warned, were menacingly reminiscent of political trials in the 1930s. Many of the petitions were couched in unflinching language, "We demand" or "we insist," and their demands included not only a review of the cases by the Supreme Court and new trials for the defendants, but also punishment for the officials who were responsible for the illegalities. For many dissident intellectuals, the initial insistence upon artistic freedom had either converged with or at times even been subordinated to a demand for change in political practices they deemed oppressive.

The Sinyavsky-Daniel case also had an impact upon the political authorities and the conservatives in the literary establishment. Their initial reaction—prompted by a desire to meet foreign criticism and to reduce the fears of the liberals—was to insist that the two writers were not being punished for "a special artistic style" but only for their "deliberate calumny against the Soviet

Union."[30] This sophistical response, however, was hardly adequate for the serious problem the regime faced.

An answer to the question of how to deal effectively with enraged intellectuals probably came hard for political leaders who were not used to such recalcitrance. After all, most of them had served their apprenticeship during the Stalin era. It is not surprising, therefore, that, although the regime officially continued a somewhat ambivalent policy toward literature, it prepared the ground for harsh measures against the conspicuous dissenters.[31] After the Sinyavsky-Daniel trial, the government reorganized the police ministries and then issued a severe decree aimed at controlling "hooliganism," a vague term which could be used to cover incidents arising out of street demonstrations. This enactment, applicable to people above the age of sixteen, strengthened the hands of the police in dealing with public disorder, and encouraged ordinary citizens to help them. It provided penalties for "exceptional cynicism or special insolence" and for resistance to those attempting to quell the disturbance. An individual convicted of "hooliganism" faced a regimented existence during imprisonment—no messages or parcels, no smoking, and very skimpy rations.

In another decree, which would affect writers after their release from prison, the authorities ordered strict supervision by the police of individuals returning from penal servitude, including regulation of their place of residence, visitation at any time of the day or night, and registration for travel. For the enforcement authorities to declare that young writers could not return to Leningrad or Moscow after having served out their terms would be bitter medicine. In order to deal more effectively with demonstrations and underground activities, the regime in September 1966 amended the Criminal Code; it was under the new provisions that Bukovsky and his colleagues were tried. A change in the conscription law, under which the draft age was lowered and a system of pre-conscription training introduced, was designed in part to develop habits of discipline among the youth.

Another feature of the regime's coercive strategy was to subject the rebels to public ostracism in an effort to bring them into line. Propaganda campaigns were launched to warn citizens that enemy intelligence services were seeking to undermine the Soviet system by subtle means, and that they must be ever vigilant in ferreting out "weak and politically immature" people who were being exploited for subversive purposes. In these campaigns, the authorities tried to destroy the reputation of artists whose published works had been used abroad; they were "scribblers," not really writers in a professional sense. Although the regime experienced difficulty in getting reputable intellectuals to support its propaganda campaign against the imprisoned authors, the

[30]*Pravda*, 22 February 1966, translated in *Current Digest of the Soviet Press* 18, no. 7 (9 March 1966): 9.

[31]The decrees discussed in this section can be found in *Current Digest of the Soviet Press* 18, nos. 30 (17 August 1966) and 41 (2 November 1966); 19, nos. 42 (8 November 1967) and 45 (29 November 1967); 20, nos. 22 (19 June 1968) and 48 (18 December 1968).

old guard writers in the literary bureaucracies denounced nonconformity and censured those who had come to the aid of the defendants.

OUTLOOK FOR THE FUTURE

As the struggle between the protesters and the political and literary stand-patters gathers momentum and becomes linked with other festering problems (such as the minority nationalities and religion), only the most hardened Kremlinologists would attempt to predict the outcome. The unexpected outburst touched off by the Sinyavsky-Daniel case and the regime's response to it have incited the younger rebels to register demands that are unacceptable to the political authorities. These have been countered by an official crackdown on the dissenters which is more severe than any since Stalin's death. Thus the chasm between the regime and segments of the intellectual community grows wider.

Communist leaders are alarmed by the collapse of discipline among the intellectuals. Especially disturbing was the discovery that some intellectuals, including a few party members, knew about the activities of Sinyavsky and Daniel but failed to report them. The Soviet rulers view this as another indication of a breakdown in their control system, and they are determined to protect the power structure against further sagging. Implicit in their statements is the view that to give in to the writers' demands for more latitude would encourage the spread of poisonous ideas and weaken the ideological underpinnings of the system.

The question of how to deal with the literary people is, of course, an aspect of a broader problem with which the regime has to wrestle as Soviet society grows more complex: How much leeway must the state give to functional specialists in order to minimize their frustrations and keep them performing effectively in their prescribed roles, yet at the same time prevent forces for change from creeping into the system? In the case of the writers, Communist leaders probably feel that concessions were made to the artistic impulse in the latter part of the Khrushchev tenure, and yet the dissenters were not satisfied. Confronted now with demands it cannot afford to meet, the regime may consider that its options have been reduced and that it must continue to stamp out dissent, at least among the extremists.

On the one hand, if they decide to administer heavy doses of coercion for a lengthy period, the Soviet authorities have sufficient means available: the party apparatus, the police agencies, the communications media, the system of rewards and denials (including job assignments). The authorities control the levers of power, and it will be difficult for intellectuals marked by the regime to stand up against coercive measures operating in full volume. For reasons already given, however, this approach involves potential costs on the domestic scene and in the conduct of foreign policy; it is a risky undertaking at a time when the Soviet rulers need the cooperation of their people and are becoming more dependent upon outside contacts. But, at least in the short run, the regime appears willing to run the risks, as evidenced by the resort to harsh measures against its own rebels and against the liberal forces in Czechoslovakia. In the longer time span, however, it is doubtful that progressive ideas at home or in a "satellite" area can be entirely rooted out by forceful means. The costly attempts to do so are likely to impair the achievement of the country's economic objectives.

On the other hand, even though repressive measures may temporarily immobilize the dissident writers and drive them deeper into the underground, such action only strengthens their conviction that a wider range of freedom is necessary. The open defiance of authority by the young writers is partly a reflection of the "generation gap," and is not easily brushed aside. Many of the rebels who were teen-agers or small children when Stalin died never experienced the severity of his control system. To them, even the prescriptions of the Khrushchev era were excessive, and they regard the regime's treatment of the artists since the autumn of 1965 as intolerable. When their older colleagues remind them that, compared with Stalinist times, artists enjoy relative freedom, the young writers respond that this is still not good enough. Moreover, the younger set perceives itself as being excluded from the structure of literary authority—an outlook that has evidential support. In 1968, for example, only 3 of the 260 poets in the Moscow organization were under the age of thirty, and only 8 writers (out of 473) who served as delegates to the Fourth Writers Congress were in this age bracket.[32]

Not only do the younger writers have higher expectations than those who survived Stalinism, but they also perceive that, measured against previous decades, they are in a better position to realize their objectives. The young people anticipate that the USSR will have to enlarge its contacts with other countries in Eastern Europe and with the West, and that resulting linkages with foreign intellectuals will help to enrich their own creative work and support them in their demands against the regime. They also view with confidence the growing solidarity of the Soviet intellectual community; with so many notables in so many fields being moved to open protest, they see a bank of support which the silent opposition in the Stalin era never had. All of this has bolstered their courage to pursue a cause to which they are devoted. Given these feelings, it is not surprising that when some of their colleagues are hauled off to prison, others move in to replace them on the literary barricades and in the demonstrations in the public square.

But bravery and numbers are hardly sufficient to prevail against the massive power the authorities are able to mobilize against them. Besides, the protest movement suffers from important liabilities. The congregation of dissenters is not a cohesive group, and its moving spirits are young and inexperienced in political combat. Under present circumstances, the protesters are extremely

---

[32]See *Literaturnaya gazeta,* 29 May 1968, condensed and translated in *Current Digest of the Soviet Press* 20, no. 22 (19 June 1968): 32; Report of Credentials Committee, Fourth Writers Congress, *Literaturnaya gazeta,* 31 May 1967, condensed and translated in *Current Digest of the Soviet Press* 19, no. 22 (21 June 1967): 21.

vulnerable to police suppression, and their displays of strength can readily be dispersed by the regime's onslaughts.

In the long run, the fate of the dissident writers is probably linked with that of other functional specialists who are demanding a wider range of autonomy in the performance of their tasks. If enough people in the centers of power eventually come to realize that the technical specialists must be given freer rein to keep the society moving forward, it may be difficult for them to deny the writers a wider field of maneuver. In the decades ahead, the Soviet rulers will be challenged to make their system flexible enough to adjust to the expectations of thoughtful and talented people whose services are needed in its operation.

In the foreseeable future, a "muddling through" type of policy can probably be expected to prevail. Before very long, the authorities are likely to realize that the current wave of repression will have to be eased, and they may hit upon a policy that will allow the writers some room for literary experimentation provided that they stay away from "political" themes. However, the line between "political" and "nonpolitical" is hard to draw, especially in the Soviet system, and in trying to apply the rule, the regime may find itself returning to the zigzag pattern, with cycles of "thaw" and "freeze" as in the past. Ambiguous answers to the problem, of course, are satisfying neither to the diehards nor to the determined protesters.

Some of the young dissenters face onslaughts courageously and sometimes even talk about the "brighter tomorrow." Others brood in an atmosphere of pessimism. The poet Yevtushenko is overcome by neither mood. He recognizes that the pace of change will be slow, but he clings tenaciously to the belief that it must eventually come:

> Oh, those who are my generation!
> We're not the threshold, just a step.
> We're but the preface to a preface,
> a prologue to a newer prologue![33]

bibliography

GEHLEN, MICHAEL P. "The Soviet Union: Literary Conflict and the Sinyavsky-Daniel Affair." In *Politics and Civil Liberties in Europe,* edited by Ronald F. Bunn and William G. Andrews. Princeton: D. Van Nostrand Company, 1967.

GINZBURG, ALEXANDER, ed. *Belaya kniga po delu A. Sinyavskogo i Yu. Danielya* [White Book on the Affairs of A. Sinyavsky and Yu. Daniel]. Frankfort, Germany: Posey-Verlag, 1967.

HAYWARD, MAX. *On Trial: The Soviet State versus "Abram Tertz" and "Nikolai Arzhak."* New York: Harper and Row 1966.

"In Quest of Justice." *Problems of Communism,* Part I, July–August 1968, and Part II, September–October 1968.

JOHNSON, PRISCILLA. "The Regime and the Intellectuals." *Problems of Communism,* Special Supplement, September–October 1963.

————, and LABEDZ, LEOPOLD. *Khrushchev and the Arts: The Politics of Soviet Culture, 1962–1964.* Cambridge, Mass.: The M.I.T. Press, 1965.

LUCKYJ, GEORGE, "Turmoil in the Ukraine." *Problems of Communism,* July–August 1968.

McCLURE, TIMOTHY. "The Politics of Soviet Culture, 1964–1967." *Problems of Communism,* March–April 1967.

SWAYZE, HAROLD. *Political Control of Literature in the USSR, 1946–1959.* Cambridge: Harvard University Press, 1962.

UNITED STATES SENATE, Committee on the Judiciary. *Aspects of Intellectual Ferment and Dissent in the Soviet Union.* Washington: Government Printing Office, 1968.

DAVID J. DANELSKI

8

THE CHICAGO
CONSPIRACY TRIAL

The roots of the Chicago conspiracy trial are deep in the 1960s—in the hopes and failures of the civil rights movement, in the frustration and despair of the peace movement, in the fear of ghetto riots, in the rise of black militance, and in the flowering of a youth counterculture. As the 1960s drew to a close, dissent escalated, became more militant, and tended to converge. The political and cultural watershed of the decade was 1967, and Chicago lay just beyond the divide.

THE MOVEMENTS CONVERGE

On New Year's Day of 1967 two young black men in Oakland, California —Bobby Seale and Huey P. Newton—painted a sign that said BLACK PANTHER PARTY FOR SELF DEFENSE and placed it in the window of an office they had rented.[1] The Black Panther Party, with Seale as chairman and Newton as minister of defense, held its first meeting a week later.

On 15 April Martin Luther King, Jr., Dr. Benjamin Spock, and Harry Belafonte led a march of 100,000 persons through Manhattan's streets to the United Nations Plaza, where King and Stokely Carmichael, among others,

---

[1] Bobby Seale, *Seize the Time* (New York: Random House, 1970), pp. 77–78. Seale was born in Dallas, Texas on 22 October 1936 and grew up in Berkeley. Released from the air force with a bad conduct discharge, he had difficulty finding employment and went to Merritt Junior College in West Oakland with hopes of becoming an engineer. There he met Huey Newton in the early 1960s and largely through his influence acquired political consciousness.

denounced the Vietnam war. Some of the young marchers carried daffodils and shouted "Flower power!" There were also shouts of "Hell no, we won't go!" and "Hey, hey, L. B. J., how many kids did you kill today?" The demonstration, which was peaceful, had been organized by David T. Dellinger,[2] a radical Christian pacifist and disciple of the late A. J. Muste. Soon thereafter Dellinger organized the National Mobilization Committee to End the War in Vietnam.

On 19 April Congressman Bill Cramer, a Republican from Florida, rose in the House of Representatives to denounce Stokely Carmichael. It was time, he said, to put out of business men like Carmichael, who traveled from state to state with the intention of inciting riots. He reminded his colleagues of his bill that would make such activities a crime. What Carmichael is doing, he said, "is un-American and he should be put in jail."[3] In June there were racial disturbances in Tampa, Cincinnati, and Atlanta. H. Rap Brown, who had succeeded Carmichael as chairman of the Student Nonviolent Coordinating Committee, had been in those cities just before or during the disturbances.

On 12 July the Newark riots began. Five days later, twenty-three persons —twenty-one blacks and two whites—were dead. On 19 July, without administration support, the House of Representatives passed Cramer's anti-riot bill by a vote of 347 to 70.

In August a group of hippies led by Abbie Hoffman,[4] a self-styled cultural revolutionary, threw money away at the New York Stock Exchange. It was "a gesture of love," said Hoffman, but most of the stockbrokers and clerks on the floor of the exchange jeered, pointed, and shook their fists at the hippies.

In early October it was announced that the Democratic Party would hold its next convention in Chicago; discussions began immediately in the National Mobilization Committee for massive demonstrations in Chicago to protest the Vietnam war.

On 21 October Dellinger, with the assistance of Jerry Rubin,[5] a political hippie from Berkeley, coordinated a mass march on the Pentagon. The government hesitated to issue a permit for the march, but at the last minute one was negotiated. At the Pentagon the demonstrators physically confronted military police and federal marshals; some 600 persons were arrested. It was

[2]Dellinger was born in Wakefield, Massachusetts and graduated from Yale *magna cum laude* in 1936. During the Spanish Civil War he drove an ambulance for the Friends; during World War II he refused to register for the draft and served two prison terms, although as a student at Union Theological Seminary he could have claimed exemption.

[3]U.S., *Congressional Record*, 90th Cong., 1st Sess., 1967, CXIII, pt. 8, 10083–84.

[4]Hoffman was born in Worcester, Massachusetts on 30 November 1936. He received a B.A. from Brandeis in 1959 and spent a year at Berkeley doing graduate work in psychology. After brief employment as a psychologist at a Massachusetts state hospital, he worked with SNCC in Mississippi and then came to New York's Lower East Side.

[5]Rubin was a reporter for the *Cincinnati Post and Times-Star*, attended Oberlin College, graduated from the University of Cincinnati, began graduate work at Berkeley, got involved in the Free Speech Movement, dropped out of school and "out of the White Race and the Amerikan nation." *Do It!* (New York: Simon and Schuster, 1970), p. 13.

"a mixture of Gandhi and guerilla," said Dellinger later, and it was planned that way.[6]

Early in the morning of 28 October Huey Newton was involved in a shoot-out with two Oakland policemen. When it was over, one policeman was dead; the other officer and Newton were seriously wounded, and Newton was charged with first-degree murder.

Sometime in December, Abbie Hoffman, Jerry Rubin, and Paul Krassner met at Hoffman's Lower East Side apartment, where they discussed going to Chicago the following summer to have a Festival of Life (in contrast with the "Festival of Death"—the Democratic National Convention), and, in the course of their discussion, the Yippies were born. Hoffman tells it this way: "There we were, all stoned, rolling on the floor . . . yippie! . . . Somebody says oink and that's it, pig, it's a natural, man, we gotta win . . . Let's try success, I mean, when we went to the Pentagon we were going to get it to rise 300 feet in the air . . . so we said how about doing one that will win. And so YIPPIE was born, the Youth International Party."[7]

GETTING IT TOGETHER

In the early months of 1968 the National Mobilization Committee held many meetings about possible activities in Chicago but could reach no decision.[8] It had, however, opened a Chicago office headed by Rennie Davis,[9] a former SDS community organizer who had gone to North Vietnam the year before and joined the National Mobilization Committee upon his re-

[6]Daniel Walker, *Rights in Conflict: A Report Submitted to the National Commission on the Causes and Prevention of Violence* (New York: Bantam Books, 1968), p. 22, hereinafter referred to as the *Walker Report.*

[7]Ibid., p. 43.

[8]Because the government and defense versions of what happened in Chicago during the week of the Democratic National Convention read like tales told by characters in Akutagawa's *Rashomon,* I have, in an effort to be objective, summarized the events of that week as described in the *Walker Report,* noting especially all references to the defendants. The *Walker Report* is the most comprehensive and objective study of the Chicago disorders. It is based on 3,437 statements of eyewitnesses and participants, 180 hours of motion picture film, 12,000 still photographs, and the official records of the FBI, the Chicago Police Department, and the National Guard. Daniel Walker, who supervised the study, is a prominent attorney and president of the Chicago Crime Commission, a highly regarded private organization. The study group consisted of 90 full-time and 121 part-time investigators, many of whom were lawyers or were trained by the FBI. Although the *Walker Report's* conclusions have not been universally accepted, the facts contained in the report are generally acknowledged as accurate. For other views on the Chicago disorders, see John Schultz, *No One Was Killed* (Chicago: Big Table Publishing Co., 1969), and Jeffery St. John, *Countdown to Chaos* (Los Angeles: Nash Publishing Corp., 1969). Schultz generally sides with the demonstrators. St. John presents a view from the right and reprints, in an appendix, a large portion of *The Strategy of the Confrontation: Chicago and the Democratic National Convention,* which was put out by the City of Chicago a week after the convention.

[9]Davis was born in Lansing, Michigan on 23 May 1940. At the time his father was an economics professor at Michigan State University. Davis graduated from Oberlin College and received a master's degree in labor and industrial relations from the University of Illinois.

turn. The Yippies were more decisive; they were coming to Chicago and had already contacted a number of folk singers and leaders of rock groups who tentatively agreed to participate in the Festival of Life. The Yippies were also acquiring notoriety in their attempts to freak out the system. They staged a raid on the State University of New York's Stony Brook campus soon after a police narcotics raid at that school, and held a midnight party at Grand Central Station attended by 5,000 persons. The latter affair resulted in a confrontation with New York police, fifty arrests, and many injuries.

Meanwhile, a civil rights housing bill was progressing slowly through the Senate. When the bill was debated in early March, Senator Strom Thurmond offered his "Rap Brown" amendment, which was in effect Cramer's "Stokely Carmichael" bill, and the Senate passed it by an overwhelming 84–13 vote.

In late March the National Mobilization Committee held a conference at Lake Villa, Illinois, to discuss the coordination of various protest organizations —especially the black liberation and peace groups—and the proposed Chicago protest that summer. Dellinger chaired the meeting and Hoffman and Rubin were present. Tom Hayden,[10] an SDS founder and New Left theoretician, collaborated with Rennie Davis on a position paper presented at the conference. The paper outlined a plan for a funeral march to the Chicago Amphitheatre while President Johnson was being renominated at the Democratic convention. Retired generals, admirals, and Vietnam veterans might lead the march followed by people from various constituencies. Spring and summer would be devoted to local organizing, wrote Davis and Hayden, and "the summer would be capped by three days of sustained, organized protests at the Democratic National Convention, clogging the streets of Chicago with people demanding peace, justice, and self-determination for all people." The paper clearly stated: "The campaign should not plan violence and disruption against the Democratic National Convention. It should be nonviolent and legal."[11]

After the Lake Villa conference a number of things happened in rapid succession on the national scene: President Johnson suspended the bombing of North Vietnam and declared he would not seek renomination; Eugene McCarthy and his "Children's Crusade" scored primary election upsets in New Hampshire and later in Oregon; Martin Luther King, Jr., was assassinated; in response to riots in the ghetto areas of Chicago, Mayor Richard J. Daley made his shoot-to-kill-rioters-and-maim-looters statement; the Civil Rights Act of 1968 (with Senator Thurmond's Rap Brown amendment in it) was approved by the House and became law; Robert Kennedy was assassinated on the night of his California primary victory; and Hubert H. Humphrey declared his candidacy for the presidency. During April and May few political activists seemed interested in a demonstration in Chicago. Rough handling

[10]Hayden is the same age as Davis. He was born in Michigan and graduated from the University of Michigan, where he was editor of the *Michigan Daily*. He worked with SNCC in Mississippi in the early 1960s.

[11]Quoted in the *Walker Report,* p. 27.

of demonstrators during a peace march in Chicago on 27 April reinforced negative notions about demonstrations in August. But Kennedy's assassination and Humphrey's candidacy revived interest on the part of those who had earlier considered various ways to focus mass protest on Chicago during the week of the Democratic convention.

Yippie spokesmen and Mobilization leaders sought permits from the city for their festival, marches, and demonstrations. A permit was especially important for the Yippies, because without it the big rock bands would not participate in the festival. The Yippies also wanted permission for their followers to sleep in Lincoln Park. There was an ordinance against this, but there were precedents for exceptions. The Mobilization's chief demand was a line of march that would bring demonstrators within eyesight of the Amphitheatre. Hoffman and Davis negotiated with Deputy Mayor David E. Stahl. Hoffman told Stahl that the Festival of Life would be such a good thing for Chicago that the city should pay $100,000 to have it put on. For $200,000, Hoffman added, the Yippies would drop the whole thing and leave town. Having heard of the Yippie's Grand Central party and having seen some of the pre-festival literature referring to nudity, open lovemaking, and drugs for all in Lincoln Park, Chicago officials saw the Yippies and the festival as nothing but trouble, and found it impossible to permit a march to the Amphitheatre. So they delayed a decision. The Yippies and the Mobilization leaders thought that permits would be granted but, as in the march on the Pentagon, at the last minute.

On 18 August hippies and other protesters began arriving in Chicago, and still there were no permits. On the next day the Yippies and the National Mobilization filed suits in the United States District Court to require the city to grant permits. The National Mobilization case was heard by Judge William J. Lynch, a former law partner of Mayor Daley. Judge Lynch decided against the National Mobilization and the Yippies withdrew their suit. Thus matters stood on the eve of the Democratic National Convention.

CONFRONTATION

A week before the convention Davis and Hayden began recruiting and training marshals for Mobilization demonstrations. Marshals were told that their function was to protect the demonstrators, keep them nonviolent, maintain order, and prevent clashes with the police. Emphasis was placed on what to do in event of disorder. If the police charged, marshals were instructed to stall them so that demonstrators could escape. Marshals were required to accept the nonviolent tenets of the Mobilization; at least two marshals resigned during the training sessions on the ground that they could not accept such principles.

News media people, police officers, and undercover agents came to Lincoln Park to observe the training of marshals. Demonstrators practiced the *wasshoi* (Japanese snake dancing), a maneuver supposed to be effective for getting through police lines, but they were so inept at it that the maneuver was never used during convention week. There were also self-defense sessions in which karate and judo were demonstrated.

On Friday 23 August Jerry Rubin went to a pig farm, purchased a 400-pound porker, dubbed him Pigasus, and declared him a presidential candidate. While Rubin and a group of Yippies sang "God Bless America," Pigasus was released in Chicago's Civic Plaza. Rubin and some of the Yippies were arrested and Pigasus was taken into custody.

On Saturday 24 August Rubin, Hoffman, Krassner, Ed Sanders, and Allen Ginsberg met and discussed their position concerning remaining in Lincoln Park after 11 P.M. After the meeting Rubin and Hoffman stated jointly that if the police demanded it, the people should leave the park rather than be arrested or beaten. "We, not they," said the statement, "will decide when the battle begins. . . . We are not going into their jails and we aren't going to shed our blood. We're too important for that."[12] At 11 P.M. the police cleared the area. When a crowd gathered outside the park, the police tried to disperse it. Police cars were stoned and eleven persons were arrested for disorderly conduct.

On Sunday 25 August there was a peaceful march from Lincoln Park to Chicago's Loop. The marchers passed the Palmer House Hotel shouting "Free Huey!" When police gave the marchers instructions, they complied, but the police did not harass or intimidate them. That afternoon a newsman overheard Abbie Hoffman say in Lincoln Park: "If the pigs come into the park tonight we are not going to stay. But we don't want to get trapped or forced into any mass arrest situation. Everybody knows what the police are planning."[13]

Later in the afternoon a disagreement occurred between police and Yippies concerning the use of a flatbed truck in the entertainment area. Hoffman worked out a compromise with the police, but it was not communicated to the crowd, and during the confusion which followed the police used their clubs on the demonstrators. Prior to the incident a number of police officers removed their badges and nameplates.

A few hours later another confrontation took place. During this incident Hoffman, negotiating with a police commander, said the demonstrators would test their right to remain in the park after 11 P.M.; the commander said they would be arrested. "Groovy," answered Hoffman. When the police tried to clear the park many demonstrators refused to follow the instructions of the marshals and shouted obscenities at them. "Daley gives orders," one demonstrator said. "Don't give us orders, you fascist!" Hundreds of demonstrators surged from the park into the streets. A march began, but the police stopped it. Some windows were broken. More than a thousand demonstrators returned to the park. Tear gas was used, and demonstrators, newsmen, and bystanders in the area adjacent to the park—Old Town—were chased and clubbed by the police.

On Monday 26 August the police arrested Tom Hayden and Wolfe Low-

12Ibid., pp. 136–37.
13Ibid., p. 142.

enthal in Lincoln Park, charging them with resisting arrest and letting the air out of the tires of a police car. Rennie Davis immediately led a march to the police station to protest the arrests. About 400 marchers went to the Conrad Hilton Hotel, chanting: "What do we want?" "Revolution!" "When do we want it?" "Now!" Joined by other demonstrators, the marchers paraded around the statue of General Logan in Grant Park. Some of them climbed the statue, and the police broke the arm of a demonstrator as they pulled him off.

By 8:30 that evening Hayden and Lowenthal had been released on $1,000 bonds. At that time in Lincoln Park, Abbie Hoffman told a group, "We are not here to fight anybody. If we are told to leave, then leave."[14] From 9 P.M. on, Old Town was chaotic. Crowds of up to 2,000 streamed along the streets; some persons threw bottles and other objects, some walked on the roofs of cars. At 10:45 a group of clergymen entered the park to act as a buffer between police and demonstrators. A barricade made of park benches and trash baskets was set up, and demonstrators taunted the police from behind it. When the demonstrators began to throw rocks and bottles, the police charged the barricade shouting "Kill, kill, kill!" Again demonstrators, newsmen and bystanders were clubbed by the police as the park and the Old Town area were cleared.

On Tuesday 27 August several peaceful marches and demonstrations took place. In the afternoon Jerry Rubin told a crowd in Lincoln Park that they should picket the Chicago Transit Authority bus garages in support of striking black bus drivers. In the evening, at approximately 7 P.M., Bobby Seale spoke to a crowd of some 1,500 persons in the park. According to a witness who took notes on his speech, he called for a revolution in the United States. "We will go forward," he said,

> as human beings to remove pigs and hogs that are terrorizing people here
> and throughout the world. . . . If a pig comes and starts swinging a club, then
> put it over his head and lay him to the ground. It's the same thing for other
> groups in a similar situation when pigs will attack. If you're getting down
> to the nitty-gritty, you'll have some functional organization like ours to take
> care of pigs in a desired manner. [Seale urged blacks to] get your shotguns,
> get your .357 magnums and get your .45's and everything else you can get.
> . . . Large groups are wrong. Get into small groups of three, four and five.
> Be armed and spread out so we can "stuckle" these pigs. . . . If the pigs treat us
> unjustly tonight, we'll have to barbecue some of that pork.[15]

Rubin also spoke, saying whites should take the same risks as the blacks. "If they try to keep us out of the park," he said, "then we'll go to the streets."[16] A little after midnight the police began clearing the park, this time using tear gas dispensed from a truck. The crowd in the streets was smaller than the previous night, but there was more violence. Police cars

[14]Ibid., p. 167.
[15]Ibid., p. 187.
[16]Ibid.

and CTA buses were stoned, bottles flew at the police, and the police, now relying on tear gas to disperse the crowd, chased demonstrators and often clubbed them. Some officers brandished shotguns and revolvers, and that in itself usually dispersed small crowds. Order was not restored until about 3 A.M. There were more than 100 arrests; seven police officers had been injured and nine vehicles damaged.

That same evening an "unbirthday party" for President Johnson was celebrated at the Coliseum, an auditorium about a half mile from Grant Park. About 3,000 persons listened to rock groups and speeches. Dellinger announced there would probably be an attempt to march to the Amphitheatre the next day. Just before midnight a crowd of about 2,000 marched from the Coliseum to the Hilton. Earlier, another group had gone there from Lincoln Park. When the Coliseum group arrived, marshals, drawn from the ranks of the demonstrators, were kneeling with their arms locked facing the police, who lined the street for an entire block. At 1:35 A.M., the demonstrators were told by the deputy superintendent of police that they could remain in the park if they stayed across the street and were peaceful. At 2:10 A.M., the National Guard relieved the police. At about 4:30 A.M. Hayden spoke to the demonstrators, saying that he had "gone underground, to get the pig off my back."

Wednesday 28 August was the most violent day of the convention week. Abbie Hoffman was arrested while eating breakfast with his wife; he was charged with having an obscene word written on his forehead. Early in the afternoon Bobby Seale made a speech in Grant Park to approximately 700 persons. He demanded that Huey Newton be freed and was quoted as saying "Burn the city . . . tear it down."[17]

At an afternoon rally, presided over by Dellinger, marshals were recruited and trained for an unsanctioned march to the Amphitheatre. During one of the speeches a young man shinnied up the flagpole near the bandshell; there were shouts from the crowd: "Tear down the flag!" Dellinger took the microphone and asked instead that the flag be lowered to half-mast in honor "of the wounded, loyal demonstrators."[18] The young man was arrested; the crowd roared "Pigs! Pigs!" and began throwing things at the police officers. Suddenly a half-dozen young men went up to the flagpole, lowered the flag, and ran up a red cloth or a woman's slip. Immediately several policemen pushed through the crowd to arrest the youth who had raised the red "flag." The crowd shouted obscenities at the police, who were freely swinging their nightsticks. When Rennie Davis started toward the flagpole in an effort to quiet the demonstrators, the police yelled: "Get Davis!" As the police left the flagpole, they were pelted with stones, bottles, and other objects. Dellinger asked the people to sit down, saying, "There's much more of the program to come. Be calm! Don't be violent!"[19] The marshals, arms locked,

[17]Ibid., p. 216.
[18]Ibid., p. 222.
[19]Ibid., p. 226.

stood between demonstrators and police. "At first," a St. Louis newspaper-man said,

> the police stepped forward in unison, jabbing in an upward motion with their nightsticks. . . . Suddenly they stopped the unison and began flailing with their clubs in all directions . . . People scattered . . . some went down, screaming and cursing and moaning. I saw a number of women . . . literally run over. In the wink of an eye, the police appeared to have lost all control.[20]

Some demonstrators hurled pieces of concrete at the police, shouting "Death to the pigs!" and "Fascist bastards!" The melee lasted about twenty minutes. For some time Allen Ginsberg had been chanting *Om;* gradually the crowd joined in, and the rally resumed. Dick Gregory made a biting speech, calling Mayor Daley a "fat, red-faced hoodlum." "The cops aren't respon-sible," he said, "the real blame goes to Daley and the crooks downtown."[21]

At approximately 4:30 P.M. Dellinger told the crowd that he would at-tempt to lead a nonviolent march to the Amphitheatre. "If you are looking for trouble," he said, "don't come with us. We don't want violence." Dellinger was interrupted; after holding a brief conference at the speakers' stand, he said: "I am told by some that there is a group which intends to break out of the park and that will be violent. Anyone who wishes to go with that group may, but the group I'm leading will be non-violent."

"Tom Neuman got up," an eyewitness said, "and indicated that he felt his place in society had been taken away and that he was ready to go to the streets to get it back. He was obviously trying to arouse the crowd."[22] Some demonstrators followed him into the streets, but a crowd estimated at between 5,000 and 6,000 persons lined up for the Amphitheatre march. Negotiations dragged on for more than an hour while the crowd waited. Per-mission for the march was denied, and at approximately 6 P.M. one of the march leaders informed the crowd that there would be no march and asked everyone to disperse and regroup in front of the Hilton Hotel. Frantically, people tried to leave the park, which was surrounded by the police and National Guard. The guardsmen used tear gas and marshals lost control of the situation. Some four to five thousand persons had converged at the Hilton Hotel. Dodging rocks and bottles the police went through the demon-strators, clubbing them and shouting "Kill, kill, kill!" The crowd chanted: "The whole world is watching. The whole world is watching."

On Thursday 29 August Dellinger, Davis, Hayden, and Rubin asked a crowd of 2,000 in Grant Park to remain there and to march to the Amphitheatre later in the day. Hayden said, "We should be happy we came here, fought and survived. If we can survive here, we can survive in any city in the country." He went on to say: "When they injure us, we will be warriors.

[20]Ibid., p. 228.
[21]Ibid., p. 230.
[22]Ibid., pp. 230–31. Although the *Walker Report* does not mention it, Rubin and Hayden also spoke at the rally.

When they gas us, they will gas the rooms in their own hotels. And when they smash blood from our heads there will be blood from a lot of other heads."[23] Abbie Hoffman led a group of demonstrators from the park, but was stopped by National Guardsmen. Later, Dick Gregory spoke to a group at the Logan statue and introduced Deputy Superintendent of Police Rocheford, who said the police would stop any march to the Amphitheatre, but that those who stayed in the park would not be arrested. Gregory then invited demonstrators to march to his southside home, which would take them to areas prohibited by the police. A march got underway but was blocked by National Guardsmen; a number of demonstrators were arrested. When bottles were thrown, guardsmen responded with gas. This was the last major incident of the convention week. The next day there were a few speeches in Grant Park, and then the last of the protesters returned home.

THE CHICAGO EIGHT

During the next few weeks attorney General Ramsey Clark came under considerable political pressure to prosecute the Chicago demonstrators. A study by his staff indicated, however, that it was the Chicago police who had rioted and that there were no grounds for a federal indictment of the demonstrators. Clark instructed Thomas A. Foran,[24] the United States Attorney in Chicago, to initiate an investigation of police behavior during the convention week with a view toward prosecution.

But Chicago would not let Washington determine the matter. On 9 September Chief Judge William J. Campbell,[25] of the Federal District Court in Chicago, an old friend of Mayor Daley, took the rather unusual step of convening a federal grand jury to investigate the demonstrations. He charged the jury specifically to investigate allegations of an interstate conspiracy to incite a riot and police violations of the civil rights of demonstrators. Judge Campbell made it clear to Foran that he did not want the Justice Department involved in the grand jury proceedings. What evidence was to be presented, he said, and who should be prosecuted, would be determined solely by the grand jury, not the Justice Department. He followed the grand jury's work closely, reading the transcript of its proceedings each day and frequently

---

[23]Ibid., p. 337.

[24]Foran was born in 1924. He received a bachelor of philosophy degree from Loyola in Chicago and a law degree from the University of Detroit. He was a close political associate of Mayor Daley and in Chicago was regarded as a liberal Democrat and an able United States Attorney.

[25]Judge Campbell was born in Chicago on 19 March 1903. A protégé of Bishop B. J. Sheil, he served as his personal attorney and as counsel and director of the Catholic Youth Organization, one of the bishop's major interests. Bishop Sheil was a political liberal and a friend of Franklin Delano Roosevelt, and Campbell apparently benefited from the friendship. In 1935 he became Illinois administrator of the National Youth Administration, in 1938 United States Attorney, and in 1940, at the age of 37, a United States District Judge.

summoning "the jurors before him to deliver instructions on what they should consider and in what light they should consider it."[26]

Judge Campbell was taken aback when the *Walker Report* was made public on 1 December. The report was based on an extensive study of the Chicago disorders at the request of the National Commission on the Causes and Prevention of Violence. In its summary section the report stated:

> During the week of the Democratic National Convention, the Chicago police were targets of mounting provocation by both word and act. . . . The nature of the response was unrestrained and indiscriminate police violence on many occasions, particularly at night. That violence was made all the more shocking by the fact that it was often inflicted upon persons who had broken no law, disobeyed no order, made no threat. . . . Newsmen and photographers were singled out for assault, and their equipment deliberately damaged. Fundamental police training was ignored; and officers, when on the scene, were often unable to control their men. . . . To read dispassionately the hundreds of statements describing at firsthand the events . . . is to become convinced of the presence of what can only be called a police riot.[27]

Judge Campbell questioned both the objectivity of the report and the timing of its release.

When the *Walker Report* was published, Richard M. Nixon was president-elect, and Ramsey Clark was preparing to leave the Justice Department. When asked whether he had changed his mind about not bringing charges against the Chicago demonstrators, he said: "No, and if the new administration does prosecute them, that will be a clear signal that a crackdown is on the way."[28] In the new administration as Clark's successor was John Mitchell, Nixon's campaign manager. One of the main themes of the presidential campaign was law and order; some observers expected the new administration to prosecute the Chicago demonstrators, not to help Mayor Daley save face by providing scapegoats, but as a show of support for the police throughout the country.

A couple of months after Mitchell took office he had two visitors from Chicago—Thomas A. Foran and one of his assistants, Richard G. Schultz.[29] After they went over the testimony heard by the Chicago grand jury, Mitchell asked a number of questions and then agreed that certain demonstration

---

[26]Richard Harris, *Justice* (New York: E. P. Dutton, 1970), p. 70.

[27]*Walker Report*, pp. 1–5.

[28]Harris, *Justice*, p. 70.

[29]Schultz was born in 1938, attended the University of Illinois, received his law degree from DePaul University, and did postgraduate work at New York University Law School. Though he had been a member of the bar less than five years, he had acquired considerable skill as a trial lawyer and originally was to try the Chicago conspiracy case by himself. He had worked with the grand jury, written the indictment, and mastered the details of the case so well that Tom Hayden would later say that he "was an overcharged computer, a structure freak [he wore gray flannel suits and gray ties] who knew the exact details of 'criminal' meetings we had long since forgotten." "The Trial," *Ramparts* IX (July 1970), p. 26.

leaders and policemen should be prosecuted. On 20 March eight demonstration leaders and eight policemen were indicted.

"Politics, pure and simple," said Clark when he heard of the indictments. "The eight-to-eight balance makes that clear. Also, the same lawyers in the Department who reported to me that proceedings against the demonstrators could not be justified must have reported the same thing to Mitchell. But with the same information he reached a different conclusion."[30] Mitchell, however, according to an assistant United States Attorney, had more information than Clark—specifically, the expected testimony of certain Chicago undercover policemen.

The eight demonstration defendants—instantly tagged the Chicago Eight —were (in order named in the indictment) David Dellinger, Rennie Davis, Tom Hayden, Abbie Hoffman, Jerry Rubin, Lee Weiner, John Froines, and Bobby Seale. All were charged with conspiracy to cross state lines with intent to cause a riot, to interfere with law enforcement officers and firemen in the performance of their duties, and to teach and demonstrate the use of incendiary devices.[31] Twelve alleged co-conspirators were also named but not indicted. Weiner and Froines were charged with teaching and demonstrating the use of incendiary devices,[32] and the remaining defendants were charged with violating the Rap Brown law: crossing state lines with intent to cause a riot.[33] Except for Weiner and Froines, the defendants were well known.

Weiner[34] was a research assistant and Ph.D. candidate in sociology at Northwestern University; Froines,[35] an assistant professor of chemistry at the University of Oregon, had returned from England and stopped off in Chicago to spend the summer with his wife's parents. Both had been marshals in the demonstrations. One writer called them "small shots"; they had seemed so unimportant that the *Walker Report* had not even mentioned them.[36] One hypothesis for their inclusion in the indictment—which would

[30]Harris, *Justice*, p. 181.
[31]In violation of 18 U.S.C. §§ 231 (1) and (2), and 2101.
[32]In violation of 18 U.S.C. § 231 (1).
[33]In violation of 18 U.S.C. § 2101, which provides: "Whoever travels in interstate or foreign commerce, including, but not limited to, the mail, telegraph, telephone, radio, or television with intent (A) to incite a riot; or (B) to organize, promote, encourage, participate in, or carry on a riot; or (C) to commit any act of violence in furtherance of a riot; or (D) to aid or abet any person in inciting or participating in or carrying on a riot or committing any act of violence in furtherance of a riot; and who either during the course of any such travel or use or thereafter performs or attempts to perform any other overt act for any purpose specified . . . shall be fined not more than $10,000 or imprisoned not more than five years, or both."
[34]Weiner was a native of Chicago who had received a B.A. from the University of Illinois and a master's degree in social work from Loyola University.
[35]Froines was born in Oakland, California, on 13 June 1939. After graduating from Berkeley in 1962, he spent a summer working in a black voter registration project in Louisiana and then went to Yale, where he received a Ph.D. in chemistry. While at Yale he joined SDS and worked in a black community project in New Haven. His SDS affiliation led to friendships with Davis and Hayden.
[36]Nicholas Von Hoffman, "The Chicago Conspiracy Circus," *Playboy* XVII (June 1970), p. 94.

be asserted later by their lawyers—was that the indictment was a crackdown on dissent, and Weiner and Froines represented dissent in the academic community. Another hypothesis was that their inclusion gave some substance to the government's case, for without the count involving incendiary devices, the indictment charged little more than thinking, speaking, and associating—activities generally regarded as protected by the First Amendment. Still another hypothesis was that they were included in order to provide some basis for negotiation during jury deliberations.

The defendants' names were not listed in alphabetical order. Perhaps Dellinger's name was first because, at fifty-two, he was the eldest (the others ranging in age from twenty-eight to thirty-two), and hence, in the government's view, the architect of the alleged conspiracy. It was not because the evidence against him was strongest; in many ways it was the weakest. The order of the defendants' names was perhaps not as significant as the essential mixture of political styles they represented, a mixture consistent with the explanation that the indictment was a crackdown on various kinds of dissent: Dellinger, radical pacifism; Davis and Hayden, the New Left; Hoffman and Rubin, political hippies; Weiner and Froines, academic dissent; and Seale, black militance. Seale's inclusion in the conspiracy charge made no sense to him or the other defendants; he had not met any of the defendants, except Rubin, before the trial. Moreover, during the convention week, he had been a last-minute speaking replacement for Eldridge Cleaver.

In the random assignment of cases in the United States District Court in Chicago, Judge Campbell drew *United States of America* v. *Dellinger et al.,* but he disqualified himself on the ground that he had worked intimately on the case with the grand jury. The case was returned for reassignment, and on 1 April it was assigned, again presumably in a random manner, to Julius Jennings Hoffman,[37] a seventy-three-year-old, conscientious, pro-government judge who had been appointed by President Eisenhower. "Hoffman," said a Chicago lawyer, "regards himself as the embodiment of everything Federal. So in criminal cases . . . he tends to see the defense and their attorneys as the enemy."[38]

NO SPEECHES, NO EMBELLISHMENTS

On 9 April the defendants were arraigned. When defense counsel— Charles R. Garry, William Kunstler, Michael J. Kennedy, Gerald B. Lefcourt, Leonard I. Weinglass, and Dennis J. Roberts—were introduced as lawyers

---

[37]Judge Hoffman was born in Chicago on 7 July 1895. He received his legal education at Northwestern University, graduating in 1915. He practiced law until 1936 when he became secretary and counsel of the Brunswick-Balke-Collender Company, a corporation belonging to his wife's family. In 1944 he returned to law practice, contributed large sums of money to the Republican Party, and in 1947 became a judge in the Superior Court of Cook County. Six years later he was appointed to the federal bench.

[38]*New York Times,* 9 October 1969, p. 30.

from California, New York, and New Jersey, Judge Hoffman asked, "These men are taking bread out of the mouths of our Chicago Bar here?"[39]

The first defendant—Dellinger—was then asked to plead. "Obviously not guilty," said Dellinger, expressing the moral outrage he would later show from time to time during the trial. "The guilty parties have not been indicted." Refusing the plea, Judge Hoffman asked Dellinger again how he pleaded. Dellinger responded: "I said obviously not guilty." Again the plea was refused. "Once more," said the judge, "how do you plead?" And Dellinger answered: "I thought I made myself clear. I said not guilty." The plea was refused a third time and the judge asked Dellinger's lawyer to advise him how to plead.

KENNEDY: He has pleaded.
JUDGE HOFFMAN: He has not pleaded.
KENNEDY: He has pleaded not guilty.
JUDGE HOFFMAN: He has not pleaded, sir. All he has to say is not guilty or guilty. I don't care which. No speeches. No embellishments. How do you plead, sir?
DELLINGER: Not guilty.[40]

When Jerry Rubin was asked to plead, William Kunstler[41] began, "Just for the record—" but was interrupted by the following exchange:

JUDGE HOFFMAN: Everything we do is for the record, Mr. Kunstler.
KUNSTLER: Of course, Your Honor.
JUDGE HOFFMAN: That is why the government pays a high salary for an official reporter. I am not frightened when you say "for the record."
KUNSTLER: Yes, Your Honor—
JUDGE HOFFMAN: You see this lady. She is a very competent reporter. Anything you say and I say, or anybody says, is for the record. You have my assurance.
KUNSTLER: Your Honor, I was not trying to put the Court in terror, as you know.
JUDGE HOFFMAN: Perhaps even way out in New York you have found that I don't frighten very easily.
KUNSTLER: Maybe that works both ways.

At that point Garry intervened:

GARRY: But I do, Your Honor.
JUDGE HOFFMAN: What did you say?

[39]Trial Transcript of the Record in the Case of *United States of America* v. *David T. Dellinger et al.*, p. A71, hereinafter referred to as Trial Transcript.
[40]Ibid., pp. A77–A78.
[41]Kunstler was born in New York City on 7 July 1919. He graduated *magna cum laude* from Yale in 1941. He wrote poetry as a young man and privately published a book of verse entitled *Our Pleasant Vices*. He graduated from Columbia Law School in 1948, underwent executive training with Macy's, and then practiced law and worked as a writer to earn a living, writing mostly books on important trials. In 1961 he defended the Freedom Riders in Jackson, Mississippi, and thereafter represented Martin Luther King, Jr., Ralph Abernathy, H. Rap Brown, and other civil rights leaders. See his book *Deep in My Heart* (New York: William Morrow, 1966).

GARRY: I get frightened.
JUDGE HOFFMAN: Well, we will try to put you at ease.
GARRY: Thank you, Your Honor.[42]

Rubin then raised a clenched fist and pleaded not guilty.

JUDGE HOFFMAN: Let the record show that the defendant Rubin pleaded
   guilty raising a clenched fist.
KUNSTLER: I have to object to that, Your Honor. He pleaded not guilty.
JUDGE HOFFMAN: Oh, he pleaded not guilty.
KUNSTLER: A Freudian slip.
JUDGE HOFFMAN: I thought with that clenched fist, he was going to change
   the order of things. Not guilty?
KUNSTLER: Not guilty.
JUDGE HOFFMAN: Your plea is not guilty?
RUBIN: Not guilty with a clenched fist.
JUDGE HOFFMAN: You see, I got frightened of that, Mr. Kunstler. I don't know
   whether that fist was directed at me or not.
KUNSTLER: No, Your Honor, it is a symbol of defiance against certain things
   which the defendants believe are wrong.
JUDGE HOFFMAN: Not against me. He doesn't think I am wrong yet, does he?
KUNSTLER: I won't even answer that question.[43]

The other lawyers who spoke in court that day fared not much better than
Kunstler. After the arraignment, Kennedy argued a motion to grant the defense six months in which to prepare pretrial motions. In view of the com-
plexity of the case, the large number of defendants and counsel, and the
fact that the government had already worked on the case for six months,
he thought the defense request was reasonable. Judge Hoffman asked Foran
for his views. Foran suggested the defense be given thirty days to prepare
pretrial motions and the government twenty in which to answer. Judge
Hoffman ruled accordingly and set the trial for 24 September, which flabber-
gasted Kennedy. "Your Honor, most respectfully," he said, "has hamstrung
us. . . . There is no opportunity for us to defend our clients when we have but
thirty days to draw together this incredible mass of information, and slightly
over three months to prepare for trial." "I never hear arguments after I
rule, sir," answered Judge Hoffman. "You will learn that when you come
to try this case, if you come to try it."[44]

Garry tried to get a clarification of the ruling, but Hoffman did not under-
stand him. When he tried to explain, the judge would not listen. He said to
Garry: "You have tried [to explain], and you have failed. The order stands."[45]
In regard to other motions, including permission for the defendants to travel,
Judge Hoffman insisted that defense lawyers work out the matter by stipula-

[42]Trial Transcript, pp. A82–A83.
[43]Ibid., pp. A83–A84.
[44]Ibid., pp. A94–A95.
[45]Ibid., p. A100.

tion with the government. At first Kunstler refused; later, however, seeing they could get nowhere with Judge Hoffman, the defense lawyers worked out stipulations with the government.

GARRY DROPS OUT

Defendants and lawyers alike were sorely disillusioned by Judge Hoffman. "From the very first moment of our arraignment we realized," Hayden said bitterly, after the trial, "that our fates were to be decided by a madman, Judge Julius J. Hoffman."[46] In May Kunstler filed an application asking the judge to disqualify himself. He said it was his distinct impression from the tenor of the judge's remarks, his attitude toward the defendants, and his rulings that he had a personal bias either against the defendants or for the government. This was the first of several such motions the defense made, all of which were denied. One of them irked Judge Hoffman so much that he impounded it for further action, presumably as evidence of contumacious conduct.

In July Judge Hoffman heard arguments on pretrial motions, all of which he subsequently denied. One of the most important was a motion to suppress evidence obtained by electronic surveillance. Michael Tigar, an expert on the subject, joined the defense to argue the motion. His command of the law and style of argument, a blend of grace and deference, impressed the judge. Arguing the same motion, Leonard Weinglass flatly criticized the government for wiretapping, saying that the attorney general admitted that by engaging in wiretapping the government committed criminal acts against its citizens. "Did he say that?" asked the judge sharply. "Did he use that language?" Weinglass read the attorney general's affidavit that stated federal agents had monitored telephone conversations of the defendants in order to gather intelligence for reasons of internal security.

> JUDGE HOFFMAN: You were slightly in error when you said the affiant . . .
> said that the government "commited criminal acts." That is not the
> language of the affidavit, is it?
> WEINGLASS: That was the justification for the wiretap and I put this question
> to the Court—
> JUDGE HOFFMAN: I just don't like a lawyer to stand before me and say a
> document contains certain language when it does not.
> WEINGLASS: The fact of the matter is—
> JUDGE HOFFMAN: I won't argue that with you because it doesn't, and you
> know it doesn't. You said it did and it doesn't.[47]

Judge Hoffman carried a negative impression of Weinglass throughout the trial. He referred to him out of court as "this wild man Weinglass," and

---

[46]Hayden, "The Trial," p. 25.
[47]Trial Transcript, pp. A296–97.

during the trial he addressed him variously as Feinglass, Weinrob, Weinstein, Feinstein, Weinrus, Weinberg, Weinramer, and once even Mr. What's Your Name. At the end of the trial, when Weinglass was sentenced for contempt of court, he mentioned Judge Hoffman's slighting him and said: "I was hopeful when I came here that after 20 weeks the Court would know my name and I didn't receive that which I thought was the minimum."[48]

Fifteen days before the trial was scheduled to begin, Garry, ill with an infected gallbladder, requested a six weeks' continuance so that he might have his gallbladder removed. His participation in the trial, he said, was of the utmost importance to the defendants because he was their chief counsel and because he was the only lawyer who had Bobby Seale's confidence. "I make this statement," he concluded, "in as serious a request as I have ever asked of a court."[49] The government strongly opposed Garry's motion. When Judge Hoffman noted that a number of lawyers had filed appearances for the defendants and that the designation of chief counsel was not recognized in the United States Code, Garry tried to explain that many of the lawyers had appeared only to prepare and argue pretrial motions or to fulfill the requirements of local counsel under the court's rules. But that made no difference to Judge Hoffman. He denied Garry's motion and issued an order requiring Bobby Seale to be brought from California, where he was in custody, for trial on 24 September. "And," Garry interjected, "he will be without counsel at that time, your Honor."[50]

On 24 September only Kunstler and Weinglass, in addition to the two local attorneys, were in court. Kennedy, Roberts, and Tigar had wired Foran stating their desire to withdraw from the case; and Lefcourt, Kunstler explained, had to take his place in the New York Black Panther trial. Kunstler told the court that he and Weinglass would each represent four defendants and had filed appearances for them that day; but, he added, the defendants took the position that they were not fully represented because Garry was not present. Foran had no objection to Kunstler and Weinglass representing all the defendants. He did object, however, to the failure of Kennedy, Lefcourt, Roberts, and Tigar to appear for the trial. In his opinion their withdrawal was "incredibly irresponsible and unprofessional."[51] But he said that the government would not ask that they be ordered to appear immediately if the defendants would represent to the court that they were satisfied with counsel then in court; he further requested "that they waive any claim that their Sixth Amendment rights are abridged." "A disgraceful suggestion," Kunstler replied.[52] Judge Hoffman responded by issuing bench warrants for the arrest of the four lawyers. Two days later they were held in contempt of

---

[48]Ibid., p. 21808. Weinglass was born in 1933. He received a B.A. from George Washington University and a law degree from Yale. Admitted to the New Jersey bar in 1959, he opened an office in Newark where he represented mostly the poor and the indigent and where he met Tom Hayden.

[49]Ibid., p. A343.

[50]Ibid., p. A368.

[51]Ibid., p. A389.

[52]Ibid., pp. A391–92.

court, but there was such a protest among lawyers throughout the country that the judge was persuaded to vacate the contempt findings and permit the lawyers to withdraw.

FREE THE JURY

For selection of the jury, the defendants were moved to a larger court-room where three hundred prospective jurors were waiting. The defendants felt uneasy as they studied the predominantly white, middle-aged, middle-class citizens who were supposed to be their peers. They looked, wrote Hayden, "like a Republican State Convention. It was the Silent Majority making a rare public appearance. . . . There was hardly a black or a young person in the room."[53] The defense challenged the use of voting lists in selecting the venire on the ground that it systematically excluded racial minorities, the young, the mobile, and those alienated from traditional electoral politics. The challenge was overruled and the judge read the indictment to the jurors.

Judge Hoffman had ruled earlier that there would be no *voir dire* examination of prospective jurors, but that the defense and the government could submit questions which he would consider. He accepted a few of the government's questions but virtually none of the defendants'. Among those excluded were: "Do you believe that young men who refuse to participate in the armed forces because of their opposition to the war are cowards, slackers, or unpatriotic?" "Do you have any hostile feelings toward persons whose life styles differ from your own?" "Would you let your son or daughter marry a Yippie?" The one defense question accepted in substance was whether the prospective jurors had any close relatives and friends who were law enforcement officers or employees of the city, state, or federal governments.

Judge Hoffman began by asking each prospective juror whether he could be impartial in the case. The first nineteen veniremen answered, without exception, that they could not. They were excused; the judge asked the remaining veniremen to rise if they felt they could not be impartial. Thirty-eight men and women rose, and they were also excused. Individual examination of prospective jurors was surprisingly brief. The examination of Mrs. Mildred Burns was typical:

Q. What is your family situation?
A. I have a husband and one married son.
Q. Your husband's business or occupation?
A. He is a planning engineer at Argonne Laboratories.
Q. That is an agency of the government, isn't it?
A. No, it is run by the University of Chicago.

---

[53]Hayden, "The Trial," p. 35.

Q. University of Chicago. Is that where Mr. Fermi started?
A. Yes.
Q. How long has he been at Argonne?
A. Twenty-one years.
Q. Are you occupied with anything?
A. Part time, on and off.
Q. What did you say?
A. Part time. A friend of mine has a bakery and I help her once in a while.
Q. Selling?
A. Yes, cashier.[54]

The defense accepted Mrs. Burns as a juror, perhaps because of the mention of the University of Chicago and Mr. Fermi. As it turned out, she was one of the "hardliners" for conviction of all defendants on all counts. More, of course, was involved than what the prospective jurors said. "You scan the face and clothing," wrote Hayden, "try to catch a vibration or two, listen to the tone of voice as he answers the simple questions."[55] As the defendants participated in selection of the jury their behavior must have puzzled, if not appalled, many of the jurors. "What a scene it must have been," recalled Hayden. "Eight madmen in bright clothes passing notes, climbing over the table, whispering, laughing, arguing over the appearance of the jurors. We were judging them, putting them down, shaking our heads, looking sharply at them, yet we were the ones on trial."[56]

The defense had seventeen and the government had six peremptory challenges for twelve jurors, and each side had two peremptory challenges for four alternate jurors. The government was willing to go to trial with the first twelve jurors in the box and tendered them to the defense. Kunstler attempted to challenge for cause jurors whose friends or relatives were police officers. Since those jurors said they could be impartial, Judge Hoffman denied the challenge. Kunstler then challenged them peremptorily. More veniremen were called and the government challenged two of them peremptorily—one a recent chemistry graduate from the University of Illinois, the other an elderly black electrician who had recently lost his job with the Pullman Company after thirty-one years of employment.

After the first few hours of jury selection, the defense felt optimistic; it had used only eight challenges, and it had accepted at least two or three jurors it believed it could count on. One was Mrs. Jean Fritz, a DesPlaines housewife, who had been seen carrying a book by James Baldwin. Another was Kristi King, a customer's representative from Crystal Lake. At twenty-three, she was the only young person on the jury, but just as important as her age was the fact that she had a sister who had worked for VISTA. And there were two black women: Mrs. Mary Butler, a widow and retired cook whose son was a food service worker at the Playboy Club, and Mrs. Evelyn

---

[54]Trial Transcript, pp. A597–98.
[55]Hayden, "The Trial," p. 36.
[56]Ibid., p. 37.

Hill, a nurse's aide with dyed red hair whose husband worked as a shipping clerk. It was difficult to tell about the others. Two were men: Edward F. Kratzke, an equipment cleaner for the Chicago Transit Authority whose wife worked as a janitress in a tuberculosis sanitarium, and John M. Nelson, a self-employed house painter with a skid row address. The remaining half dozen were middle-aged white women. Three of them—Shirley Seaholm, Ruth Peterson, and Lorraine Bernacki—had children attending college, and one, Miriam Hill, had a son serving in the navy. The remaining jurors were Frieda H. Robbins, who worked as a cashier for a public utility company, and Mildred Burns, whose husband worked at Argonne Laboratories.

At this point the defendants asked for a recess for purposes of mutual consultation. They suspected the government was deliberately saving its four remaining peremptory challenges until the defendants had used all of theirs, at which time it would challenge jurors like Kristi King and Mrs. Butler. The jury, as described, had been tendered by the government. Should the defendants, with nine peremptory challenges left, accept it? That was the question they discussed and voted upon in a conference room eight feet square. "That little room," said John Froines, "was the most tension-packed place I've been in in my life."[57] The defendants believed that they could achieve no more than a hung jury in the trial, and they felt that at least some jurors were sympathetic to them; so they voted unanimously to accept the jury.

When they returned to the courtroom four alternate jurors were still to be chosen. They were regarded as important, because the trial would be a long one, and some of the alternates were likely to be regular jurors by the time the verdict was reached. Kunstler noticed that among those called as prospective alternates were a young woman, Kay S. Richards, and a black woman, Mrs. Wafer Fisher; he used the two defense challenges in a way that secured both. Thus the jury was selected, and in record time for such a case—less than a day.

During the first witness's testimony something happened which affected the composition of the jury and perhaps the outcome of the case. The families of two of the jurors—Kristi King and Ruth Peterson—had received notes saying "You are being watched. The Black Panthers."[58] The notes were reported to the FBI, and Judge Hoffman met with counsel in chambers to decide what should be done about the matter. Neither judge nor government counsel wanted the existence or contents of the notes made public, because the other jurors might learn of them. Kunstler informed Seale of the notes and told him that Foran and Schultz did not want the notes publicized. "Don't want publicity about it?" Seale retorted. "We're not going to send any stupid notes like that, man. Somebody's railroading us."[59] Seale wrote a statement for the press that was given to Hayden. Later at a press con-

<hr>

[57]Quoted in John Schultz, "The Struggle for the Laugh in the Courtroom," *Evergreen Review* XIV (June 1970), p. 73.
[58]Trial Transcript, pp. 458–59.
[59]Seale, *Seize the Time*, pp. 329–30.

ference, Hayden told reporters of the notes and said: "What we are facing here is a frame-up on trumped-up charges." He then read from Seale's statement: "There is a plot by the FBI and other lackey pig agents to tamper with the jury and then try to blame it on the Black Panther Party."[60] When the judge heard of the press conference, he immediately ordered the jury sequestered.

Judge Hoffman questioned jurors King and Peterson about the notes. Miss King was given the note and asked if she had seen it. She said she had not. He asked if any member of her family had brought it to her attention, and she again said no. He then said: "All right. Read it, Miss King. Read it, please." After she read it aloud he asked whether, having read the note, she could continue to be fair and impartial in this case. She stared at Bobby Seale and, on the verge of tears, said, "No, sir."[61] Kunstler objected to the revealing of the contents of the note to Miss King, but it was too late. She was excused as a juror, and Kay Richards, a twenty-three-year-old computer operator, took her place. Mrs. Peterson said she had seen the note but it did not affect her impartiality. She also said she had mentioned the note to her roommate, Mrs. Burns. The latter said the note would not affect her impartiality, and both women remained as jurors. The jury was complete and underwent no further changes.

Far more was involved in this incident than the replacement of a juror. For the next four-and-a-half months the jury was to be sequestered—shut up with each other and federal marshals in hotel rooms, away from their families and loved ones. Perhaps such measures were inevitable, but they were a blow to the defense, because jurors often blame the defendants for their plight. Indeed, the jurors envied the defendants' freedom—all but Seale were out on bail during most of the trial—and at least one of them appreciated the sentiment of a sign Lee Weiner held up one day outside the courtroom as the jury boarded the bus for its hotel. It said: "Free the jury."[62]

A FREE, INDEPENDENT BLACK MAN

During the selection of the jury, Bobby Seale sat somewhat apart from the seven other defendants. He was waiting for word from Garry, who he still hoped would come to Chicago to defend him. Meanwhile Kunstler had filed two appearances for Seale—one on 22 September simply for the purpose of seeing Seale, who had just been brought cross-country in shackles and was being held incommunicado; the other a general appearance filed two days later when Kunstler and Weinglass divided the defendants among them. Seale maintains he had not agreed to be defended by Kunstler at

[60]*Chicago Tribune*, 1 October 1969, p. 1.
[61]Trial Transcript, pp. 457–59.
[62]Kay S. Richards, "Chicago 7 Verdict: Step by Step," *Boston Globe*, 23 February 1970, p. 5.

that or any other time.[63] On the afternoon the jury was selected—25 September —Warden Moore of the Cook County Jail put in a phone call to Garry's office for Seale, and Barney Dreyfus, Garry's law partner, told him that Garry was going to the hospital the next day and could not come to Chicago to defend the Panther leader. Seale told Dreyfus that he would ask Judge Hoffman to postpone his part of the case until he could have Garry, because he could not function without him. "Let Garry know what I am doing," he said, "and then maybe after he gets out of the hospital he can go on."[64]

That night Seale, thinking about how Malcolm X and Huey Newton wanted to be lawyers and how Huey had once defended himself in California, drafted his first legal motion.[65] On a legal yellow pad, he wrote:

> I submit to Judge Julius Hoffman that the trial be postponed until a later date when I, Bobby G. Seale, can have the "legal council of my choice who is effective," Attorney Charles R. Garry and if my constitutional rights are not respected by this court then other lawyers on record here representing me, except Charles R. Garry, do not speak for me, represent me, as of this date 9-26-69. I fire them now until Charles R. Garry can be made chief counsel in this trial. . . .

When Seale signed the motion, he added, "Chairman, Black Panther Party."[66]

On the morning of the twenty-sixth, before the court session began, Seale told Kunstler he was firing all the lawyers and gave him his motion to read. "Man," said one of the defendants, "that's going to make it look like all of the defendants are splitting." No, Seale assured them. His situation was simply different than theirs; he needed Garry "and everybody knows it."[67] When the court convened, Seale walked up to the attorney's lectern and began reading his motion. Near the end of his statement, he read:

> If I am consistently denied this right of legal defense counsel of my choice who is effective by the Judge of this Court, then I can only see the Judge as a blatant racist of the United States Court.
> JUDGE HOFFMAN: Just a minute. Just a minute.
> SEALE: With gross prejudicial error toward all defendants and myself.
> JUDGE HOFFMAN: Just a minute. What did you say? Read that, Miss Reporter.
> SEALE: I said if my constitutional rights are denied as my constitutional rights have been denied in the past in the course of this trial, et cetera, then the tenor is the act of racism and me a black man, there seems to be a form of prejudice against me even to the other defendants on the part of the Judge.[68]

[63]Seale, *Seize the Time*, pp. 323–25; Trial Transcript, p. 5363.
[64]Seale, *Seize the Time*, pp. 323–25.
[65]Bobby Seale, "A Personal Statement" in *The "Trial" of Bobby Seale* (New York: Priam Books, 1970), p. 121.
[66]Motion of Defendant Bobby G. Seale, 26 September 1969, File 69 CR 180, United States District Court, Chicago, Illinois.
[67]Seale, *Seize the Time*, p. 325.
[68]Trial Transcript, p. 5416.

Judge Hoffman was stung. He said he was a friend of the Negro people and referred more than once to his 1968 South Holland decision, the first, he pointed out, requiring school desegregation in the North. Seale's motion was denied, but that did not end the matter, for Seale fully intended to defend himself. That same day, after the government and defense attorneys made their opening statements, Seale rose to reply to some statements Schultz had made about him. "Just a minute, sir," the judge said. "Who is your lawyer?" "Charles R. Garry," Seale answered.[69] The judge then said that Kunstler might make another opening statement in behalf of Seale. Refusing, Kunstler said: "Your Honor, I cannot compromise Mr. Seale's position." Later, Kunstler made it clear that he was not directing Seale in any way. "He is," said the lawyer, "a free, independent black man who does his own direction."

> JUDGE HOFFMAN: Black or white, sir—and what an extraordinary statement, "an independent black man." He is a defendant in this case. He will be calling you a racist before you are through, Mr. Kunstler.
> KUNSTLER: Your Honor, I think to call him a free, independent black man will not incite his anger.[70]

Although there were references in the newspapers to Seale's disruptions, the record shows that he seldom spoke unless statements were made about him or the Black Panthers, and when he spoke, he reiterated that he had fired Kunstler and wanted to exercise his right to defend himself. If a witness testified against him, he would wait until the lawyers finished their examinations, then rise to cross-examine when he thought it was his turn. Judge Hoffman refused to let him speak, much less defend himself, and the intensity of the exchanges between the two men escalated. When Seale rose to speak, the judge often excused the jury. Seale claims that Hoffman would say deliberately in an overly loud voice: "Take the jury out! Take the jury out! I don't want to hear this man. Mr. Marshal, set that man down!" so that the reporter could not record Seale's words. "But," Seale said, "I got hip to him. I saw the tactics he was using, so every time he started raising his voice I'd raise my voice up too."[71] As time went on, Seale also used more invective, calling Judge Hoffman a fascist and a pig as well as a racist.

Eventually Schultz and Foran also felt the sharp edge of Seale's invective. On 22 October Schultz marked a photograph for identification that showed a boy wearing a sweatshirt with a clenched black fist on it, which Schultz referred to as the "black power symbol."

> SEALE: It's not a black power sign. It's a power to the people sign, and he is deliberately distorting that and that's a racist technique.

[69]Ibid., p. 76.
[70]Ibid., pp. 78, 699.
[71]Seale, Seize the Time, p. 329.

SCHULTZ: If the Court please, this man has repeatedly called me a racist—
SEALE: Yes, you are. You are, Dick Schultz.
SCHULTZ: And called Mr. Foran a racist—[72]

Some observers of the trial, acknowledging that Seale was disrespectful to Judge Hoffman, said he acted with enormous dignity in asserting what he honestly believed to be his constitutional rights. All during the trial he was imprisoned (due to his scheduled appearance at another trial in New Haven on a charge of murder) and a good part of the time he was ill. The other defendants could hold press conferences and speak to groups throughout the country, but Seale's only forum was the courtroom. It is not clear whether he deliberately used the courtroom as a means of speaking to the people outside. But in asserting the right to defend himself, he spoke of many things that bothered him. Two examples:

> You denied me the right to defend myself. You think black people don't have a mind. Well, we got big minds, good minds, and we know how to come forth with constitutional rights, the so-called constitutional rights. I am not going to be quiet. I am talking in behalf of my constitutional rights, man, in behalf of myself. . . .[73]

> You have George Washington and Benjamin Franklin sitting in a picture behind you, and they were slave owners. That's what they were. They owned slaves. You are acting in the same manner, denying me my constitutional rights . . .[74]

By 29 October Judge Hoffman was at wit's end. He could no longer tolerate Seale's calling him a racist, a fascist, and a pig and thus ordered him bound and gagged—measures that only exacerbated an already impossible situation. When Seale tried to rise and, through his gag, object, black marshals were ordered to quiet him, and their manner was not gentle. Even the cold words of the official record give a vivid picture:

> KUNSTLER: Your Honor, are we going to stop this medieval torture that is going on in this courtroom? I think this is a disgrace.
> RUBIN: This guy is putting his elbow in Bobby's mouth and it wasn't necessary at all.
> KUNSTLER: This is no longer a court of order, Your Honor; this is a medieval torture chamber. It is a disgrace. They are assaulting the other defendants also.
> RUBIN: Don't hit me in my balls, mother fucker.
> SEALE: This mother fucker [referring to the gag] is tight and it is stopping my blood.
> KUNSTLER: Your Honor, this is an unholy disgrace to the law that is going on in this room and I as an American lawyer feel a disgrace.

[72]Trial Transcript, pp. 3599–3600.
[73]Ibid., p. 4344.
[74]Ibid., p. 4720. Seale's statements are remarkably similar to certain passages of Eldridge Cleaver's Soul on Ice (New York: Delta, 1968). See, for examples, pp. 162–63.

FORAN: Created by Mr. Kunstler.
KUNSTLER: Created by nothing other than what you have done to this man.
ABBIE HOFFMAN: You come down here and watch it, Judge.
FORAN: May the record show the outbursts are the defendant Rubin.
SEALE: You fascist dogs, you rotten, low-life son-of-a-bitch. I am glad I said
    it about Washington used to have slaves, the first President—
DELLINGER: Somebody go to protect him.[75]

The defendants were sensitive men who had been in the civil rights movement from its earliest days. Being activists and protesters, they felt they should
do something to express their moral outrage, and they did. On at least one
occasion, Dellinger threw his body between the marshals and Seale in an effort
to protect him, and once when the jury entered the courtroom, Davis ran up
to it and said that the marshals had tortured Seale. On 28 October, Seale refused
to rise when Judge Hoffman entered and left the courtroom, and the defendants
did the same. But Seale wanted this form of protest to be his own, and after a
couple of days told the white defendants, through his gag, to rise. Near the end
of October, Judge Hoffman told them that if they did not cease supporting Seale,
he would revoke their bail. Kunstler answered that the defendants would not
let a threatened loss of their liberty stand in the way of Seale asserting his constitutional rights. Nothing further was said of the matter, and the defendants'
bail continued.

Seale had a profound effect on the jurors, most of whom were frightened of
him. Kay Richards said she was so afraid that she could not have convicted him.
Mrs. Peterson, who received one of the threatening notes, was also "terribly
afraid, no matter what she told the judge." Mrs. Fisher, a black alternate juror,
told Miss Richards that after the trial was over she was afraid that Seale would
pay her a visit. Mrs. Butler sympathized with Seale and tried to understand his
behavior. "She didn't know why he made those outbursts but she didn't feel
that he should shut up. She felt he had a reason for doing it."[76]

Binding and gagging Seale was no solution; with Judge Hoffman's consent,
Hayden and Weinglass went to San Francisco on 31 October to consult Garry
and to determine whether he could still defend Seale. Garry said he was still
too weak after his operation, and that it was too late for him to enter the case.
Nonetheless, Judge Hoffman decided there would be no more bonds or gag
for Seale. There had been no deal.

Seale sat quietly as government witnesses took the stand until a deputy sheriff
from San Mateo testified about Seale obtaining an airline ticket to come to
Chicago in August of 1968. Seale then said he would like to approach the lectern. "You may not cross-examine, sir," the judge replied. But Seale rapidly
asked the witness a series of questions punctuated by Judge Hoffman's repeated
plea: "Mr. Seale, I ask you to sit down." Seale continued: "Why did you follow
me . . . at the airport?" "Have you ever killed a Black Panther Party member?"

[75]Trial Transcript, pp. 4815–16.
[76]Richards, "Chicago 7 Verdict," Boston Globe, 24 February 1970, p. 24.

"Have you ever been on any raids in the Black Panther Party's offices or Black Panther Party members' homes?"[77]

Again, Judge Hoffman went over the old arguments about whether Kunstler was Seale's lawyer and whether Seale had a constitutional right to defend himself. The judge then recessed the court, and when he returned, found Seale guilty of sixteen instances of contempt. Before sentencing him, he said that Seale might speak. "For myself?" asked the defendant. "This," said Hoffman crisply, "is a special occasion." Seale repeated what he had said throughout the trial: he wanted either to have Garry defend him or to be allowed to defend himself; and he insisted that his requests were not contemptuous. "If a black man stands up and speaks," he explained, "if a black man asks for his rights, if a black man demands his rights . . . what do you do? You're talking about punishing. If a black man gets up and speaks in behalf of the world—" Judge Hoffman interrupted to note that if Seale was addressing him, he would have to stand. Seale retorted that earlier he was prevented from standing, and now he was required to do so. He gave up; he would go to a higher court. Judge Hoffman abruptly sentenced him to four years in prison for contempt of court and declared a mistrial in the case. "You can't call it a mistrial," said Seale. "I'm put in jail for four years for nothing? I want my coat." The audience cried "Free Bobby! Free Bobby!"[78]

THE INFORMANTS TESTIFY

When Seale was taken from the courtroom the government was in the middle of its case. David Stahl and a lawyer for the City of Chicago had testified about permit negotiations with Hoffman, Davis, and Dellinger. They told the jury that city officials had taken seriously the Yippies' plans for body painting, nude-ins at the beaches, and public fornication. Stahl also said he had taken seriously Hoffman's statement that the Yippies could call off the Festival of Life for $100,000.[79] According to Stahl, during the negotiations Hoffman had said he was prepared to tear up Chicago and the convention and even die in Lincoln Park; Davis had observed that the city's failure to grant permits was an invitation to violence; and Dellinger, who made it clear that he was not interested in violence or in disrupting the convention, had said that he believed in civil disobedience—a remark the government presumably thought incriminating.

The heart of the government's case was the testimony of three undercover policemen—Robert Pierson, William Frapolly, and Irwin Bock—and a journalism student, Dwayne Oklepek, who had been paid by a Chicago newspaper columnist to infiltrate the Mobilization. Pierson, posing as a member of a motorcycle gang, had acted as Jerry Rubin's bodyguard, and had played his part

[77]Trial Transcript, p. 5404.
[78]Ibid., pp. 5475–84.
[79]Hoffman said the figure he mentioned for calling off the festival was $200,000.

with enthusiasm, calling his fellow officers pigs, throwing rocks at them, even being clubbed by them. Frapolly had posed as a student radical. He had joined SDS at Northeastern Illinois College and played his undercover role so well that he was expelled from the school. Bock, a navy veteran, had joined Veterans for Peace and worked himself up in the Chicago peace movement, claiming all along that he was a United Airlines employee. He did not shed his cover until after he had been interviewed by Weinglass as a possible defense witness.

Pierson testified mostly about Hoffman's and Rubin's aggressive rhetoric. "Last night's confrontation was a pretty good one," the undercover agent said to Hoffman on Monday 26 August. "Last night," Hoffman is supposed to have answered, "they pushed us out of the park, but tonight we are going to hold the park." Then Pierson said Hoffman used a "foul word": "We're going to 'F' . . . up the pigs and the convention." Schultz told Pierson to say the "foul word." He said it.

> SCHULTZ: Then what did he say, please?
> PIERSON: He said that "If they push us out of the park tonight, we're going to break windows," and again he used a foul word.
> SCHULTZ: The same word?
> PIERSON: Yes.[80]

When Hayden and Lowenthal were arrested later that day, Pierson claimed to have heard Rubin say: "We're going to get even with the 'F' . . .'n pigs . . . We're going to hold the park, if we're pushed out, we're to 'F' . . . up the Old Town area."[81] The next day, Pierson said, Rubin showed him a newspaper picture of a policeman with a nightstick in his hand. "Look at that fat pig," Rubin said. "We should isolate one or two of the pigs and kill them." Pierson said he had agreed.[82] That night Rubin and Pierson ran through the streets together, and, according to Pierson, each of them threw a small bottle at a police car. And on Wednesday, during the flagpole incident, as demonstrators jumped up and down on a police car, Pierson said he heard Rubin yelling: "Kill the pigs! Kill the cops!"[83]

Bock, Frapolly, and Oklepek testified that on 9 August they had attended a marshals' meeting at which the Mobilization's plans for the convention protests were discussed. Their versions differed somewhat but were generally consistent. According to their narratives, all of the defendants, with the exception of Seale and Rubin, were present at the marshals' meeting. The major topic of discussion was a planned march to the Amphitheatre on 28 August. Davis explained the plan for the march, and Hayden said that he, Davis, and Hoffman had worked on plans for diversionary tactics during the march. Those tactics, Davis said, involved breaking windows, pulling fire alarms, and setting small

---

[80] Trial Transcript, pp. 1359–60.
[81] Ibid., pp. 1371–72.
[82] Ibid., p. 1403.
[83] Ibid., p. 1459.

fires. After further discussion of the march, Dellinger said he agreed with the plans and would report them to the Mobilization Steering Committee.

The undercover agents said that a discussion of Lincoln Park produced a plan to "lure" McCarthy kids and other young people into the park with sex and music and keep them after the 11 P.M. curfew; if the police used violent measures and some of the young people were injured, sympathy would be generated for the Mobilization. Hoffman said he wanted Mobilization marshals to help defend the park on 25 August. Davis said he would have them and referred to "the perimeter of defense of Lincoln Park." He expected the police to drive the demonstrators out of the park sometime after midnight; at that time, they should regroup and march south to the Loop to "tie it up and bust it up." When someone asked what would happen if the police would not let the demonstrators leave the park, Davis replied: "That's easy. We just riot." Davis also talked about a mill-in in the Loop on 26 and 27 August that would involve blocking pedestrian and motor traffic, smashing windows, running through stores, and generally shutting things down. On the last day of the convention Davis proposed a demonstration that would send the protesters home in a proper frame of mind, "if," he was quoted as saying, "there was anyone left."[84]

Of the three witnesses, Bock was the most impressive—and his testimony the most damaging. After describing the 9 August meeting, he told the court of a meeting on 21 August, when Davis again discussed the Amphitheatre march. Davis allegedly said the Mobilization had four alternatives: One, have the march as announced. Two, have a rally in Grant Park. Three, have the rally and a confrontation. And four, have the rally and take over some buildings in the Loop. These alternatives were discussed by some of the marshals later that evening at Froines's apartment. Weiner favored the fourth alternative: there should be some speeches at Grant Park inciting the crowd and then the Conrad Hilton—at least a floor of it—should be seized. The other marshals, including Froines, agreed. On 26 August Davis told a group which included Weiner, Froines, and Rubin that "the people are now ready for a little bit more. . . . We should have a wall-to-wall sit-in in front of the Conrad Hilton. . . . When the police come to break these people up, they would break into small bands and go directly into the Loop causing disturbances . . . break windows, pull fire alarm boxes, stone police cars, break street lights." Rubin added that "they could start fires in the Loop."

At a meeting on 28 August, Dellinger was said to have reported that the city would not grant a permit to march to the Amphitheare. "If the city doesn't give in to our demands," Hayden responded, "there would be war in the streets and there should be." On 29 August Weiner told Bock, Froines, Lowenthal, and a student named Craig Shimabukuro (an unindicted co-conspirator) that they had needed Molotov cocktails the night before. "They're easy to make," Weiner said. "All it takes is gasoline, sand, rags, and bottles." Next they discussed the possibility of firebombing the Grant Park Garage. No such

[84]Ibid., pp. 2496–99, 4265–67, 6212–16.

bombing occurred, but the next day at a Mobilization picnic near Morton Grove, Weiner, who believed that Shimabukuro had been arrested, said that if the police had waited five minutes longer they would have caught him with all the necessary materials for making Molotov cocktails.[85]

Frapolly also testified about the abortive plan to firebomb the Grant Park Garage. At the picnic, according to Frapolly's account, Froines said he had purchased butyric acid (a harmless, foul-smelling chemical) and given it to some girls who had used it the night before. Expanding on the subject, Froines talked about the need for chemists in the movement—then the protesters "could have the formulas for making tear gas, Molotov cocktails, MACE and other devices."[86]

Scores of additional government witnesses testified about statements made by the defendants. On the evening of 27 August Abbie Hoffman was allegedly overheard telling demonstrators that they were going to storm the Hilton Hotel and that they should bring rocks, bottles, and bricks. On 29 August he supposedly approached a black undercover agent and asked if he would help capture Deputy Superintendent Rocheford, who at the time was negotiating with Dick Gregory in Grant Park. Paid informers testified that Hayden made speeches in March and July in which he talked about disrupting the convention. A paid informer also testified that Dellinger told students at San Diego State College in July: "Burn your draft cards. Resist the draft. Violate the laws. Go to jail. Disrupt the United States Government in any way you can to stop this insane war." After being loudly applauded, Dellinger said "I am going to Chicago to the Democratic National Convention where there may be problems. I'll see you in Chicago."[87]

Tape recordings of speeches given at the Grant Park rally on Wednesday 28 August and films of marches were presented to the jury. The defendants could not understand why the films were offered until they saw that a number of Viet Cong flags were shown in them. Later, in his argument to the jury, Schultz would say: "And the crowd charged up the hill with their flags, red, black and Viet Cong flags. You saw films of this incident."[88]

The defendants maintained that most of the testimony concerning their conversations was fabricated or greatly distorted. Cross-examination, however, did not show that government witnesses were lying, and only occasionally exposed distortions.[89] This might be attributed to the fact that cross-examination was neither Kunstler's nor Weinglass's forte. Originally Garry was to handle this part of the defense; his absence from the trial was in this respect a great loss to the defendants. Furthermore, Judge Hoffman interpreted the rules of evidence rigorously against the defendants and generously for the government.

[85]Ibid., pp. 6286, 6468, 6476, 6484.
[86]Ibid., p. 4381.
[87]Ibid., pp. 2913–16.
[88]Ibid., p. 20552.
[89]In cross-examining Frapolly, Weinglass was able to get him to admit that in the same conversation in which Molotov cocktails were discussed, Froines had said that he did not know how to make them.

Weinglass's repeated complaints about this double standard served only to increase Judge Hoffman's hostility toward him. And seldom did the judge explain his rulings, even when requested to do so by counsel. This gave defendants and spectators the impression that he was being arbitrary; Dellinger, for example, referred to him as the chief prosecutor in the case. At the end of the trial Judge Hoffman told Schultz: "I shall not restrict you to do something that the other side insists be done all the time. We will handle each objection as it is made."[90]

The defendants, believing they were being treated unfairly and frustrated by the failure of cross-examination to bring out what they thought was the truth, sometimes charged in open court that witnesses were lying. When Frapolly was on the stand, for example, Dellinger asked if Foran believed the witness's testimony. Then he said to Judge Hoffman: "I asked Mr. Foran if he could possibly believe one word of that. I don't believe the witness believes it. I don't think Mr. Foran believes it."[91]

Another defense response to government testimony was laughter. At one point Bock mistakenly referred to Weiner instead of Froines, and Schultz asked him a question so that he might correct himself. The defendants and their lawyers burst into laughter. Schultz appealed to Judge Hoffman, who warned the defendants that they were in a United States District Court, "not a vaudeville theatre." "But your Honor," replied Kunstler, "we are human beings, too, and when remarks are made from the witness stand which evoke laughter, I don't think it can be helped. You can't make automatons out of us or robots; we are human beings and we laugh occasionally, and if it comes irrepressibly, I don't see how that really becomes a court matter." Schultz accused Kunstler of laughing to influence the jury by creating the impression that Bock's testimony was absurd, and Kunstler answered: "I agree with Mr. Schultz. I happen to think it is absurd, and sometimes when the absurdity becomes too much, I laugh."[92]

POLITICAL THEATRE

The laughter and outbursts in court, the defendants maintained, were almost always spontaneous. There were, however, three deliberate incidents. The first occurred on 15 October when the defendants, in observance of the nationwide War Moratorium, wore black armbands and draped Viet Cong and American flags over the defense tables. When Judge Hoffman entered the courtroom, Dellinger addressed him: "Mr. Hoffman, we are observing the moratorium."

JUDGE HOFFMAN: I am Judge Hoffman, sir.
DELLINGER: I believe in equality, sir, so I prefer to call people Mr. or
by their first name.

[90]Trial Transcript, p. 20441.
[91]Ibid., p. 4372.
[92]Ibid., pp. 6288–89.

JUDGE HOFFMAN: Sit down. The clerk is about to call my cases.
DELLINGER: I wanted to explain to you we are reading the names of the war dead.
MARSHAL: Sit down.
DELLINGER: We were just reading the names of the dead from both sides.[93]

The marshals removed the flags; when the jury was brought in, Dellinger rose and asked for a moment of silence.

The second incident occurred a week later when the defendants asked if they might present a birthday cake to Bobby Seale. The cake was taken by marshals at the courtroom door and Davis announced loudly: "They have arrested your cake, Bobby. They arrested it."[94] The third incident took place during the final days of the trial. Angered by the revocation of Dellinger's bail, Hoffman and Rubin appeared in court the next day attired in judicial robes. While the judge watched, they threw the robes on the floor and wiped their feet on them. These acts were not mere theatre; each had an intended message, but it was not necessarily the message the jury received.

One of the reasons more such incidents did not occur was that the defendants did not need the court as a forum. During the trial they held press conferences, appeared on television, and spoke on college campuses throughout the nation. Kunstler and Weinglass did the same—to the consternation of Judge Hoffman, Foran, and Schultz. When the government suggested that such appearances were improper, Kunstler and Weinglass maintained they were simply exercising their First Amendment rights.

WOODSTOCK NATION FOR THE DEFENSE

In his opening statement at the beginning of the trial Kunstler had said: "We hope to prove before you that the evidence submitted by the defendants will show that this prosecution which you are hearing is the result of two motives on the part of the government—"

SCHULTZ: Objection as to any motive of the prosecution, if the Court please.
KUNSTLER: Your Honor, it is a proper defense to show motive.
JUDGE HOFFMAN: I sustain the objection. You may speak to the guilt or innocence of your clients, not to the motive of the Government.
KUNSTLER: Your Honor, I always thought that—
SCHULTZ: Objection to any colloquies, and arguments, your Honor.
JUDGE HOFFMAN: I sustain the objection, regardless of what you have always thought, Mr. Kunstler.[95]

Apparently the motives Kunstler intended to mention were the government's attempt to stifle dissent in the nation and to make the defendants scapegoats for Chicago's police riot during the convention.

[93]Ibid., p. 2425A.
[94]Ibid., p. 3640.
[95]Ibid., pp. 34–35.

The defense was never able to present its case concerning the government's motives. It tried when it called as witnesses former Attorney General Ramsey Clark, two of his aides—Wesley Pomeroy and Roger Wilkins—and Mayor Richard J. Daley. Pomeroy and Wilkins testified that they had consulted Daley and Foran in an effort to encourage permit negotiations between the city and the Mobilization; but government objections prevented them from saying more than that. Clark was not even allowed to take the stand. Daley testified, but Judge Hoffman refused to declare him a hostile witness, which prevented Kunstler from cross-examining him. Direct examination was fruitless. When Daley was asked about his relationship with Foran, the mayor said that Foran was one of the finest attorneys in the country. A question about the relationship between Daley and Judge Campbell was ruled objectionable, as were some eighty-two other questions. Kunstler renewed his motion to declare Daley a hostile witness but the judge denied it a second time.

Since Kunstler and Weinglass had made their opening statements, the defendants had discussed at length the kind of defense case they wanted. Hoffman and Rubin argued for imaginative theatre while Hayden advocated a fairly straight legal defense; the result was a compromise. The defense set out to do principally two things: One, show the jury (and, beyond the jury, the country) the kind of people the defendants were—their life styles, their heroes, their political views, their hopes for the future. Two, prove that they had come to Chicago to protest peacefully and that the police and their superiors were responsible for the violence during the week of the convention. The defense sought to make its case by calling three types of witnesses: rebuttal witnesses, political witnesses, and theatre witnesses.

The vast majority of defense witnesses spoke in rebuttal. Some testified that the defendants who had planned the Mobilization protests and the Festival of Life—Dellinger, Davis, Hayden, Hoffman, and Rubin—had said before the convention that they wanted no violence. The testimony of others constituted a replay—with emphasis on police violence—of the events in Lincoln Park and Grant Park during the week of the convention. Still others took the stand to rebut specific remarks made by government witnesses.

Among the political witnesses were the Reverend Jesse Jackson, Arthur Waskow, Mark Lane, Julian Bond, and Bobby Seale. By describing conversations with the defendants and reporting remarks made in their presence, they presented the defendants' political views—views with which they sympathized. Expert witnesses were also called to testify about the original meaning of the First Amendment, racism in the Democratic Party, and repression of the youth counterculture, but the jury was not allowed to hear their testimony.

Among the theatre witnesses were Arlo Guthrie, Judy Collins, Pete Seeger, and Jacques Levy. Guthrie told the story of "Alice's Restaurant," Judy Collins recited the words of "Where Have All the Flowers Gone," and Pete Seeger began reciting but finished almost singing "Wasn't That a Time." The defendants wanted the songs sung in order to give the jury some notion of their feelings and hence their intentions, but Judge Hoffman would not allow any singing. When Levy testified, the judge reminded him: "You are not in a theatre now, sir." And Foran stressed the fact that the nudity in Levy's *Oh, Calcutta!* had caused the musical to be shut down in Los Angeles.

Allen Ginsberg was, to the defendants, an ideal witness. He testified as to Abbie Hoffman's peaceful intentions and spoke for the counterculture the defendants saw themselves representing:

> He [Hoffman] said that politics had become theatre and magic; that it was the manipulation of imagery through the mass media that was confusing and hypnotizing the people in the United States and making them accept a war which they did not really believe in; that people were involved in a life style which was intolerable to the younger folk, which involved brutality and police violence as well as larger violence in Vietnam, and that ourselves might be able to get together in Chicago and invite teachers to present different ideas of what is wrong with the planet; what we can do to solve the pollution crisis, what we can do to solve the Vietnam war, to present different ideas for making the society more sacred and less commercial, less materialistic, what we could do to uplevel or improve the whole tone of the trap that we felt ourselves in as the population grew and as politics became more violent and chaotic.[96]

One reporter called Foran's cross-examination of Ginsberg a form of fag baiting. Foran wanted to know how "intimate" Ginsberg's relationship was with Rubin and Hoffman, and asked about the religious significance of some of Ginsberg's sexual poems which he was asked to read to the jury. The defense decided that if the government wanted poetry, the jury should hear something relevant. Weinglass asked Ginsberg to recite the poem "Howl." "I saw the best minds of my generation destroyed by madness," the poet began as the courtroom fell silent. As he cried "Moloch! Moloch! Nightmare of Moloch!" even Judge Hoffman seemed affected. And when he finished—"They saw it all! the wild eyes! the holy yells! They bade farewell! They jumped off the roof! to solitude! waving! carrying flowers! Down to the river! into the street!" —the defendants were in tears.[97] Foran declined to cross-examine again. He stared at Ginsberg and muttered: "Damn fag."[98]

Some of the defense witnesses actually may have helped the government's case before the jury. The cross-examination of Linda Morse is perhaps the best example. Armed with an interview she had given to *Playboy*, Schultz began by showing her a photograph of a machine gun and asking her if she knew its caliber. Even Judge Hoffman was a little shaken by the question and reminded Schultz that the proceedings were not *voir dire*. Schultz, confident, assured the judge and pushed on:

SCHULTZ: You practice shooting an M-1 yourself, don't you?
MORSE: Yes, I do.
SCHULTZ: You also practice karate, don't you?

[96]Ibid., pp. 10661–62.
[97]From "Howl," in *Howl and Other Poems*, by Allen Ginsberg. Copyright © 1956, 1959 by Allen Ginsberg. Reprinted by permission of City Lights Books.
[98]Hayden, "The Trial," p. 23.

MORSE: Yes, I do.
SCHULTZ: What else do you practice?
MORSE: Just those two things.
SCHULTZ: That is for the revolution, isn't it?
MORSE: After Chicago I changed from being a pacifist to the realization that we had to defend ourselves. A non-violent revolution was impossible. I desperately wish it was possible.[99]

Schultz explored her political views and got her to admit that when the revolution came, people would gain control of American cities the way the National Liberation Front did in Vietnam. Schultz refused to accept certain answers on the ground that they were not responsive.

KUNSTLER: Your Honor, they are intensely political questions and she is trying to give a political answer to a political question.
JUDGE HOFFMAN: This is not a political case as far as I am concerned.
KUNSTLER: Well, Your Honor, as far as some of the rest of us are concerned, it is quite a political case.
JUDGE HOFFMAN: It is a criminal case. There is an indictment here. I have the indictment right up here. I can't go into politics here in this court.
KUNSTLER: Your Honor, Jesus was accused criminally, too, and we understand really that was not truly a criminal case in the sense that it is just an ordinary—
JUDGE HOFFMAN: I didn't live at that time. I don't know. Some people think I go back that far, but I really didn't.
KUNSTLER: Well, I was assuming Your Honor had read of the incident.[100]

The defendants decided among themselves that Abbie Hoffman and Rennie Davis would testify. Rubin very much wanted to testify and the rest of the defendants, with one exception, were willing to do so. The possibility that Dellinger might take the stand was discussed, but the defense case took so much time that the defendants decided to go to the jury with only the testimony of Hoffman and Davis.

"My name is Abbie," Hoffman told the jury. "I am an orphan of America. . . . I live in Woodstock Nation. . . . It is a nation of alienated young people. We carry it around with us as a state of mind in the way the Sioux Indians carried the Sioux nation around with them. It is a nation dedicated to cooperation versus competition, to the idea that people should have better means of exchange than property or money, that there should be some other basis for human interaction." He said he had not come to Chicago intending to encourage or incite anyone to commit an act of violence. When asked if he had entered into an agreement with the other defendants to encourage violence during the convention week, he answered: "An agreement? We couldn't agree on lunch."[101]

[99]Trial Transcript, pp. 11352–53.
[100]Ibid., pp. 11359–60.
[101]Ibid., pp. 12397–400, 13003, 13005.

Schultz cross-examined Hoffman on the Yippies' plans for nude-ins and public fornication at Lincoln Park. He dwelt especially on the latter until Kunstler called him a dirty old man. Schultz asked Hoffman about the plan for Yippies to assist in diversionary tactics. Hoffman answered: "Yippies would assist in diversionary tactics. . . . Never. No. That kind of an agreement with the Mobilization? We had a closer agreement with the Mayor than with the Mobilization."[102] When asked if he wanted to make it appear that the convention was being held under military conditions, Hoffman answered: "You can do that with a Yo-Yo in this country. That's quite easy. You can see just from this courtroom. Look at all the troops around. Right?"[103]

Twice Hoffman took the Fifth Amendment but changed his mind both times and answered the questions. The first time he said: "This might be incriminating. . . . Why don't I take the Fifth Amendment? I always wanted to."[104] The second time he took it in protest to a ruling by Judge Hoffman. When he answered the question he said: "All my years on the witness stand, I never heard anything like that ruling."[105] Schultz then questioned him about his statement in Grant Park about trying to capture Deputy Superintendent Rocheford. In his book, *Revolution for the Hell of It*, Hoffman had mentioned the incident, but maintained, on redirect examination, that he never intended to kidnap Rocheford. Hoffman often distinguished between what he had said and what he had written in the book.

> ABBIE HOFFMAN: Did you ask me if I had the thoughts or if I wrote I had the thoughts? There is a difference.
> SCHULTZ: It is a convenient difference, isn't it, Mr. Hoffman.
> ABBIE HOFFMAN: I don't know what you mean by that, Mr. Schultz. I have never been on trial for my thoughts before.[106]

Davis took the stand to describe the events leading up to the Mobilization's decision to hold a protest demonstration in Chicago. When he testified about the Lake Villa conference, Weinglass offered in evidence the position paper Davis and Hayden had written. The government objected on the ground, among others, that it was self-serving, and Judge Hoffman sustained the objection. "Your Honor has read the document?" asked Weinglass. "I have looked it over," the judge said. "You never read it," Davis interjected. "I was watching you. You read two pages."[107] That exchange earned Davis a two month sentence for contempt. Davis was able, however, to testify that the paper stated that any demonstration in Chicago "must be legal and nonviolent." The permit negotiations were covered in detail; Davis maintained that he sincerely sought the permits because he and the Mobilization wanted a legal, nonviolent demonstration.

102 Ibid., p. 13233.
103 Ibid., p. 13108.
104 Ibid., pp. 13314–15.
105 Ibid., p. 13340.
106 Ibid., p. 13328.
107 Ibid., pp. 17443–44.

Davis testified about his discussions with demonstration marshals, giving a different version than that supplied by Oklepek, Frapolly, and Bock. He said that on 2 August, Bock had suggested that a balloon filled with helium be sent over the Amphitheatre. When Davis asked what it would carry, Bock answered "Anything." He told of the marches he led on Sunday and Monday and the events he observed during the rest of convention week. He also told of two beatings he received at the hands of the police.

Foran cross-examined Davis for two-and-a-half days, and admitted later that it was one of the most difficult cross-examinations in his career. Davis refused to be held to yes-or-no answers and sought to explain his responses. Foran was not always in control, which exasperated him. When he asked if Davis had heard Bock's testimony, Davis shot back: "I heard him testify falsely, yes, sir."[108] But eventually Foran got what he wanted:

> FORAN: And what you want to urge young people to do is to revolt, isn't that right?
> DAVIS: Yes, revolt. That is probably right.
> FORAN: And you stated, have you not, "that there can be no question by the time that I am through that I have every intention of urging that you revolt, that you join the movement, that you become part of a growing force for insurrection in the United States"? You have said that, haven't you?
> DAVIS: I was standing right next to Fred Hampton when I said that, and later he was murdered.[109]

On Friday 30 January Kunstler said the defense had no more witnesses and would rest its case on Monday. Over the weekend he learned that Ralph Abernathy, who had been co-chairman of the Mobilization and in Chicago during the Democratic convention, had returned to the country and was willing to testify. But Judge Hoffman would not permit him to do so, and told Kunstler to rest the defense case as he said he would. Kunstler refused:

> You can't tell me that Ralph Abernathy cannot take the stand today because of the technicality of whether I made a representation. That representation was made in perfect good faith with your Honor. I did not know that Reverend Abernathy was back in the country. We have been trying to get him for a week and a half. . . . I have sat here for four and a half months and watched the objections denied and sustained by your Honor, and I know that this is not a fair trial. I know it in my heart. If I have to lose my license to practice law, and if I have to go to jail, I can't think of a better cause to go to jail for and to lose my license for—
> VOICE: Right on!
> KUNSTLER:—than to tell your Honor that you are doing a disservice to the law . . . everything I have learned throughout my life has come to naught, that there is no meaning in this court, and there is no law in the court—
> VOICES: Right on!
> KUNSTLER:—and these men are going to jail by virtue of a legal lynching—

[108]Ibid., p. 18055.
[109]Ibid., p. 18243.

VOICES: Right on!
KUNSTLER:—and Your Honor is wholly responsible for that, and if . . . this is
what your pride is going to be built on, I can only say to Your Honor,
"Good luck to you."
JUDGE HOFFMAN: Every one of those applauders—
VOICES: Right on! Right on!
JUDGE HOFFMAN: Out with those applauders.[110]

Kunstler refused to rest the defense's case without Abernathy's testimony;
so Judge Hoffman stated for the record that the defense had rested.

WHO WAS LYING?

In the government's rebuttal case, Deputy Police Chief Riordan gave testimony that suggested that Dellinger had committed violent acts after his attempted march to the Amphitheatre on 28 August was prohibited. "Oh, bull
shit," Dellinger burst out. "That is an absolute lie. Let's argue about what I
stand for and what you stand for, but let's not make up things like that."

JUDGE HOFFMAN: I have never heard in more than a half century of the bar
a man using profanity in this court or in a courtroom.
ABBIE HOFFMAN: I've never been in an obscene court, either.
JUDGE HOFFMAN: I never have as a spectator or as a judge. I never did.
KUNSTLER: You never sat here as a defendant and heard liars on the
stand, Your Honor.
SCHULTZ: Now, Your Honor, I move that that statement—How dare Mr.
Kunstler—
KUNSTLER: I say it openly and fully, Your Honor.
SCHULTZ: Your Honor, we had to sit with our lips tight, listening to those
defendants, to those two defendants, Mr. Hayden and Mr. Hoffman,
perjure themselves.
JUDGE HOFFMAN: Don't, please.
SCHULTZ: I mean Davis and Hoffman.
KUNSTLER: A little Freudian slip, Your Honor.[111]

For that outburst, Dellinger's bail was revoked. Angered by the action, the
defendants had long discussions concerning what they should do about it.
Hayden argued for keeping cool. Hoffman and Rubin disagreed, and the next
day they appeared in court dressed in judicial robes.

Bock, recalled, testified that he had never made a statement to Davis about
a balloon carrying anything. In fact, he said, he had not even seen Davis on
2 August, the day the conversation was supposed to have occurred. Weinglass
did his best during cross-examination to shake Bock's testimony. He asked if

[110]Ibid., pp. 19109–13.
[111]Ibid., pp. 19669–70.

Bock had seen Davis on 27 July, but Schultz objected on the ground that the question went beyond the scope of direct examination. When the judge sustained the objection, Weinglass complained that the rules of evidence were being read restrictively against the defense. The most Weinglass was able to elicit from Bock was a statement that while he was in the navy he had heard of the balloon technique for rescuing downed flyers. In answer to a question by Kunstler, Bock said that he had not read about Davis's testimony in the newspapers. Later, Kunstler asked him whether he knew that Davis had testified.

> BOCK: I knew that he had testified, yes, sir.
> KUNSTLER: How did you find it out?
> BOCK: I read it in the paper.[112]
> With that answer, Kunstler sat down.

THE LIGHTS IN CAMELOT

The government's position throughout the trial had been that the case was criminal, not political. Yet in the government's opening argument to the jury, Schultz made it sound as though the defendants were being tried because they were revolutionaries:

> The point is that they came here wanting a riot, wanting people to be injured
> —not because they liked people being hurt, people, whether they be
> policemen or demonstrators, but by creating a situation of violence, where
> it would appear that the demonstrators were being oppressed, people would
> be magnetized, would be polarized, would join in with the demonstrators,
> and a national liberation front would be started. People would start taking
> to the streets to overthrow, to revolt, as Davis now uses the word—he is calling
> for a revolution and insurrection; this was to be the beginning.[113]

In his concluding remarks to the jury Weinglass sought to put the case in historical and political perspective. "Throughout history," he said, "it has always been easy to go along. They did it at the Salem Witch Trials. They went along in Jerusalem—"

> SCHULTZ: Oh, objection, if the court please. That doesn't belong in this
> courtroom. That is not legitimate argument and I object to that. I object
> to that. I object to that.
> JUDGE HOFFMAN: I see no relationship—
> SCHULTZ: That is grossly improper.
> JUDGE HOFFMAN: I see no relationship of the Salem Witch Trials to this
> courtroom. I don't think it is comparable. I sustain the objection.[114]

[112]Ibid., p. 20018.
[113]Ibid., pp. 20448–49.
[114]Ibid., pp. 21087–88.

Kunstler sought to explain to the jury that the right to dissent in the United States—and not merely the defendants—was on trial. "These seven men," he said, "are important to us as human beings, as clients, but they are not really sitting in the dock here. We are all in the dock because what happens to them happens to all of us. What happens to them is the ultimate answer to all of us."

> FORAN: Your Honor, I object to that. That is improper.
> JUDGE HOFFMAN: Oh, I would question the validity of that statement.
> Do you object to the statement?
> FORAN: Yes, Your Honor. I object to the statement.
> JUDGE HOFFMAN: I sustain the objection.[115]

Later Kunstler returned to the dissent theme: "The defendants are well known. They are leaders in many areas of what we call the spectrum of dissent in the United States. That is one of the reasons they are indicted, because they are such people."

> FORAN: Your Honor, I object to that. That is improper.
> JUDGE HOFFMAN: The reason for their indictment is set forth in the indictment. That indictment has been read to the jurors, and it does not contain any such statement as you have just made, Mr. Kunstler. Therefore, I sustain the objection.
> KUNSTLER: Your Honor, the real reason—
> JUDGE HOFFMAN: I direct the jury to disregard it.

Kunstler concluded. "I think if this case does nothing else, perhaps it will bring into focus that again we are in that moment of history when a courtroom becomes the proving ground of whether we do live free and whether we do die free."[116]

Foran made the government's closing argument. He said the defendants were highly sophisticated, educated, "evil men" whose intentions were obvious. "Davis," he said, "told you from the witness stand after two-and-a-half days of the toughest cross-examination I ever was involved in, because he was so smart and so clever and so alert, but at last he told you. 'Revolution. Insurrection.' "[117]

Later Foran returned to the theme of evil and its relation to the corruption of American youth by the defendants:

> Evil is exciting and evil is interesting, and plenty of kids have a fascination
> for it. It is knowledge of kids like that that these sophisticated, educated
> psychology majors know about. They know about kids, and they know how
> to draw the kids together and maneuver them, and use them to accomplish
> their purposes. Kids in the sixties, you know, are disillusioned. There is no
> question about that. They feel that John Kennedy went, Bobby Kennedy went,

115Ibid., p. 21091.
116Ibid., pp. 21110, 21222.
117Ibid., p. 21251.

Martin Luther King went—they were all killed—and the kids do feel the lights have gone out in Camelot, the banners are furled, and the parade is over, and this kind of thing. These guys take advantage of them. They take advantage of it personally, intentionally, evilly, and to corrupt those kids, and they use them, and they use them for their purposes. . . .[118]

In conclusion, Foran said:

The lights in that Camelot kids believe in needn't go out. The banners can snap in the spring breeze. The parade will never be over if people will remember, and I go back to this quote, what Thomas Jefferson said, "Obedience to the law is the major part of patriotism." . . . You people are obligated by your oath to fulfill your obligation without fear, favor, or sympathy. Do your duty.[119]

PEOPLE WILL NO LONGER BE QUIET

While the jury was doing its duty, Judge Hoffman adjudged the defendants and their lawyers guilty of 159 contempt citations and sentenced them to jail terms ranging from two months and eight days (Weiner) to four years and thirteen days (Kunstler). There was a pattern to the dates of the citations. From the time the first witness testified on 26 September until 15 October, no defendant was cited for contumacious behavior.[120] Almost half of the defendants' contemptuous acts occurred during two brief periods—28, 29, and 30 October and 4 and 5 February—during which Bobby Seale was bound and gagged and Dellinger's bail was revoked.[121] The pattern of the lawyers' citations was somewhat different. Two-thirds of the acts for which they were punished occurred for the most part during the last thirty days of the trial. In November Kunstler had a contempt-free record. That month Weinglass had only one citation, and in December, his record was free of contempt.

Before they were sentenced the defendants and their lawyers were allowed to address the court. Dellinger referred to racism and the Vietnam war in trying to explain some of his behavior. Judge Hoffman stopped him, saying he should not "talk politics." "You have tried," answered Dellinger, "to keep what you call politics, which means the truth, out of this courtroom, just as the prosecution has." The judge asked Dellinger to say no more, but he would not stop: "You want us to be like good Germans supporting the evils of our decade and . . . when we refuse . . . you want us to be like good Jews, going quietly and politely to concentration camps. . . . People will no

---

[118]Ibid., p. 21319.

[119]Ibid., pp. 21338–39.

[120]Hoffman and Hayden were each cited for contempt prior to the first witness taking the stand, but both incidents were trivial. Hoffman blew a kiss to the jury, and Hayden greeted the jury in a friendly fashion with a power-to-the-people salute.

[121]This was initially pointed out by Harry Kalven, Jr., in his introduction to *Contempt* (Chicago: Swallow Press, Inc., 1970), p. xviii.

longer be quiet. . . . I am an old man and I am just speaking feebly, and not too well, but I reflect the spirit that will echo throughout the world."

One of Dellinger's daughters applauded, and a marshal forcibly removed her from the courtroom. "Leave my daughter alone!" Dellinger cried. "Leave my daughter alone!" "Tyrants! Tyrants!" shouted a spectator.

"Heil Hitler! Heil Hitler! Heil Hitler!" Rubin yelled at the judge. And Kunstler, weeping as he hunched over the attorney's lectern, said: "What are you doing to us? My life has come to nothing. I am not anything any more. You destroyed me and everybody else. Put me in jail now, for God's sake, and get me out of this place. Come to mine now. Come to mine now, Judge, please. Please. I beg you." Judge Hoffman, his jaws working, stared straight ahead and said nothing.[122]

Davis explained that the reason for his behavior in October was Judge Hoffman's treatment of Seale. "You know what he called me," said the judge.

DAVIS: He called you a racist, a fascist, and a pig.
JUDGE HOFFMAN: Several times.
DAVIS: Many times, and not enough.
JUDGE HOFFMAN: I will ask you to sit down.[123]

Because Hayden's statement was courteous and restrained, a genuine dialogue took place between him and the judge—the first in the trial. Judge Hoffman said it pained him to be called a racist and have obscenities shouted at him; he felt he did not deserve such treatment. Both men agreed that the trial did not work the way American trials are supposed to work. "I think the difficulty," said Hayden, "is trying to try people for . . . ideological crimes. That is what brings politics and consciousness into the courtroom."[124]

Abbie Hoffman said he had no respect for the court because he did not regard it as legitimate. Rubin said that Judge Hoffman had "done more harm to this country than any other single person alive today."[125] Weiner said that Judge Hoffman saw the Chicago Seven as defendants, but "we see ourselves as revolutionaries. You see us on trial in a criminal trial. We see ourselves under the gun of a political trial being used as a weapon in the hands of the government in an ongoing political war against dissent and youth in this country."[126] Judge Hoffman almost overlooked sentencing Froines, who said: "It's part of being a media unknown that even the Judge finally forgets you're here."[127]

The lawyers were last to speak. Weinglass humbly asked Judge Hoffman for compassion, explaining that this was his first trial before a federal court.

[122]Trial Transcript, pp. 21508–10; *Chicago Sun-Times*, 15 February 1970, p. 1.
[123]Trial Transcript, p. 21541.
[124]Ibid., p. 21587.
[125]Ibid., p. 21649.
[126]Ibid., p. 21661D.
[127]Ibid., p. 21673.

With some difficulty he referred to the judge's slighting him and calling him Mr. Feinglass, but he confessed that in the heat of courtroom battle perhaps he too had argued somewhat zealously. Compassion was not forthcoming. "I am accustomed to having lawyers obey the rules," said the judge, "and that you consistently failed to do . . . As you may know—perhaps you don't —this is [your] first case in the federal court you just told me—the United States of America in this case is the plaintiff. 'The accuser'—Justice Cardozo says, 'the accuser has some rights.' "[128]

"I am going to make a rather unorthodox statement," the judge said to Kunstler. "If [crime] is on the increase, . . . it is due in large part to the fact that waiting in the wings are lawyers who are willing . . . to go beyond professional responsibility, professional rights, and professional duty in their defense of a defendant." The judge was leading up to a matter that had bothered him throughout the trial—Bobby Seale. "You represent yourself," he told Kunstler, "to be a leader at the Bar, . . . and you have never, never, made an attempt to say something like this to him, 'Bobby, hush. Cool it. Sit down now.' You let him go on. . . . You made no effort, no effort, to have him keep from calling a Judge of the United States District Court a pig, a fascist pig, a racist pig. . . . You let him continue speaking and repeating. If that is being a great lawyer, I do not share your view." To which Kunstler answered: "I am glad your Honor spoke because I suddenly feel nothing but compassion for you. Everything else has dropped away."[129]

THE JURY DEALS

Meanwhile the jury deliberated. Eight jurors were for conviction on all counts; four were for complete acquittal. Two of the four were Jean Fritz, the woman who had been seen carrying the Baldwin book, and Mary Butler, the retired cook. The other two were Shirley Seaholm and Freida Robbins. Some of the jurors favoring conviction expressed strong views. One said that "the young people who demonstrated during the convention should have been shot down by the police." Another thought "the defendants should be convicted because of their appearance, their language, and their life style." A woman juror, asked if she could understand the defendants' position, replied: "Do you want your kids to grow up that way?" John Nelson, the unemployed housepainter, thought the defendants were dangerous men who were plotting to take over the country. Mrs. Miriam Hill said she resented all war protesters because her son was in the navy.[130]

Feelings ran high between the jury's two factions. Sequestration had taken

[128]Ibid., pp. 21803–05.
[129]Ibid., pp. 21746, 21749–50.
[130]Richards, "Chicago 7 Verdict," *Boston Globe,* 22 February 1970, p. 28.

its toll; one of the jurors was willing to vote either way in order to go home as soon as possible. At one point the vote was nine to three for conviction on all counts. Then the young computer operator, Kay Richards, suggested a compromise: a verdict of not guilty on the conspiracy charge and complete acquittal of Weiner and Froines. Three of the jurors who had stood firm for complete acquittal for three days could not at first accept the compromise. They said the anti-riot law was unconstitutional. But that was not, Miss Richards explained, for them to determine; they had only to decide if the defendants had violated the law. That was the turning point; on the fourth day of deliberation, all the jurors had agreed to the compromise.

After the verdict was announced and the jury discharged, some of the jurors expressed their views on the case and the defendants. Edward Kratzke, the jury foreman, said: "I was a streetcar conductor. I've seen guys, real bums with no soul, just a body—but when they went in front of a judge, they had their hats off. These defendants wouldn't even stand up when the judge walked in. When there's no respect, we might as well give up the United States."[131] During a television interview Mrs. Ruth Peterson said the defendants "needed a good bath and to have their hair cut. . . . They had no respect for nobody, not even the marshals. When they told them to get their feet off their chairs, they just put them right back up again. I don't think that's nice."[132]

ALICE IN 1984?

Each defendant received the same sentence: five years in prison and a $5,000 fine. Court costs were also assessed against them. Before sentences were passed, each of the defendants was allowed to make a statement, his last in the trial.

David Dellinger spoke calmly. He told the judge that he felt more compassion than hostility toward him. However misguided and intolerant he thought Judge Hoffman was, Dellinger had to admit the old man had a spunky quality one had to admire. "All the way through the trial," he said to the judge, "I kept comparing you to King George III of England, . . . perhaps because you are trying to forestall a second American revolution which is in the cards."[133]

Rennie Davis was hostile. He said that from the beginning the trial was controlled by the FBI and undercover agents, and that they had lied day after day on the witness stand. "Since I did not get a jury of my peers," he said, "I look to the jury that is in the streets. My jury will be in the streets

---

[131]Hayden, "The Trial," p. 37.
[132]J. Anthony Lucas, "The Second Confrontation in Chicago," New York Times Magazine, 27 March 1970, p. 34.
[133]Trial Transcript, p. 21959.

tomorrow all across this country and the verdict from my jury will keep coming in over the next five years."[134]

Tom Hayden said:

> Our intention in coming to Chicago was not to incite a riot. . . . [It] was to see to it that certain things, that is, the right of every human being, the right to assemble, the right to protest, can be carried out even where the Government chooses to suspend those rights. It was because we chose to exercise those rights in Chicago . . . that we are here today. . . . We would hardly be notorious characters if they had left us alone in the streets of Chicago last year. . . . It would have been testimony to our failure as organizers. But instead we became the architects, the master minds, and the geniuses of a conspiracy to overthrow the government. We were invented. We were chosen by the government to serve as scapegoats for all that they wanted to prevent happening in the 1970's.[135]

Abbie Hoffman said he felt like Alice in Wonderland. "I am still waiting for the permits for Lincoln Park. I still think Lyndon Johnson is President. I don't understand what is going on in America, America with a 'k,' not a 'c.' . . . We are being tried as criminals. America doesn't have political trials. . . . This is a criminal trial. So it can't be a political trial. It was Alice in Wonderland coming in; now I feel like Alice in 1984 because I have lived through the winter in injustice in this trial."[136]

Jerry Rubin gave Judge Hoffman a copy of his book *Do It!* with this inscription: "Dear Julius, the demonstrations in Chicago in 1968 were the first steps in the revolution. What happened in the courtroom is the second step. Julius, you radicalized more young people than we ever could. You're the country's top Yippie." Rubin's final words were: "This is the happiest moment of my life." To which other defendants responded: "Right on!"[137]

Judge Hoffman had the last word. He said that the record in the trial and the defendants' remarks in the court that day showed they were "clearly dangerous persons" who should not be at large. "Therefore, the commitments here will be without bail."[138]

THE JURY IN THE STREETS

Rennie Davis had said his jury would be in the streets, and it was. Tens of thousands of young people protested the conviction of the Chicago defendants. They held rallies and marched in Boston, New Haven, New York, Washington, Chicago, Madison, Seattle, and Berkeley. More than 100 were

[134]Ibid., p. 21965.
[135]Ibid., pp. 21967–68, 21972.
[136]Ibid., pp. 21992–93, 21996, 22001.
[137]Ibid., pp. 22015, 22018.
[138]Ibid., p. 22021.

arrested and some were injured. At Drew University, student response to a speech by Senator Strom Thurmond supporting Judge Hoffman was something Abbie Hoffman might have dreamed up: they pelted Thurmond with marshmallows. The Court of Appeals for the Seventh Circuit gave the defendants their freedom pending appeal, and they and their lawyers traveled around the country speaking at colleges and universities to finance their appeal. After Kunstler spoke at the University of California at Santa Barbara, the students began a protest demonstration that culminated in the burning of a branch of the Bank of America.

Tom Hayden and several writers began books on the trial. The Toronto Workshop Company produced *Chicago 70*, a skillful blend of Chicago trial transcript and *Alice in Wonderland*. The trial had been tape recorded, and one enterprising soul bought the tapes with a view to selling recordings. A publishing house plans to print the entire transcript of the trial, some 22,000 pages. Film producers are considering making a movie of the proceedings. The trial was over, but its myth was just beginning.

THE IDEAL OF A FAIR TRIAL

Just prior to being sentenced for contempt, Bobby Seale said his case would be taken "to a higher court, possibly to the highest court in America."[139] Tom Hayden, in the same situation later, also mentioned the Supreme Court, but in a pessimistic way. He feared the trial indicated a change of direction in the courts. In support of his view he pointed to Judge G. Harrold Carswell's nomination to the Senate as a candidate for the Supreme Court, and said he doubted that a man like Carswell—who fought against "outside agitators," who was against what the defendants considered social justice, and who upheld the status quo—could overturn the rulings in the Chicago trial. "Therefore," he concluded, "for a lot of people who feel the way I do, we are in the movie Z. I mean there is not going to be a higher court."[140]

A few days after the trial ended the Supreme Court of the United States heard arguments in *Illinois* v. *Allen*,[141] a case in which a defendant charged with armed robbery acted in such a disruptive manner during his trial that the judge removed him from the court and tried him in absentia. The Court, in an opinion by Justice Black, held that the circumstances of the judge's action did not violate the defendant's constitutional rights of confrontation. In such cases, Justice Black said, "there are at least three constitutionally permissible ways for a judge to handle an obstreperous defendant like Allen: (1) bind and gag him, thereby keeping him present; (2) cite him for contempt; (3) take him out of the courtroom until he promises to conduct himself properly."[142] In deciding the *Allen* case the justices no doubt gave some

[139]Ibid., p. 5480.
[140]Ibid., pp. 21583–84.
[141]397 U.S. 337 (1970).
[142]Ibid., 343–44.

thought to Judge Hoffman's binding and gagging of Bobby Seale. Justice Douglas, who wrote a separate opinion, almost certainly had the Chicago case in mind. "Would we," he asked, apparently referring to Seale, "tolerate removal of a defendant from the courtroom during a trial because he was insisting on his constitutional rights, albeit vociferously, no matter how obnoxious his philosophy might have been to the bench that tried him? Would we uphold contempt in that situation?"[143] And for the first time in a judicial opinion Justice Douglas officially recognized political trials and identified five of them in the nation's past: those of Spies, Debs, Mooney, Sacco and Vanzetti, and Dennis.[144]

The Court's real problems, according to Douglas, do not arise in trials like Allen's, which was "the classical criminal case without any political or subversive overtones." They arise in two other types of trials. The first are political trials that involve either political indictments or political judges. The second "are trials used by minorities to destroy the existing constitutional system and bring on repressive measures." Involved in a trial of the second variety, the defendant proceeds at his peril, for "the Constitution was not designed as an instrument for a form of rough-and-tumble contest. The social compact has room for tolerance, patience, and restraint, but not sabotage and violence." In a political trial, Justice Douglas suggested, it is the government that runs the greater risk. "Problems of political indictments and of political judges," he wrote, "raise profound questions going to the heart of the social compact. For that compact is two-sided: majorities undertake to press their grievances within limits of the Constitution and in accord with its procedures; minorities agree to abide by constitutional procedures in resisting those claims." Then he asked a crucial question that the Court would one day face: "Does the answer to that problem involve defining the procedure for conducting political trials or does it involve the designing of constitutional methods for putting an end to them?" He suggested that the record in the *Allen* case was "singularly inadequate to answer those questions," and that it would "be time enough to resolve those weighty problems when a political trial reaches this Court for review." The record of the Chicago trial, if it reaches the Supreme Court, will give the justices an opportunity to consider the problems raised by Justice Douglas; clearly it was not a "classical criminal case without any political or subversive overtones."[145]

The Chicago case might never reach the Supreme Court. If it does, it is not inconceivable that it will be decided against the defendants. After all, the Court decided against Debs, Mooney, and Dennis and refused to hear the appeal of Sacco and Vanzetti. If the defendants lose on appeal, their trial may have an even greater social and political impact than if they win,

---

[143]Ibid., 355.
[144]*Spies et al.* v. *People (The Anarchists' Case)*, 122 Ill. 1, 12 N.E. 865 (1887); *In re Debs*, 158 U.S. 564 (1887); *Mooney* v. *Holohan*, 294 U.S. 103 (1935); *Commonwealth* v. *Sacco et al.*, 255 Mass 369, 151 N.E. 839 (1926), 259 Mass 128, 156 N.E. 57 (1927); *Dennis et al.* v. *United States*, 341 U.S. 494 (1951).
[145]397 U.S. at 356.

since they claimed from the beginning that the trial was political and hence unfair. "The cultural value of the ideal of a fair trial," Thurman Arnold wrote,

> is advanced as much by its failure as it is by its success. Any violation of the symbol of a ceremonial trial rouses persons who would be left unmoved by an ordinary nonceremonial injustice. . . . Harmless anarchists may be shot by the police. . . . Liberals will be sorry and forget. But let them be treated unfairly by a court . . . and, before dissatisfaction has died away, the prejudice or phobia which created the unfair atmosphere of the trial will receive a public analysis and examination which otherwise it would not get.[146]

The Chicago conspiracy trial is already a cause célèbre. Ultimately the people, not the courts, will decide whether justice was done.[147]

[146]*The Symbols of Government* (New Haven: Yale University Press, 1935), p. 142.
[147]In addition to the sources cited, this chapter is based on interviews with and observations of some of the lawyers and defendants. I discussed the case with both Weinglass and Schultz and interviewed Froines. On May Day 1970 the Chicago Seven came to New Haven; at that time I had an opportunity to observe and listen to all of them. I also spoke briefly with Davis. Earlier I heard Kunstler give a lecture at Yale on the case. Also useful were filmed interviews of Seale and his wife.

four:
"political"
trials

CARROL W. CAGLE

HARRY P. STUMPF

9

THE TRIAL OF REIES
LOPEZ TIJERINA

On 5 June 1967 a band of armed men swept into a remote northern New Mexico courthouse in search of a hated district attorney. The district attorney was not present, but two officers were wounded, the courthouse shot up, and a newsman and deputy kidnapped. Before nightfall, armored, troop-carrying vehicles of the New Mexico National Guard had fanned out across the vast, mountainous area in search of the "insurrectionists." The date has since become the most discussed and debated in the state's history.

The "courthouse raid," as it is now known, brought national reporters into Rio Arriba County in force for the first time; thus it focused national attention on the land grant issue, on fiery land grant leader Reies Lopez Tijerina, and on the plight of New Mexico's Hispanic[1] population.

Tensions produced by the violent event were to simmer without letup until 13 November 1968—the day the authorities moved the continuing struggle with the Hispanic militants into the establishment's own arena of the courtroom. There, the mercurial Tijerina—eloquent, but with little formal education, and unversed in the law—confronted the man he had sought to "arrest" a year-and-a-half earlier, District Attorney Alfonso Sanchez. The trial, whether evoking memories of Pancho Villa or Zapata, or capturing the imagination of black separatists and campus revolutionaries, was to become the nonviolent equivalent of the confrontation which never occurred at the courthouse.

---

[1]The issue of what to call New Mexico's Hispanic minority is frequently a hot one in the state. "Spanish-speaking" does not necessarily apply, nor does "Spanish-surnamed." Some prefer "Mexican-American," although others are offended by that term and prefer "Spanish-American." "Hispanic" seems the most adequate, although "Chicano" seems to be gaining favor.

THE HISPANIC LEGACY

To understand what was at stake in the flamboyant trial, it is necessary to have some knowledge of New Mexico history, of the land grant issue, and of Reies Tijerina himself. For the courtroom clash was more than a clash between a dominant, legalistic majority and an unregenerate, radical minority.

Contrary to popular belief, the settlement of New Mexico did not first occur in the 1800s with the westward push of American frontiersmen. When the wagon trains and railroads arrived, they found an already flourishing outpost of European culture. The Catholic Church, a legal system, and agricultural settlements were all ongoing operations, implanted in the vast area by earlier Spanish settlers. Starting with the *conquistador* Coronado, who moved with his men up the Rio Grande valley in 1540, the stream of Spaniards became sizeable. Santa Fe, America's oldest capital, was founded on the site of an existing *pueblo* in 1610 to administer Spanish affairs throughout the northern province. Other tiny Spanish towns sprang up—almost always with a Catholic church—along the general route of the Rio Grande. Much of this activity occurred long before the American Revolution erupted in the East.

Indeed, even the early Spanish arrivals found a well-established, civilized and humane society existing in the numerous *pueblos* along the Rio Grande. The Pueblo Indians, who had settled in their riverside apartment complexes centuries previous, already possessed an agricultural system, a religion, and amazingly sophisticated forms of art, crafts, and music.

These are not only interesting but pertinent facts, for they illustrate that American frontiersmen[2] were indeed latecomers on the scene. When they arrived, the land ownership issue and interrelated social questions already were becoming confused.

The ordinary difficulties of administering a legal system in a frontier setting, following directions from a distant governing authority in Spain, were made even more complex by two facts: that Indians already claimed substantial acreage in the Spanish domain, and that the newly independent nation of Mexico imposed yet another government over the area before the United States moved in.

Mexico, which gained independence from Spain in 1821, ruled the region which is now New Mexico until 1848, when the United States defeated the fledgling nation and took—under the Treaty of Guadalupe Hidalgo—the Southwest as new American territory.

That the Indians had bona fide land rights, even as far back as Spanish rule, is clear. Under the 1680 code, *Recopilación de Leyes los Reynos de los Indias,* "not only were the Indians to have full possession of all the area which they

---

[2]The question of what to call the "Americans" is likewise at issue, and is most frequently resolved with the term "Anglos." "Americans," of course, cannot be a distinction since all residents involved are United States citizens. "Whites" is not a proper characterization. "English-speaking" can apply to both the majority and Hispanic minority. In this account, we will use the term "Anglo" to characterize the non-Hispanic American settlers and their contemporary descendants.

used or occupied, but they were also to be given more territory if for any reason their lands were insufficient for their needs," according to New Mexico Archivist Myra Ellen Jenkins.[3] She adds: "Unfortunately, the laws were honored more in the breach than in the observance. The most influential Spaniard in the area was generally given the post of *alcalde mayor* for political favor."[4] Miss Jenkins, who has made it her career to study the tortured history of land ownership, also notes that the situation did not improve with Mexican independence in 1821: "The Pueblo Indians suffered even worse abuses under the Republic of Mexico, for now virtually all checks were removed. By the Treaty of Cordoba, Indians were granted citizenship and land rights were continued, but nothing was done to implement this provision by specific legislation or orders to the chief executives."[5]

Nor did the new Hispanic residents themselves contribute to an easing of the confusion. Their common custom was to divide landholdings among all male heirs for inheritance purposes, rather than following the English common law of primogeniture—which bestowed all the father's land exclusively on the eldest son. As one writer has observed:

> On the surface this law appears to have been hard on the younger children; but it had the effect of keeping the land in large, workable units, and also forced the younger sons to make their living in the army, the navy, or commerce. Spanish law, as practiced in New Mexico, provided for all children to share equally in the estate of their parents. The custom actually was to divide the land. There are now many tracts 50 to 100 feet wide and a half-mile to a mile long caused by such inheritance divisions. Obviously, no one can make even a bare living on such a tract.[6]

The confusing factors of Indian claims, inheritance practices, and diverse national hegemony all contributed to land disputes before the United States clashed with Mexico. As one noted New Mexico historian put it, "When the United States of America acquired New Mexico by invasion and conquest on 15 August 1846, it inherited a land grant problem of considerable magnitude."[7] The historian, William A. Keleher, reiterated points made by Miss Jenkins. "Both under Spanish rule and Mexican rule the granting of lands was not a simple transaction," Keleher wrote. "Many pitfalls stood between the grant and the final confirmation, and there was always the possibility of a revocation of the grant for legal or political reasons. Doubtless political influence, close friendship and other factors entered into the granting and holding of lands."[8]

[3]"The Baltasar Baca 'Grant': History of an Encroachment," *El Palacio* 68, nos. 1 and 2 (Spring and Summer 1961): 49.
[4]Ibid., p. 53.
[5]Ibid., p. 60.
[6]Wayne S. Scott, "Spanish Land-Grant Problems Were Here Before the Anglos," *New Mexico Business* 20, no. 7 (July 1967).
[7]William A. Keleher, *Maxwell Land Grant: A New Mexico Item* (Santa Fe: Rydal Press, 1942), p. 4.
[8]Ibid., p. 5.

The land grant problem, inherited with the war of 1846 and confirmed by the treaty of 1848, lay fallow until 22 July 1854, when the United States Congress enacted a law creating a surveyor-general for New Mexico. His obligation was to "ascertain the origin, nature, character, and extent of all claims of land under the laws, usages, and customs of Spain and Mexico." He further "was obligated to make a full report on all claims of land grants, with his decision as to the validity or invalidity of the titles."[9] It was during the period of the surveyors-general that confusion of considerable magnitude was to develop over the land grant issue in New Mexico; this in turn contributed to the development of ill feelings by Hispanic settlers toward the Anglo newcomers. Tales of shady dealings, outright thefts, and conspiratorial transactions were to be passed down—almost in the way of familial legend—to the poor Hispanic villagers of the 1960s.

It must be noted, however, that Tijerina and his *Alianza Federal de los Pueblos Libres* ("Federal Alliance of Free City-States") have mistakenly relied on the Treaty of Guadalupe Hidalgo as confirmation of the validity of current claims. The original Article X of the treaty specifically provided that Spanish and Mexican land grants would be respected as valid. The United States Senate, however, did not ratify this article. Senators apparently felt that all property rights were fully protected by other articles of the treaty, and that "Article X might be used to revive grants which had become invalid."[10] The real story of land shenanigans, during the tenure of various surveyors-general in New Mexico's territorial days (1848–1912), indicates reason enough for distress on the part of Hispanic descendants of those early settlers.

LAND GRANTS AND LAND GRABS

The wild-and-woolly frontier days ushered in by the conquest of Mexico proved to be a fertile time for land maneuverings. Newcoming Anglo frontiersmen proved, for the most part, to be more brash, acquisitive, and land-hungry than the generally placid, rural Hispanic settlers. In addition, the Americans brought with them an entirely new legal system and language—two devices which made it relatively easy for land to be gradually eased away, either illegally or through unethical practices, from the Hispanos. The shady maneuverings, and resultant chaos in land negotiations, has been well documented by officials of the period and by latter-day historians.

Territorial Governor Lionel A. Sheldon, in a report to the Secretary of the Interior for 1883, wrote:

> New Mexico is largely plastered with grants of land, real or pretended, made by the Spanish and Mexican governments. . . . In some cases the grants overlap, which leads to disputes and occasional acts of violence. . . . It is generally believed

[9]Ibid., p. 7.
[10]Jenkins, "Baltasar Baca 'Grant'," p. 88.

that errors and frauds have been practiced and apparently legalized through want of knowledge or attention to the subject.

Success in securing confirmation of grants of a doubtful character so encouraged and emboldened the covetous that it is alleged the manufacture of grant papers became an occupation.[11]

Two years later, Territorial Governor Edmund G. Ross, a one-time United States Senator from Kansas, added his appraisal to the Secretary of the Interior:

... So general and apparently well grounded is the suspicion that there has been in operation for many years a systematic and cunningly executed scheme for the manufacture of fraudulent titles to large tracts of public domain under the guise of Spanish and Mexican grants, that the public faith in all such titles has largely diminished.[12]

Later, Keleher was to write:

Mexican citizens soon found their estates in jeopardy, many of them lost their landed interests entirely, became pauperized, as the result of the failure of the promises made by [General Stephen] Kearney [commander of American forces in the area], or the failure of the United States of America to back up in good faith the assurances extended in the Treaty of Guadalupe Hidalgo. Families which had been in undisputed possession of small tracts of land for one and two centuries found themselves on the defensive. Land grant owners found their property an attractive prize to scheming Anglos.[13]

The scheming and thievery were not simply the practices of unscrupulous outlaws; indeed, the leading figures of the territorial government were known to have been involved. That this was the case was not lost on the (mainly) defenseless Hispanos of the time. Their resentment festered and was passed down through generations. The Hispanic folklore of a century later was to make it much easier for a firebrand orator like Tijerina to rally supporters behind his land-seeking Alianza.

The methods of the "Santa Fe Ring," as the Republican establishment at the territorial capital was dubbed, are also well documented by Keleher, Twitchell, and others. One historian, Frances Swadesh, describes the rough-and-ready scene this way:

In the early 1870s, representatives of highly capitalized land and livestock enterprises, spearheaded by the British land speculator, William Blackmore, and the "Santa Fe Ring" of lawyers and bankers made rapid headway in acquiring Spanish and Mexican grant lands. By paying members of some grantee families nominal sums, by representing legal clients in exchange for title to their

---

[11]Keleher, *Maxwell Land Grant*, p. 8.
[12]Ibid.
[13]Keleher, *The Fabulous Frontier: 12 New Mexico Items* (Santa Fe: Rydal Press, 1945), pp. 86–87.

land, and by other devices, fair and foul, whole grants were taken out of the hands of their rightful owners.[14]

Professor Swadesh adds, in particular reference to the Tierra Amarilla Grant, an area where Tijerina was later to appear on the scene:

> Those who were illiterate signed for a "gift," generally a horse, which would be presented to them, not knowing they were signing a deed giving away their lands.[15]

Some observers are surprised that long-ago excesses by American settlers still have the capability of arousing enmity on the part of mid-twentieth century Hispanos. If it were folklore alone that provoked contemporary wrath, one could rightly be startled. The fact is, however, that current land practices —added to those territorial shenanigans—are also a source of constant irritation to Hispanic residents in the northern part of the state. Specifically, the United States Forest Service—largest landholder in northern New Mexico—has exacerbated old wounds with its frequently changing, little understood, often irritating policies concerning grazing on federal land. The presence of large private ranches owned by Anglos—in contrast to tiny plots held by Hispanos— adds to the feelings of anger and resentment.

These later trends in land ownership are described by Professor Swadesh:

> The loss of grant lands . . . has been followed by a tendency toward monopoly of "public" lands by powerful private interests. Much of the jointly-owned range and forest lands of Spanish grants was converted into National Forest lands in the late Nineteenth and early Twentieth centuries. In the subsequent policy of leasing these range lands, preference for large, corporate leasers as against small stockraisers has all but shut Hispano stockmen out from their ancestral rangelands.[16]

The magnitude of contemporary land ownership is illustrated by the fact that 44 percent, or 33.8 million acres, of New Mexico's total acreage of 77.8 million acres is owned by the federal government.[17] Even an "establishment" publication, issued by the New Mexico State Land Office a few years ago, makes the same point frequently made by Tijerina and his followers, albeit in bureaucratic language. The Land Office report asserts that "the present magnitude of ownership of lands by the United States" should be "viewed with alarm." The practice "would not seem to be consistent with our democratic form of government."[18]

State government, too, has been remiss. It should be noted that in addition

[14]Frances Leon Swadesh, "Hispanic Americans of the Ute Frontier from the Chama Valley to the San Juan Basin 1694–1960" (Ph.D. diss., University of Colorado, 1966).
[15]Ibid., p. 99.
[16]Ibid., p. 309.
[17]Report of New Mexico Land Resources Association, "Land Resources of New Mexico" 1959, p. 75.
[18]Ibid.

to the complex land grant problem in the north, there is a highly confused land *title* situation. In some areas, even county lines are not surveyed with care. The absence of clear property boundaries naturally throws land owner-ship into doubt, making it impossible for poor residents of the area to secure equity for improvement loans. Their small plots of land are often all these residents have, but even that ownership is shaky, and they cannot parlay it into capital improvement projects. According to State Representative Finis Heidel, chairman of the New Mexico House Taxation Committee, state government could—and should—have done much to correct this situation years ago. Heidel noted a 1947 law which declares that "when the State Tax Commission finds that lands within the whole or any part of any county has never been surveyed, or that a general survey . . . affords insufficient data for a comprehensive and general assessment . . . the commission is authorized to make an actual survey of all lands within the whole or part of any county." Heidel told his audience: "Since 1947, no one has had the political guts to assess or have surveys of land made. . . ." If assessments and surveys had been made, he added, "we wouldn't have all the [land] problems we have."[19]

Finally, there was the fact that taxes under United States rule were levied against land grants as an entirety. But rights to grants were vested in dozens—perhaps as many as a thousand—of heirs. "Thus," says a state government report, "before the 20th Century was well under way, tax sales, forced sales of land to raise cash in the new money economy, and commercial rather than subsistence use of the [area] had deprived the Spanish-American settlements of much of their traditional range and land resource base. For the first time in centuries, many of the Spanish-Americans were forced to leave their native villages. . . ."[20]

All these diverse elements, along with a myriad of social, economic, and cultural deprivations, combined to make northern New Mexico of the 1960s fertile ground for the militant activity of Reies Tijerina. Although many young men leave the area—for Denver, Albuquerque, Los Angeles—to seek jobs, the predominantly old who remain are susceptible to pleas for direct action, especially if the pleas are as eloquent as those of Tijerina. However complex the analysis of New Mexico's land issue, it is imperative to review some of these facts in order to understand the rise of Tijerina.

A LEADER APPEARS

What then, led to the 1967 courthouse raid and the subsequent courtroom engagement between Tijerina and the New Mexico establishment? What manner of man was able to draw to him an unlikely group of would-be revolutionaries around the unlikely issue of land grant restoration?

[19]Finis Heidel, quoted in *Albuquerque Journal,* 27 August 1967.
[20]"Embudo, Pilot Planning Project for the Embudo Watershed of New Mexico," published by the Interagency Council for Area Development Planning and the New Mexico State Planning Office, 1961, p. 23.

"Tijerina's character," writes a journalist who knows him as well as anyone, "contains something of the archetypal Robin Hood style of social bandit. Conflicting with his idealistic platform and his expressed adherence to nonviolence is an obvious pride in his wiles as a fugitive. His statements reveal an enjoyment of contests with the law. In this life-gambling some observers have sensed a fatalism, an embracing of the encounter to have done with it, a desperate leap to unload some private demon from his back. Tijerina says it is the concept of Justice which drives him with such unrelenting force."[21] Tijerina, adds the journalist, "became a catalyst for a variety of frustrations he was never fully to comprehend."[22]

Tijerina was born in Falls City, Texas, on 21 September 1926, one of seven children of poor migrant farm workers. He says he picked cotton himself during the Depression, roamed for a time, and ended up at age nineteen in the Latin American District Council of the Assemblies of God Church at Ysleta, Texas. There, he studied to be an evangelist. The superintendent of the fundamentalist school remembers young Tijerina as being "sincere" but "fanatical."[23]

"He was fanatical, more peculiar in his thoughts, I guess," recalls the superintendent. "When he went to school he was a very sincere student. I don't know, when he left school he began to get these rather far out ideas about how people ought to conduct themselves." By 1950 Tijerina's ministerial license and credentials had been revoked because of his "unorthodox attitude." The intense, eloquent young man then wandered around Arizona, Utah, and other states "trying to start up religious movements." During one period in his life he spent some time around the Tierra Amarilla area of northern New Mexico, trying to organize a religious sect and "talking to the old people and learning about their land." Fifteen years later, he was to return with his ideas for a solution to the land problem.

After an attempt to start a utopian religious colony near Florence, Arizona, and several scrapes with the law there, Tijerina says he spent time in Mexico—until 1963—doing research into the laws of the Spanish empire and the background of land grants. New Mexicans first became aware of his presence in the state in 1963 and 1964, when he was organizing the *Alianza Federal de Mercedes* ("Federal Alliance of Land Grants"). This organization, made up of alleged heirs to ancient Spanish grants, later was changed to *Alianza Federal de los Pueblos Libres* ("Federal Alliance of Free City-States"). Most, including Tijerina, simply refer to the organization as the "Alianza."

Tijerina is frequently and accurately described as a "fiery land grant leader." His eloquence, especially in the Spanish language, would be difficult to surpass. He has an intense quality about him, even when relaxed, and his eyes are piercing.

[21]Peter Nabokov, "Reflections on the Alianza," *New Mexico Quarterly* XXXVII, no. 4 (Winter 1968): 351.

[22]Ibid., p. 349.

[23]These and other details of Tijerina's early life are based on conversations with Tijerina himself and with Peter Nabokov, and on numerous press accounts.

In his attempts to organize the poor Hispanos of northern New Mexico, he seized an ideal issue: land.

Land was only a code word, a symbol, for deeper social problems facing the Hispanos of northern New Mexico. Governor David F. Cargo told a congressional subcommittee after the raid that "a century of broken promises led to the rebellious act in northern New Mexico." "These people," the governor added, "are losing faith in the democratic process."[24] At another time, Cargo explained: "Contrary to what people have said, the whole thing does not turn around the matter of land grant rights. It involves a hundred other problems . . . from grazing on national forests to disrepair of roads. All he [Tijerina] did was set it off."[25] One of the authors, a Santa Fe journalist at the time, observed: "Underneath, waiting for years to be played upon, were resentments resulting from generations of putting up with unpaved roads, run-down schools, sorry health facilities, and politicians who played upon ignorance."[26]

During 1966 and early 1967 Tijerina and his Alianzans were involved in several confrontations with authorities. Most, such as the attempt to take over a Forest Service campground at Echo Amphitheater and the corresponding "arrest" of Forest Rangers, were designed to dramatize the Alianza's claims to land. Specifically, Tijerina claimed for the Alianza the so-called San Joaquin del Rio de Chama grant in northern Rio Arriba County. As June 1967 approached the Alianza planned a large meeting of land grant "heirs" at the tiny community of Coyote. The night before the meeting, however, a number of Alianza members were arrested on various charges.

As a direct result of the arrest—and also to demonstrate the Alianza's authority in matters of law—members of the organization, including Tijerina, swooped down on the pink adobe courthouse at Tierra Amarilla. They sought to "arrest" District Attorney Alfonso Sanchez, who had carried on what they saw as a vendetta against Tijerina.

The courthouse was shot up, its occupants held captive for some two hours, two officers were shot and wounded, and a deputy and a United Press International newsman were kidnapped. The raiders then fled into the mountainous countryside—all without encountering District Attorney Sanchez, who was in Santa Fe at the time. The "raid" and its aftermath became the biggest story in New Mexico. Reporters from the two Albuquerque dailies, the national networks, and national publications such as the *New York Times* drove into the north, looking bewildered. The National Guard, called out by a jittery Lieutenant Governor E. Lee Francis in the absence of Governor Cargo, swarmed over the region in armored vehicles—most unsuitable for conducting a manhunt in the vast, almost roadless, area. The reaction to the manhunt and to the actions of officers was almost as strong as reaction to the raid itself. While most New Mexicans used terms like "insurrection" and "shocking outlawry," Professor Clark Knowlton, a scholar of Hispanic affairs, shot back the charge "that the National Guard and State Police violated the Spanish-Americans' civil rights

[24]*Albuquerque Journal*, UPI, 15 June 1967.
[25]*Santa Fe New Mexican*, 8 June 1967.
[26]Ibid., 16 June 1967.

. . . when they 'systematically broke into homes, lined the people up, searched them and confined men, women, and children for many hours in a dirty sheep pen.' "[27] In Denver, Hispanic militant Rudolph "Corky" Gonzales said the use of troops was "an act of imperialistic aggression."[28]

District Attorney Sanchez, who all along had been citing "evidence" of "Communist influence" in the Alianza's actions, felt he had been vindicated. Among items confiscated when Tijerina and his colleagues were finally captured were maps of the area showing "prime objectives for seizure," an organization chart, gas masks, guns, books including *Rise and Fall of the Third Reich* and *Ché Guevara on Guerrilla Warfare*.[29]

COURTROOM CONFRONTATION

What the *Albuquerque Journal* called "one of the state's most noted criminal cases" got under way on 12 November 1968, in a paneled, carpeted, heavily guarded courtroom of the Bernalillo County Courthouse in downtown Albuquerque. Reporters, visiting high school classes, hangers-on, and Alianza sympathizers packed the galleries. District Court Judge Paul Larrazolo, a slight, nervous man whose father had once been governor of New Mexico, was plainly ill at ease. He had reason to be. Assembled before him were District Attorney Sanchez and his assistants, Tijerina and nine of his co-defendants, and a diverse array of defense lawyers. In addition to court-appointed New Mexico attorneys, there was legal counsel representing the nation's radical community, whose attention Tijerina had drawn: Beverly Axelrod, one-time friend of Eldridge Cleaver, and bearded, booming, California civil liberties lawyer John Thorne.

It was obvious from the first that confusion would reign. Even technical questions as to juror exclusion (How many challenges would be permitted? What about disagreements among defense lawyers?) began to bog down the proceedings as soon as they got under way. Ethnic composition of the jury was raised as an issue (and ultimately left unresolved). Excessive publicity—resulting in prejudice on the part of potential jurors—was argued by Thorne and Axelrod as grounds for dismissal of the trial. Each morning and each afternoon, one of these two would wave the latest edition of the *Journal* or *Tribune* in front of Larrazolo and call for a mistrial. Each time, Larrazolo would decline. With as many lawyers as defendants, with Tijerina himself jockeying for verbal position, with every technical procedural point immediately and sharply challenged, Larrazolo found himself befuddled and seemed to wish the trial would dissolve of its own accord.

Tijerina and the other nine defendants were to be tried on three charges each: kidnapping (which carries a possible death penalty), assault on the Rio

[27]*Albuquerque Journal,* UPI, 17 June 1967.
[28]*Albuquerque Tribune,* UPI, 8 June 1967.
[29]Ibid., 7 June 1967.

Arriba County jail, and false imprisonment of Deputy Sheriff Daniel Rivera. The other defendants were Jerry Noll (self-styled "King of the Indies"); Tijerina's son, Reyes Hugh Tijerina of Albuquerque; Baltazar Martines, Moises Morales, Juan Valdez, Tobias Leyba, and Solomon Velasques of Canjilón; Jose Madril of Velarde; and Esequiel Dominguez of Bernalillo.

One of us talked with Tijerina at his cavernous Alianza headquarters in Albuquerque an hour before the trial began. He was plainly nervous, uncertain of what would happen and of his own capability in the new, legalistic arena. He made it clear that he regarded the trial as but one more instrument in the establishment's arsenal. The whole procedure, he said, "was only one more act in the oppression of the Spanish people." Stirring restlessly in his chair, Tijerina seemed alternately remote, distracted, then excitable. He appeared uncomfortable in his green sport coat, green tie, and white shirt. Somewhat incongruously, he also wore slightly scuffed, high-topped, black work shoes.

His discomfort appeared to increase once he entered the courtroom. By contrast, his old adversary "Al" Sanchez—the district attorney who regards Tijerina as a Communist and worse—seemed quietly efficient, almost smug. Finally, after more than three years of inconclusive jousting, Sanchez had Tijerina before the bench—required to answer for his militant activities and his continuing challenges of the status quo.

The trial was important beyond the specific charges involved. First, it pitted Tijerina and his archenemy Sanchez in direct battle. Long the most vociferous critic of Tijerina and his Alianza, Sanchez had called loudly and frequently for the land grant leader's detention, and had spread by means of various news media his belief that Communistic influences were at work. Tijerina, for his part, regarded Sanchez (and United States Senator Joseph Montoya) as the Hispano who had "sold out," who had abandoned his heritage to "make it" in the Anglo establishment. Worse, he had turned on *los pobres* ("poor Hispanos") rather than championing their cause.

Second, public opinion throughout the state was enraged by the raid. Editorial writers and citizens in the street called for Tijerina to be "locked up," legal niceties and procedural detail notwithstanding. Tijerina became the target for reactionary denunciations from law officers, public officials, and New Mexico citizens who were disturbed about urban and campus rebellion elsewhere around the country. He was the local manifestation of hated and feared revolution, the antithesis of law, order, and complacency. Having declined to petition for grievances within normal channels, Tijerina must now submit to the awesome judgment of the law. Thus, the trial became the arena for the protectors of the status quo to assert their full authority over the unregenerate minority.

The trial, then, was for Reies Tijerina a personal confrontation (with Sanchez) and another contest in his continuing struggle against the establishment. Placed in formal, almost austere surroundings, denied the friendly atmosphere of rural Rio Arriba County, denied even his most formidable weapon—the use of fiery Spanish-language rhetoric—Tijerina obviously did not relish the encounter.

The confrontation became direct four days after the trial opened as Judge Larrazolo announced his decision to sever Tijerina's trial from those of the nine co-defendants. He acted on the strength of a memorandum from Robert Singer, assistant district attorney in Albuquerque, which concluded that the court could—and should—sever the cases. "The antagonisms developing between prosecuting attorneys and the numerous counsel for the defendants, and among the defense attorneys themselves, seem to foreshadow irreconcilable conflicts at the trial," the memorandum stated. "The situation, if left unaltered, will surely prevent both the state and the defendants from obtaining a fair trial."[30]

Four days of argumentation, motions, and jury selection were thrown out when the announcement came. The Tijerina-State of New Mexico battle was stripped of its distracting elements. "I've given a lot of thought about the manner in which we are progressing on a joint basis in selecting a jury," the judge said. "The court has come to the conclusion that there is a tremendous imposition on court-appointed counsel to continue with this case on a joint basis, that the cost to the State of New Mexico is not justifiable, that even perhaps the interest of all the defendants from the point of view of getting a fair trial all together is not the best."

District Attorney Sanchez declared that the severance was granted "over strenuous objections from the state." But Larrazolo, harassed to his wit's end by the jumble of defense motions, intramural arguments, and disputes over even the most minute points by the battery of lawyers, welcomed the opportunity to sever the cases.

Tijerina, it should be noted, preferred the severance. Although he did not say so publicly, he indicated indirectly that he was beginning to feel more confident. After four days of watching the powerful legal apparatus of the state become entrapped in a morass of technical confusion, Tijerina appeared to be gaining confidence that he could, just perhaps, beat the state with the force and clarity of his own eloquence.

TIJERINA FOR THE DEFENSE

Two days later, the showdown became even more direct: Tijerina announced abruptly what he had only hinted at before—that he would act as his own attorney in the trial. The announcement came after more than a week of desultory maneuverings, and yet before jury selection had been completed. It obviously caught Tijerina's attorneys by surprise. "The job of a lawyer is to represent his client and I want time to discuss this with Mr. Tijerina," attorney Thorne told Larrazolo. The judge agreed to allow Tijerina to defend himself, but ordered that court-appointed attorneys Beverly Axelrod and Gene Franchini remain as advisers. The ever-more-confident Tijerina objected to this, too. He said he was "reserving my right to dismiss these attorneys at any time."

[30]*Albuquerque Journal,* 19 November 1968.

The one-time migrant cottonpicker and wandering evangelist obviously was regaining his composure, losing his fear of the formal surroundings, and finding himself eager to test his powers of oration in the courtroom. Severing of the trial, he announced, had made his attorneys "obsolete." But he insisted that he needed "a few days" to prepare his case.

Larrazolo, growing increasingly impatient with the slow pace of the exasperating trial, told Tijerina sharply: "I don't want to hear any speeches from you. I just want to know if you want to represent yourself." When Tijerina said he would "give my answer in a few days," Larrazolo retorted that the land grant leader would have exactly thirty minutes to respond. Added prosecuting attorney Jack Love, assistant to Sanchez: "We can't wait until Tijerina learns how to conduct a criminal case."

Surprisingly, Alfonso Sanchez did not seem to jump at the chance of meeting his old adversary face-to-face in his, Sanchez's, own arena. During most of the trial, in fact, Sanchez sat quietly, making notes and conferring with E. E. Chavez and Jack Love, his assistants. Love, indeed, carried most of the load in arguments and cross-examination. Sanchez perhaps was reluctant to meet Tijerina in a test of oratorical ability; or perhaps he simply was so confident of victory that he preferred to sit quietly and not rock the boat. In such a way, the drama between Tijerina and Sanchez actually was heightened: Tijerina, self-assertive, growing more confident—perhaps cocky—pacing, using the rhetoric that evoked images of tent revivals and migrant farm camps; Sanchez, quiet, with an air of condescension, making his little notes and appearing serene, no matter what was happening within. One thing he did not attempt to hide was his ever-prevalent, intense personal dislike of Tijerina.

Peter Nabokov, author of *Tijerina and the Courthouse Raid*,[31] who knows both Tijerina and Sanchez well, described the confrontation this way:

> To appreciate the irony of Tijerina and Sanchez confronting each other, it must be recalled that . . . the "citizens' arrest" of Sanchez had been the sole reason for the courthouse blitz.
>
> The district attorney apparently had inflamed some local citizens by threatening imprisonment to anyone attending an Alianza "convention" the weekend before. In hot retaliation for his . . . "persecution" the raid was staged, and Tijerina was fingered as its architect.
>
> Now the two men, the . . . raid's object and its . . . alleged perpetrator, were facing each other in the polite and equal footing of opposing barristers—arguing a case from which they were anything but removed and cool legal minds.[32]

After the stage was set for direct battle, the trial took a meandering course. Reporters, including one of the authors, found it extremely difficult to predict a possible outcome. As Peter Nabokov wrote, Judge Larrazolo "apparently felt his court sinking into a legal bog." Tijerina surprised almost everyone with his

---

[31] Peter Nabokov, *Tijerina and the Courthouse Raid* (Albuquerque: University of New Mexico Press, 1969).

[32] *Sacramento Bee*, 24 November 1968.

adroit handling of the case—aided, to be sure, by Thorne, Miss Axelrod, and close legal adviser William Higgs. But it was Tijerina himself who, through shrewd cross-examination, succeeded in making the state's case appear a bit shaky. Sanchez and Chavez, probably more familiar than any lawyers with the entire case, never seemed to get the prosecution rolling. Jack Love, the bright and able assistant who had recently joined the case, was not as well prepared as he should have been.

One of the prosecution's main witnesses was Pete Jaramillo of Espanola, now sheriff of the county, the deputy who was held hostage during the raid. Jaramillo, in his testimony, placed Tijerina at the scene. He said Tijerina held a rifle to his ribs and gave orders to other armed men at the courthouse. "Reies Lopez Tijerina came behind me and put a gun in my ribs and said 'Where's Alfonso Sanchez? Tell me, you son-of-a-bitch, or I'll kill you,'" Jaramillo testified.

But Tijerina, throughout the days of testimony, sought to place doubts about the time he actually arrived at the courthouse (he said it was after the raid had begun), and whether he was—beyond doubt—guilty of the specific charges brought by the state.

In a more interesting tactic, he continually advanced the notion that citizens may make "arrests" of guilty persons—even authorities themselves (such as Sanchez). His deeper point was not missed by the intent Hispanos who sat in the gallery: that, in the land grant areas, the Alianza—not the state—is the law. If men got shot and a courthouse damaged in the process of making a legitimate "arrest," that was too bad.

Tijerina drew out this contention further when cross-examining State Policeman Juan Santistevan. The officer had testified he was approaching the courthouse on 5 June when men started shooting at him. A bullet hit the windshield of his car; he backed the vehicle behind a house and ran for cover.

"Did you know that citizens of the United States could arrest an officer if they believed they had a grievance against him?" Tijerina asked. "No," replied Santistevan. "Isn't it possible," asked Tijerina further, that "these people, pushed to the brink of desperation, had to teach you a lesson, teach you what you were not taught by your superiors?"

Undaunted, Tijerina did not miss an opportunity to pursue this point throughout the trial. He knew that if the "citizen's arrest" theory could be vindicated, it would have the short-range practical effect of making the raid—in search of Sanchez—plausible. Further, it would secure him a valuable legal weapon in his efforts to secure Alianza hegemony over territory within the "free city-states." As every witness ascended to the paneled witness stand, he hammered home his point as to the plight of a people "pushed to the brink of desperation" and using the common law right available to every citizen to obtain redress.

To make matters worse for Sanchez and the prosecution, witnesses at the courthouse failed to come through with the clear-cut, dramatic testimony that was expected. On 3 December, in fact, when the state rested its case, a Rio Arriba County undersheriff seemed to take the steam out of an already sputtering prosecution case. The undersheriff, sixty-eight-year-old Daniel Rivera, told the jury he had not heard Tijerina order him to be pistolwhipped. "I'm not blaming you for anything, sir," he told Tijerina.

LAST-MINUTE SPECULATION

As the trial proceeded into December and neared a close, it became even more difficult to predict the outcome. National attention was focused on the trial. The state press, particularly the Albuquerque dailies and television stations, provided extensive and daily coverage. Although editorial comment was not forthcoming, those familiar with New Mexico newspapers know there was strong sentiment among editors for a conviction on all three counts. If hallway talk was a fair indication, New Mexico reporters at the scene seemed to feel the state could get a conviction on only one or possibly two charges— not all three. Meanwhile, the nation's underground and left-wing press were keeping a close watch on Albuquerque. The *National Guardian,* a leftist publication, wrote on December 14: "The trial of Tijerina for crimes supposedly committed in the Tierra Amarilla courthouse 'raid' of 5 June, 1967, finally got down to the real issues: the oppression and exploitation of the Indo-Hispano people. At the same time, Tijerina's legal chances also seemed to be improved." The *Guardian* also cast aspersions on District Attorney Sanchez's refusal to take the witness stand himself, at Tijerina's request. It noted with approval this vignette, which occurred on 5 December: "A group of young people including members of Los Comancheros del Norte [a rural version of the Brown Berets] picketed outside the courthouse with signs saying 'Sanchez is afraid of Tijerina.' These signs were seized by the state to be entered as evidence. Then, in a dramatic courtroom scene, a Comanchero strode up to the judge to demand their return—and got them."[33]

Finally, on Friday the thirteenth, after a month of seemingly inconclusive testimony, Judge Larrazolo prepared to instruct the jury. His instructions, although perhaps not directly affecting the jury's verdicts, certainly were regarded with amazement by New Mexico legal practitioners, and with delight by Tijerina and his sympathizers in the state and around the country. The instructions seemed to give particular sanction to the concept of "citizen's arrest."

Those instructions read:

> The Court instructs the Jury that citizens of New Mexico have the right to make a citizen's arrest under the following circumstances:
>
> (1) If the arresting person reasonably believes that the person arrested, or attempted to be arrested, was the person who committed, either as a principal or as an aider and abettor, a felony; or

[33]*National Guardian,* 14 December 1968.

(2) If persons who are private citizens reasonably believe that a felony has been committed, and that the person who is arrested or attempted to be arrested was the person committing, or aiding and abetting, said felony.

The Court instructs the Jury that a citizen's arrest can be made even though distant in time and place from the acts constituting or reasonably appearing to constitute the commission of the felony. The Court further instructs the Jury that a citizen's arrest may be made whether or not law enforcement officers are present, and, further, may be made in spite of the presence of said law enforcement officers.

The Court instructs the Jury that anyone, including a State Police Officer, who intentionally interferes with a lawful attempt to make a citizen's arrest does so at his own peril, since the arresting citizens are entitled under the law to use whatever force is reasonably necessary to defend themselves in the process of making said citizen's arrest.[34]

These words were startling enough to the courtroom observers, but in a few hours they were overshadowed by the surprise verdict: "not guilty" on all three counts.

Tijerina, his young wife Patsy, and the devoted Hispano followers who had sat through the trial were elated. The vigorous land grant leader immediately began bubbling over with future plans. Among other things, he would write a book, a "New Science" on how the "browns" (Hispanos) could bridge the widening gap between whites and blacks in America. Shortly, he announced plans to "organize" Albuquerque's garbage collectors and to sue the Albuquerque Board of Education for discrimination against "Indo-Hispano" students.

When Tijerina first returned to Tierra Amarilla after the trial, he told his followers: "When the jury brought in its verdict that Tijerina was innocent, the justice of God and of you who struggle fell on the heads of the powerful . . . the sky fell on their heads!" Noting national publicity of the verdict, he added: "Many of you, who are not lawyers, may not realize the effect of this victory on the judges, officials, everyone." He later told the audience, "We don't believe in violence, but we believe in Jesus Christ. The revolution of Tierra Amarilla was like Christ entering the temple and cleaning out the Pharisees."[35]

Later, in a talk with one of the authors at a Santa Fe cafe, Tijerina talked further about his court victory:

"First, it was a great example for a terrified people who had been in captivity for more than 470 years." The state, he said, "threw all the organized power that the taxpayers have built up to crack the people of the mountains. They got me into court. I took it on myself to beat them in their own game. Now everyone knows that the cops are subject to citizens' arrest, just like criminals. The establishment is cracked already—it's like the Liberty Bell. They

[34]Quoted in full, The New Mexico Review and Legislative Journal, 30 January 1969, p. 3.
[35]Ibid., p. 4.

thought I was going to break down under court entanglements, court threats, court action. But I didn't. I go for court action now. I love it!"[36]

He vowed to carry on with his land grant activities, claiming his (almost) single-handed victory in the courts had increased his popularity among northern Hispanos. He gleefully told the *New York Times*: "My philosophy is that of the cricket against the lion. The cricket is the king of the insects and the lion is the king of the beasts. The cricket had no chance against the lion, so he jumped into the lion's ear and tickled him to death. That's what we're going to do to the United States—we're going to tickle him to death."[37]

Tijerina's friends and associates were likewise jubilant. *El Grito del Norte* ("The Cry from the North"), an unofficial publication of the Alianza published in Espanola, noted the expressions of shock from officialdom. It quoted Jack Love as saying, "the verdict came as a complete shock. Never can I remember so completely misreading what the mood of a jury seemed to be." It also mentioned comments by Rio Arriba County Sheriff Benny Naranjo and others, then commented: "These men just couldn't tolerate the fact that Reies Lopez Tijerina, a man with few years of formal education behind him and many years of poverty, had defeated the power structure on its own grounds, by its own rules, and in its own language—which is his second language."[38]

Underground publications elsewhere also applauded the acquittal. Typical was the *Berkeley Barb*:

> 'Amazing, amazing and beautiful,' is how San Francisco lawyer Harold McDermid described the freeing of Reies Tijerina from the manacles of New Mexican pigs. Tijerina, Mexican-American leader of the liberation struggle of the brown people from the repressive economic and educational system in New Mexico, was charged with kidnapping District Attorney Alfonso Sanchez. . . . Actually, Tijerina was making a citizen's arrest of Sanchez. . . . The beauty of the decision that freed Tijerina is that it upholds the right of a citizen to make an arrest of anyone, even the police, who deprives him of his constitutional rights.[39]

If there was jubilance among the militants, there was consternation among New Mexico officials and middle class citizens. Reporter Ed Meagher, who covered the trial for the *Los Angeles Times-Washington Post* service, wrote: "New Mexico was in a state of shock . . . following the acquittal . . . of Reies Lopez Tijerina."[40] The *Washington Post* account read: "The acquittal of Reies Lopez Tijerina . . . has stunned New Mexico's officialdom."[41]

The *New Mexican*, a Santa Fe daily, editorialized: "The recent trial . . . was a travesty on our New Mexico system of law enforcement. The lengthy and costly trial did little, if anything, to uphold law and order in New Mexico.

[36]Interview with Carrol W. Cagle in Santa Fe, New Mexico, 27 May 1969.
[37]*New York Times*, 19 December 1968.
[38]*El Grito del Norte*, 11 January 1969.
[39]*Berkeley Barb*, 27 December 1968.
[40]*San Francisco Sunday Examiner & Chronicle*, 22 December 1968.
[41]*Washington Post*, 16 December 1968.

And, perhaps worst of all, it will lend encouragement to men like Tijerina to stir racial unrest and hatred."[42]

UNOFFICIAL REBUTTAL

Alfonso Sanchez was a beaten man, and did not hide it. The previous August, he had been defeated in the Democratic primary election, thus he knew that the Tijerina case would be his last one as district attorney. Voters apparently were strongly dissatisfied with Sanchez's poor performance in a highway scandal case (he lost on a legal technicality), and with his intemperate but incompetent attack on the Alianza. Rather than lash out bitterly, Sanchez remained quiet, as if in a state of shock. About the only public comment he made was to tell the Associated Press a few days later that the state should have the right to appeal questions of law in criminal cases. Speaking of the defendants, Sanchez said: "Law forces us to give everything to them and they don't have to reciprocate."[43]

Sanchez, in a later interview with one of the authors after leaving office, went into further detail on the trial. "Everything is over-balanced in favor of the defendant," he said. He cited what he called "sympathy" for Tijerina on the part of jurors.

Then he detailed his contention that the Tierra Amarilla raid did not have to occur in the first place. He recalled that, before the raid, Tijerina already was wanted on another warrant, but had not been picked up. "I knew that as long as Tijerina was out, that someone was going to do something," Sanchez said. "I could just tell that man had a one-track mind." Sanchez explained that he had learned the morning of 5 June that Tijerina was at the home of Tobias Leyba in Canjilón. He called State Police Chief Joe Black and urged an arrest to be made.

Black replied, according to Sanchez, that he would have to have search warrants to go to Leyba's house. The warrants were ready by noon, but never were picked up, Sanchez said. "That's where Cargo came in, you know. They were wheeling and dealing," Sanchez declared. He refused to elaborate, but indicated that the governor—who had long disputed Sanchez's tactics concerning the Alianza—refused to enforce the law strictly, and instead intervened to try to "cool things off." Such tactics, Sanchez said, do not work with Tijerina.

"History proves I was right," said Sanchez. "Tierra Amarilla shouldn't have happened, really. This guy is crazy and I've said that all along." He said he told Governor Cargo the morning of 5 June: "Look, you're dealing with a crazy man. You don't know what you're dealing with."

Asked what he sees next for Tijerina, Sanchez replied: "A guy like that has got a one-track mind. He's built a monster and doesn't know how to handle it."[44]

[42]*Santa Fe New Mexican,* 16 December 1968.
[43]*Albuquerque Journal,* 18 December 1968.
[44]Interview with Carrol W. Cagle in Santa Fe, 15 June 1969.

Although Tijerina took the "citizen's arrest" instructions of Larrazolo to heart (in June 1969 he tried unsuccessfully to arrest Cargo, Los Alamos atomic scientists, and Chief Justice Warren Burger), there is evidence that the jurors themselves paid little heed to the instructions as such. Instead, the majority seemed to feel that the state failed to prove beyond doubt that Tijerina was guilty of the specific charges involved. Only one juror indicated that the state absolutely proved its case, but said it was impossible to try to convince his colleagues. These comments were published 22 December 1968, in the *Albuquerque Journal*.

Jury foreman Charles Burand was quoted as saying: "I think the general consensus of the jury . . . was that there was not enough evidence and so much of the evidence was in conflict, that we thought we could not convict him beyond a reasonable doubt."

Another juror, Mrs. Willard Tennison, said, "We read the instructions over and over. We discussed each one and finally all decided there was not enough evidence to convict." She added that no one seemed to arrive at his or her decision on the basis of "fear." "A lot of people think that we did it because we were afraid," she said, "but none of us felt that way at all." Three jury members, said the *Journal*, believed Tijerina was completely innocent. But most, the newspaper said, shared the feeling of Mrs. Andrew Johnson: "We thought he was behind it, but there was nothing we could do about it. We tried awfully hard but couldn't come up with a thing as far as the charges on which he was tried were concerned. That's what made us so sick."

Many agreed that Tijerina was a "pretty good" attorney for himself. Mary Hochstatter put it this way: "The man has a fantastic mind, and he did an unbelievable job for not being an attorney."[45]

A BOOST FOR THE ALIANZA

The acquittal seemed, at first, to provide a much-needed boost for the Alianza and for Tijerina personally. The land grant issue had begun to drag, and Tijerina spent much of his time involved in numerous state and federal court proceedings stemming from several minor confrontations. But the surprising acquittal seemed to give the land grant leader new strength. Smiling broadly, pacing frantically, he tossed out ideas for new Alianza programs. In addition to announcing plans to organize garbage collectors and sue the board of education, he was sharply critical of the 1969 Legislature for forcing New Mexico out of Medicaid, the health care program for the poor.

Still, Tijerina seemed to lack enthusiasm for these more "acceptable" goals. He seemed to yearn to get back to the land grant issue, but months went by before the Alianza returned to the north in numbers.

Then, on 5 June 1969—the second anniversary of the raid—some one hundred Alianzans began a camp-out near Coyote in Rio Arriba County. Signs appeared on boulders near roadways and on makeshift signboards proclaiming "San Joaquin: A Free City-State." Armed members of the Brown Berets, a militant band of youthful Hispanos, guarded the entrance to the secluded campground. Tijerina and a few others sported big, colorful, Zapata-style *sombreros*. Shotguns and pearl-handled revolvers were in evidence.

One of the authors camped with the Alianzans, and heard Tijerina explain his summer goals: a cattle drive across Forest Service land to dramatize Alianza land claims, construction of a "municipal building" for the San Joaquin Free City-State, organization of a private "security force" to enforce Alianza laws within the area. He warned that interlopers could be treated "severely." "There's no way," he said, "the government or the state can interfere with our police. Any state policeman interfering or questioning our police will be in violation of the law. He will be considered a threat. . . . These guys will be subject to immediate arrest. We're serious. We will act immediately and severely. We're not going to start any trouble, but we're not going to stand for any foolishness either." Underscoring his claims to the land, he declared: "If you have private land, you have the absolute right to protect it."[46]

Still, there seemed to be an irresolute, desultory atmosphere about the gathering. Tijerina and those close to him kept intimating that "something" would happen, without specifying what. The much-mentioned cattle drive never became reality.

Finally, on Saturday afternoon, 7 June, there seemed to be a rapid change of mood. Apparently tiring of doing nothing, and realizing that the news play of his camp-out was dropping off, Tijerina announced abruptly that the Alianza would make "arrests" of Governor Cargo and an unspecified number of atomic scientists at nearby Los Alamos. Tijerina was angered by Cargo's criticism of a Presbyterian national council plan to give sizeable acreage in northern New Mexico to "recognized" Hispano organizations (not the Alianza). Tijerina's logic was unclear; he seemed merely to be searching for an anti-Cargo issue. The scientists would be arrested, Tijerina explained, for their part in devising "instruments of destruction."

Thus began a tumultuous, confusing sequence of events. The two reporters on the scene telephoned the story to their Albuquerque offices; Tijerina's announcement was being broadcast and published within an hour. State Police whisked Cargo—who was not even at the state capital—away by airplane to an undisclosed place. Los Alamos authorities prepared for trouble. As the twenty-five-car Alianza caravan pulled out of the campground, the situation began to develop aspects of a slapstick comedy. First, Tijerina's car radio picked up the news that Cargo, their first target, had been spirited away. So the caravan pulled over while discussions took place as to what to do next. It was decided to go instead to Los Alamos to arrest the unnamed "scientists." When the caravan stopped temporarily because of car trouble, one of us asked Tijerina how he expected to find atomic scientists and to know who they were. "We'll just have to go door-to-door, I guess," he replied.

[46]Interview with Carrol W. Cagle near Coyote, 7 June 1969.

It sounded like a joke, but it might not have been. Upon arriving in the scientific research town, the curious-looking caravan wandered aimlessly for a
time and then ended up at the laboratory's museum. Tijerina was met by the
chairman of the county council, Del Sundberg, who explained that he would
like to help but there were no scientists around. It was, after all, a Saturday
afternoon, he explained.

Tijerina told Sundberg he had a "warrant" for the arrest of scientists, but
didn't know who should receive it. Sundberg told Tijerina the director of the
laboratory, Norris Bradbury, would be the logical person, but that he did not
know where to find him. With that, Tijerina and his ragtag caravan drove off,
searching for a telephone booth and a directory to ascertain Bradbury's address. Once this was accomplished, the Alianzans discovered they had no idea
where the address was located, so a helpful group of curious Los Alamos
teenagers agreed to lead the caravan. The situation did not improve once the
caravan and its entourage of hangers-on reached Bradbury's residence. Tijerina
strode to the door, knocked purposefully, and waited confidently while news
cameras whirred. No one answered. He knocked again. Still no one. He rang
the door bell. It was obvious that if anyone were home, the door was not
being answered. With that, Tijerina was reduced to placing the "warrant" in
Bradbury's mail box and leaving. The caravan dissolved. "Ludicrous," reporters
said. Neighbors shook their heads in wonderment.

Before the weekend had ended, Tijerina was arrested on a minor charge
when his wife, Patsy, set fire to a Forest Service sign. And he ended in federal
detention, at least temporarily, when bond for a previous offense was revoked.
There were signs that the movement was losing steam, and, worse, credibility.
Tijerina seemed to recognize this, but did not know how to cope with the
flagging effort. It would be a mistake, however, to count the fiery orator out as
a bona fide leader of the poor Hispanos of northern New Mexico. Those who
love him really love him. And he is a magnetic, engaging man with many
appealing qualities. The question now is whether he can translate his personal
strength into a viable, vital movement. Land is his dream, and the dream of his
followers. His slogan, starkly presented on posters, may someday become
reality. The posters say: *Tierra o Muerte*, "Land or Death."

SAMUEL KRISLOV

10

THE HOFFA CASE

the criminal trial as a process of interest group leadership selection

It is no doubt an exaggeration to suggest, as one wag has, that American liberals lean to the view that it is unconstitutional ever to convict anyone of a crime. Neither is it clear that all those who call for stronger measures against crime are ready to abandon the Constitution. The issues run deeper than superficial slogans.

The Hoffa case is an interesting one in which to examine some of these competing values. This was no run-of-the-mill police court action against an obscure or ill-advised defendant. Rather, it was a concerted, juggernaut massing of governmental legal power against the leader of one of the nation's most powerful unions, a man who was a past master of legal technicalities, a juggler of legal talent not necessarily inferior to that commanded by the government, and one who did not exhibit fastidiousness in his own use of the legal, fiscal, and physical power embodied in his leadership.

The government's efforts—it is not too much to say the efforts of John and Robert Kennedy and their close associates—were designed to free willy-nilly those in apparently happy thralldom to Hoffa. To execute this program extreme pressure was mounted, somewhat shady practices occasionally countenanced, and the resources of government utilized in prosecution and in legislation all aimed "to cut Hoffa to size."

In a sense this case differs from others in this volume in that crimes were proven with evidence of reasonably impressive calibre, of the type appellate courts normally sustain and leave to the jury. Nor, except with respect to certain investigatory techniques, is there any question of lack of due process. Hoffa not only exhausted his remedies, he also wore down his prosecutors and kept his lawyers busy indeed.

Rather it is on the less legalistic level that the Hoffa story becomes a political case. On the more prescriptive level of what government should or should not do, the question becomes how much—if we be permitted pietistic phrasing—the forces of light should be permitted to take on the shading of their opponents?

The issue becomes more complex still when we realize the responsibilities imposed upon government in regulation of labor unions—in some ways special charges of the National Labor Relations Board, and the federal government generally. What then is owed the general public, or the union member? And what are the limits imposed by our concept of limited government and individual privacy?

THE BEGINNINGS

The New Deal years had strengthened and dignified labor, but at the same time had socialized it. The Wagner Act gave leverage to the unions as a phalanx against management, but left the individual worker dependent for his rights upon an internal democracy which was characteristic of only a handful of unions. (And that is a euphemistic estimate—one national union held no elections for three decades!) All too often not only democracy but even honesty has been lacking. Racketeering has always been a by-product of American unionism; Hoxie, writing in 1917, included in a typology of unions, "guerrilla unionism" and "predatory unionism." But now governmental power was involved to aid the growth of labor, maximizing the opportunities for a "new class" of privileged union leaders.

This corruption came under attack in the post-World War II period. The Taft-Hartley Act of 1947, among other things, required certain fiscal reports from unions and forbade some internal practices, for example, the use of dues for political contributions. Yet little change actually ensued, although a climate in which labor union evils could be discussed was created. Of course, the discussion was principally carried on by enemies of the labor movement generally, a fact which made reforms more difficult and the discussion protracted, acrimonious, and not always particularly informative.

The issue of crime and the unions was prominently raised first in connection with the Longshoreman's Union. Besides the movie *On the Waterfront,* governmental investigations resulted in closer regulation and some reform. As early as 1953 a House investigation led by Congressman Clare Hoffman, a right-wing Republican from Michigan, suggested some corruption in the Teamsters. The accusations included charges with which others were later to prove Hoffa's downfall. Perhaps due to the source, these accusations attracted little attention.

In 1957 Robert Kennedy was a relatively unpublicized staff investigator for the Senate Committee on Governmental Operations, originally a seemingly unimportant committee which had for a brief period been made most salient by the spectacularly expansive and irresponsible conduct of its former chairman, Joseph McCarthy. McCarthy's censure by the Senate largely ended his flamboyant activities, and the committee drifted without much purpose or direction for a time. The shift of control of the Senate—and the committee— from the Republicans to the Democrats accentuated Robert Kennedy's desire to find some major role for the committee.

Kennedy was pressed into dealing with labor racketeering from two sources. Clark Mollenhoff, of Cowles Publications, had already covered enough hearings and gathered enough information to conclude that evil in the Teamsters was a reality. His almost monomaniacal interest was later to yield him a Pulitzer Prize. One of his major accomplishments in this area was convincing Kennedy to undertake an investigation of the Teamsters.

The role of another man in prompting closer scrutiny of the Teamsters is more difficult to assess. Kennedy and Edward Bennett Williams, the gifted attorney, became friends in 1959. They even talked of the possibility of becoming partners. Williams's actual partner, Eddie Chayfetz, had worked for, then split with David Beck, who then led the Teamsters. Chayfetz and Williams both suggested Teamster investigations, especially of individuals whose misdeeds would reflect upon Beck, or whose removal would further impair Beck's weakening grasp on the union presidency. Hoffa, by that time, probably had effective control of the union. But the suspicion lingers that Williams and Chayfetz were already close to Hoffa, who was probably more than willing to let outsiders administer Beck's final ouster.[1]

The decision to investigate the Teamsters was hardly precipitous. In the first place, it was somewhat imperialistic for a committee on governmental conduct to look into labor racketeering at all. Such matters rather obviously were in the domain of the Labor Committee, and senators are especially jealous of their prerogatives. The investigators gave their project semi-plausible justification by noting that presumably false reports by the unions were being filed with various governmental agencies, and no action was forthcoming, therefore government operations were at fault.[2] (Ultimately, a compromise was reached for a joint select committee to investigate the matter, with members from both the Senate Governmental Operations and Labor Committees. This meant that John Kennedy was also involved in the investigation. The Massachusetts senator chose to serve, though Henry Jackson and Stuart Symington declined.)

By this time, too, the Kennedy brothers had decided to pursue the presidency. They moved carefully, hoping to avoid actions that could lead to charges that they were anti-labor. Failure to prove their accusations against the Teamsters could irreparably damage their political ambitions.

[1]For Kennedy's relationship to Mollenhoff and Williams, see Robert F. Kennedy, *The Enemy Within* (New York: Harper, 1960) pp. 4–5; on Chayfetz, see John Bartlow Martin, *Jimmy Hoffa's Hot* (New York: Fawcett, 1959), pp. 9, 17.

[2]Kennedy, *Enemy Within*, pp. 23–24.

In the end, Clark Mollenhoff tells us, the balance of political calculations helped point the Kennedys to activism.[3] Having just been trounced in a political convention by Senator Estes Kefauver, whose national reputation had been built mainly by such hearings, they were decidedly impressed by the long-term political advantage of crime investigations.

Expecting only mild successes at local levels of the union, the investigators at first rather naïvely sought cooperation from above. They assumed prominent men were honest—or at least that they would be willing to clean house in order to preserve their organizations' reputations and their own images. Instead, the ferocity of the opposition by national leaders of the Teamsters to *any* investigation—even to the point of sending out instructions to subordinates not to cooperate—both convinced the investigators something was wrong and forced them to redouble their efforts. These attempts rather quickly and overwhelmingly pointed to a succession of delicts on the part of Dave Beck. These included the use of union funds to finance speculations; income tax evasion; and financial manipulations at the expense of his best friend's widow. The embarrassing pettiness of some of his activities left Beck as bereft of dignity as of power.

The visible deflation of Beck called further attention to the ever rising estate of Hoffa, already a kingmaker. For years Beck had bided his time waiting for the retirement of Dan Tobin, who had been president since 1907, even though Beck's control of the Western Regional Conference of Teamsters meant he was de facto the single dominant force in the union.

But Hoffa had learned the concepts of regional control and economic leverage directly from its originator, Farrell Dobbs; by the time Beck took over the presidency in 1952, Hoffa rivaled and probably even surpassed him in power. Hoffa always acknowledged his intellectual indebtedness to Dobbs, though that obligation did not hamper his practical activities. Dobbs, operating from the Trotskyite locals in Minneapolis, had shown such originality of thought and tactical effectiveness that Tobin had offered him a Teamster vice-presidency. But Dobbs had chosen to pursue Marxian orthodoxy, devoting himself to the Trotskyite Socialist Workers Party, rather than to union activity. On the eve of World War II, almost simultaneously with a federal decision to prosecute Dobbs, the Dunne brothers, and others under the Smith Act, Tobin decided that having such radicals in the union was too great an embarrassment. Among those sent by the Teamsters to Minneapolis to handle the situation was Hoffa. This proved a major step up the ladder.

Slowly but inexorably—the most thorough students of Hoffa, Ralph and Estelle James, believe rather more slowly than his official biographies acknowledge—Hoffa, who never was himself a truck driver, rose toward the top.[4] By the time Tobin was persuaded to retire, Hoffa was in a position of complete

<hr />

[3]Clark Mollenhoff, *Tentacles of Power* (Cleveland: World, 1965), pp. 3–4.
[4]Ralph C. and Estelle P. James, *Hoffa and the Teamsters* (Princeton: Van Nostrand, 1965), pp. 70–72, 75. Hoffa likes hagiography. See, for example, Jim Clay, *Hoffa: Ten Angels Swearing* (Beaverdam, Virginia: Beaverdam Books, 1965), an embarrassing work: "You might say he arrived under his own power, struggling and squalling!" p. 14.

power in the Midwest, strong enough to consider contesting heir-apparent Beck. Deciding against such a foray, Hoffa made his vital role as visible as possible. Reaching out for allies in the South, East, and West, Hoffa established the fact that he was much more than one of the Teamsters' junior vice-presidents—he had become an inexorable force in the union. By 1957 he was very nearly at the peak of his power, and was actually being given additional leverage by the McClellan hearings which were undermining Beck and his allies.

As the committee was proceeding against Beck, Robert Kennedy was called by staff member John Cye Chesty, who reported he had been asked to spy on the committee by Hoffa. Acting quickly, Kennedy called in FBI agents, who arrested Hoffa and found him in possession of committee documents he had exchanged for $18,000.

This led to the first trial of Hoffa—for attempting to corrupt a congressional staff member. The availability of good, reliable witnesses, and the fact that all the elements of the case seemed so straightforward—the FBI had observed the entire transaction at the Dupont Plaza Hotel—led to overconfidence. Robert Kennedy exclaimed in an off-the-record remark, "If Hoffa gets out of this one, I'll jump off the Capitol." (At the end of the trial, Hoffa's attorney, the ubiquitous Edward Bennett Williams, gallantly offered Kennedy a parachute.)

The audacity of the defense stunned the government. Assuming Hoffa would never dare take the stand, the prosecutor's cross-examination was weak. He failed to rebut or shake Hoffa's claim that he had no reason to fear committee revelations, and so would not have been interested in such espionage. Hoffa's story was simple: he had hired an attorney; he had not known it was committee material he was reading. The prosecutor found the story incredible, but the jury obviously did not. Hoffa's odd choice of an hotel lobby locale to pass a retainer also did not seem to upset them.

It was in this trial, in front of a predominantly Negro jury, that the famous Joe Louis incident occurred. The tactics of the defense were generally slanted to take advantage of the race issue. Only white jurors were challenged. A Negro woman attorney—later briefly married to Louis—was photographed with Williams. The picture appeared in the Negro press as well as in a full-page advertisement praising the defense as pro-Negro and suggesting prejudice on the part of Chesty and the prosecution. Williams has insisted that all this occurred without his knowledge. But he personally inserted into the trial record insinuations of prejudice on Chesty's part. And the presence of Louis and a hearty greeting for Hoffa were clearly planned, though Williams claims Louis was originally scheduled as a character witness. In any event, Kennedy and others in the prosecution regarded the failure of the government to cross-examine vigorously as more crucial than the racial tactics. (Popular mythology, however, runs the other way.)[5]

A triumphant Hoffa went on to further triumphs. At their annual convention

---

[5]See Williams, *One Man's Freedom* (New York: Atheneum, 1962) pp. 220–24; J. L. McClellan, *Crime Without Punishment* (New York: Duell, Sloan and Pearce, 1962), pp. 23–24; Kennedy, *Enemy Within*, pp. 57–60.

in October of 1957, the Teamsters elected him international president by a three-to-one margin, despite Secretary of Labor Mitchell's public appeal to the delegates not to choose Hoffa, and his warning that such a choice would lead to public pressure for anti-union legislation.[6] But the elevation to the presidency was not an unmitigated triumph. His election resulted in expulsion of the Teamsters from the AFL-CIO. (Ironically, this saved the Teamsters a million dollars in dues—approximately the annual amount used later for litigation.)[7] And a challenge to the legality of the election resulted in a court-ordered monitor system by which Hoffa shared power with a three-man body appointed by the court. This compromise also left Hoffa only with the title "provisional president." The first round was Hoffa's.

The second confrontation between Kennedy and Hoffa came directly at the committee hearings. Here the staff bore down hard on both the broad general configuration of power within the union and Hoffa's own internal union activities.

Hoffa, who had sanctioned Teamster use of the Fifth Amendment, did not personally invoke it; Robert Kennedy suggested that in 1958 Hoffa had decided to utilize the privilege, but was fearful the court-appointed monitors might use this to have him removed from the presidency. Accordingly, Hoffa relied on two major techniques: First, the averment of failure to recall, rather than a denial, which is more susceptible to perjury charges. The most famous example is his almost Freudian (or Casey Stengelian) response, "I can say here to the chair that I cannot recall in answer to your question other than to say I just don't recall my recollection." Second, a blanket statement that a domain of questions was unanswerable by him and could be responded to properly only by some subordinate, who in turn took the Fifth Amendment. The perjury charge Hoffa was risking, thereby, could be supported only by proving that he did in fact recall the matter at issue. Since human memory is notoriously fallible, prosecutors and juries would not relish arguments about burdens of proof and assumptions of innocence. Of course, the public could make a different practical judgment, but Hoffa was confident he could weather such a reaction. In any event he had to chance it.

At best, Hoffa showed indifference to the moral failings of underlings. Apparently it was sufficient for him to question the accused about alleged misbehavior (much of it misuse of union power or abuse of members), and if the official denied the matter, Hoffa announced he could do no more and ended the inquiry. When convictions resulted, he found regular due process of law was punishment enough—though labor racketeering was often the crime involved. In 1959—perhaps the high point of his cynicism—he announced a five-year rule, in conformity with the Landrum-Griffin Act. No one could hold Teamster office if convicted of a felony within the past five years. This, he announced simultaneously, would affect only five officials, all but one of whom could resume office promptly in 1960. Since these draconian measures were secured only after intensive pressure and nationwide publicity, there was

[6]New York Times, 30 September 1957, p. 1:7.
[7]New York Times, 8 June 1958, p. 45:1.

some feeling that he was not really strongly resisting corruption in his union.[8]

But the significant development was the lack of any pronounced Teamster revulsion to the sometimes murky McClellan revelations. Hoffa finished the ordeal, in the words of two sympathizers, "bruised but not beaten." Those days were touch-and-go in many ways. The battles with the court-appointed monitors were regular and intense; in seventeen instances in a few short years, court proceedings ensued—resulting in Hoffa victories in fifteen cases. A few locals broke away from the union and some leadership fights developed.

Nor was the Department of Justice completely inactive. Two different issues resulted in criminal charges. Back in 1953 Hoffa had apparently concluded some of the committee revelations came from inside his staff. A professional "electronics expert," Bernard Spindel, was engaged to install eavesdropping and wiretapping devices in the Teamster headquarters during the night, apparently to avoid alerting the staff. The wiretaps violated federal law; Hoffa admitted ordering the equipment but not the wiretapping component. The listening devices were to investigate alleged corruption, he blandly explained. Perjury charges were brought unsuccessfully against him and abandoned. On the wiretap violation charge a jury in 1957 hung 11-1 in favor of conviction, and a 1958 retrial resulted in acquittal. Finally, charges in the Sun Valley Case, which returned to plague Hoffa, resulted in an indictment. This was set aside in 1961, not on the merits but on the grounds that the Florida grand jury had improperly excluded Negroes.

In the interim, the monitor system had failed to change power relationships within the union. The courts could not indefinitely justify so costly and artificial an intervention into the operations of a voluntary organization. By the close of 1960 Hoffa secured the dissolution of the monitor system and was triumphantly reelected president; no hyphenated "provisional" label got in his way. He had emerged from a series of prosecutions and other litigations with his reputation for invulnerability intact.

But he had proven unable to affect a broader, more vital development. Hoffa committed the resources of the Teamsters to anti-Kennedy political activity, but the irresistible Kennedy charm resulted in an upset presidential victory. Even Teamster members appear to have been little swayed by Hoffa's position. In the crucial primary in West Virginia, the Teamsters did work for Humphrey. The Kennedys countered by publicizing Hoffa's role in "the gang-up against Senator Kennedy in West Virginia."[9] In the November election, Hoffa called for Kennedy's defeat, but refrained from endorsing Nixon. Teamsters as individuals—even some locals—generally supported the Democratic candidate. By 1960 Hoffa had fought off all efforts to remove him; but his very opposition to Kennedy's candidacy had been used to advantage by the new president. The New York Times wrote of Hoffa being at the peak of his powers; but the Kennedys were also at their zenith.

[8]McClellan, *Crime Without Punishment*, pp. 48–49; *New York Times*, 29 September 1959, p. 33:1.
[9]Harry W. Ernst, *The Primary that Made a President: West Virginia, 1960* (New York: McGraw-Hill, 1962), p. 27.

DECISION TO PROSECUTE

The newly chosen attorney general—for obvious reasons—took an intensively personal interest in criminal investigations into labor. The Department of Justice became an aggressively anti-Hoffa operation. The assistant attorney general in charge of the criminal division had served as an attorney for the Teamsters' monitors. A special office in the Justice Department under Walter Sheridan, a McClellan Committee investigator, had special access to Attorney General Kennedy and a specialized focus. As Clark Mollenhoff describes it: "Walter Sheridan made Hoffa a 24-hour-a-day project. He knew where Hoffa was nearly every hour of the day, or he could find out within a matter of minutes. Through informants in the Teamsters Union, Sheridan knew most of Hoffa's schedule in advance."[10]

This relentlessness produced more than one hundred convictions of Teamster officials—and eventually two convictions of Hoffa himself. The efforts of the department reflected, in part, a new strategy in the anti-Hoffa campaign. Originally the McClellan Committee expected that revelations about Hoffa would lead to an internal revolt in the union. Judge F. Dickinson Letts of the Federal District Court in Washington had assumed that the absence of democracy in selection of convention delegates represented something novel and temporary in the union and that Hoffa did not have a base of support. The monitors had been appointed to foster and prove this lack of popularity.

These efforts had all failed, and rather conspicuously so. Some individuals and locals withdrew from the union, but for the vast bulk of the membership, Hoffa's successful contract negotiations seemed to far outweigh the effect of accusations on corruption. The dominant factor was Hoffa's reputation as a doer—a man with unrivaled understanding of the industry, relentless in his quest to foster gains for those loyal to him.

The new governmental strategy was apparently designed to weaken Hoffa's hold by demonstrating his inability to protect those around him. These measures—essentially identical to guerrilla warfare strategy—involved pressing Hoffa in less direct ways. Of these, the most significant was the ruling that Teamster payment of fees to defend Hoffa in his nonunion, business capacity was subject to income taxation. This, together with pressure suggesting the executive board members might become individually liable for return of such funds, finally ended Teamster treasury subvention of all Hoffa litigation, and therefore raised the costs for him of continued intransigence.

Pressure, too, helped develop cleavages among the leadership of the union. Hoffa's notorious temper did not improve and his suspicious nature led to a growing constriction of his circle of confidantes. Disagreement with Edward Bennett Williams, who had become the Teamsters' general counsel, reached the point where Hoffa tried to fire him; Williams showed some political muscle of his own, and was ready to take the case to the executive board. Recognizing that at best a public fight could result in a Pyrrhic victory, Hoffa backed

[10]Mollenhoff, *Tentacles of Power*, p. 341.

down. A public relations aide—Sam Baron—claimed Hoffa physically beat him after a disagreement. Hoffa's growing disenchantment with Harold Gibbons and his brain trust cut him off from his most effective aides. (Gibbons at one point muttered that Hoffa's unwillingness to delegate him any authority made him the most overpaid clerk in history.) Ultimately all were to leave the Washington office over a tongue-lashing Hoffa administered to Gibbons for closing Teamster headquarters on the occasion of the assassination of President Kennedy. (It was shortly after that incredible incident that labor analyst A. H. Raskin suggested the central structure of the Teamsters had now been so weakened that the issue of Hoffa's control from prison was largely an issue of semantics.)[11]

In this atmosphere of a world closing in on him, Hoffa was forced to defend himself. Characteristically, he seems to have overreacted, exhibiting what Raskin called his Dostoevskian Character,[12] doomed by a desire to control events, yet causing his own downfall.

THE COURTROOM TANGLE

At some point, if the effort to remove Hoffa was to succeed, the government had to move directly against him. Successful convictions of minor officials had not led to any weakening of his power, nor had the noncriminal litigation and negotiation. Countenancing racketeers was not a crime promising easy convictions and had already failed to arouse the union membership. But Hoffa was vulnerable on several of his transactions on his own behalf, made more profitable by union power and control over funds. A number of those exposed during the hearing were clearly morally objectionable, but it was not clear whether a criminal case could be made to stick. With William Rogers as attorney general, the decision of the Department of Justice had been to prosecute in only a few instances. Under Robert Kennedy, more convictions were sought.

These were not fanciful cases, but rather, instances involving strong although not absolute evidence. They also depended on complicated questions of law and problems of motives and beliefs, as distinguished from questions of business judgment. Since everyone, including Kennedy, admitted that Hoffa showed consistently poor judgment as a businessman,[13] it was difficult to know whether he was committing fraud or reflecting misguided optimism. With regard to a number of Hoffa's dealings, evidence and witnesses were often hard to come by.

The record of Hoffa and the other trustees in administering the union pension fund was so bad that fraud was actually a generous verdict on their conduct; any other conclusion would reflect the business acumen of an imbecile.

---

[11]Raskin, "Is Hoffa Finished?" *Reporter*, 26 March 1966, p. 24.
[12]Ibid., p. 23.
[13]See Kennedy, *Enemy Within*, p. 113.

Loans were almost unfailingly made to poor risks—for example, to Zeckendorf's ill-fated Webb and Knapp venture into nationwide downtown-redevelopment, to the John Thomas department store in Minneapolis, and to some twenty other bankrupts—yet invariably at low rates of interest. Sometimes the Teamsters lent at rates one-third below those the borrower was paying elsewhere.

The legal battles between the Teamsters and the government were no-holds-barred efforts. No technicality was left unurged, no legal argument was undeveloped; witnesses impeached each other, and accusations against prosecutors, defense attorneys, and judges were the order of the day. Hoffa was a voracious consumer of attorneys, hiring and firing large numbers, directing, cajoling, encouraging, and baiting them. Observers talked of the "Teamsters Bar Association." His skill at utilizing this talent and his own burgeoning legal ability gained him an awesome reputation. Even as he approached the end of his string of appeals in 1966 it was reported that lawyers' gossip was confident he would still win: "In legal circles, the question is not whether Hoffa will win, but how he will win."[14]

The government officials from the beginning had an additional—and not so complimentary—explanation of Hoffa's success. They saw Chesty as merely one among many whom Hoffa's men paid to inform. His early association with electronics expert Spindel suggested that the Teamster boss might also be willing to eavesdrop on those not in his employ. As early as the wiretap case, government attorneys noted that regular attempts to contact jurors by nebulous personages were a constant feature of Hoffa's trials. They suspected tampering and eventually found witnesses—of varying repute—to bear out this possibility.

From his vantage point Hoffa saw the government as an encircling enemy. Numerous cases were filed, while others were still pending. The locale for cases varied virtually all over the country. He was forced to maintain his political power in the union while all this was going on, and legal attacks were also mounted against his chief allies. He was convinced the government was tapping his own phones, intruding upon all his conversations with attorneys in his defense, corrupting jurors through blandishments—including girls—at the trials, and harassing him with income tax and other claims while simultaneously pursuing deadly serious criminal charges.

It was in this embittered and embattled atmosphere that the Hoffa trials proceeded. There was none of the semi-camaraderie of the *Perry Mason* show. Nor was there the gentlemanly surrender of viewpoints or total confession by principals. On the contrary, each case led to another, more complex one. Confessions of perjury were common. The more cases that came up—the more claims and counterclaims, admissions and retractions that were presented—the murkier matters became. Not one trial but a series of proceedings constitutes "the Hoffa Case."

[14]Robert Cipes, "How They Got Jimmy Hoffa—Or Did They?" *Atlantic*, November 1966, pp. 118–22.

The Test Fleet Case

The Test Fleet Company leased trucks to commercial carriers for whom the truckers acted as bargaining agents. The company was established with Mrs. Hoffa and Mrs. O. B. Brennan (wife of Hoffa's longtime, self-effacing, and loyal associate) as owners of record—and in their maiden names. With such well-established contacts it is perhaps not surprising that the company was to record impressive profits—a $62,000 return in four years on an investment of $4,000. In all, alleged payoffs amounted to considerably more than a million dollars. The president of Commercial Carriers, Van Beckum, was later to testify that in their own minds the owners were convinced that this was a necessary compensation to continue to have cordial relations with the Teamsters—in crude terms, a payoff.[15] But Hoffa had legal advice to the effect that such business relations did not violate Taft-Hartley, advice which was reasonable when given, though rendered incorrect when the Supreme Court subsequently interpreted the act to prohibit all financial dealings between employers and union representatives.[16]

The Commercial Carriers Company had no apparent reason to lease trucks from another company, but it wanted good relations with the Teamsters and its president. Hoffa's use of his wife's name in this transaction undoubtedly betokened consciousness of potential conflict of interest and embarrassment, but its illegality was not as clear. The employers were willing, even eager, to indict the union leaders, though the law was equally clear on the illegality of employer action. The matter was sufficiently complex to get a jury split of 7-5 favoring exoneration. (The prosecutors were subsequently indicted, but the case was dismissed after the failure to secure Hoffa's conviction.)

However, the trial was at least as dramatic off camera as on. Close surveillance by the FBI of the Hoffa camp was the order of the day when Spindel, the electronics specialist, arrived in Nashville during the middle of the trial. Hoffa claimed proof that Walter Sheridan, the head of Kennedy's Teamster squad, was wiretapping and denying him and his attorney privacy. The Department of Justice said the close surveillance was largely limited to the comings and goings of Spindel, to prevent any chicanery.

And during the proceedings a familiar scene in Hoffa trials was reenacted. Government officials again drew the judge's attention to out-of-court action affecting a juror. But this time the officials were more confident about the source and nature of the disclosure. A jury tampering charge was to be brought against Hoffa and key associates.

The Jury Tampering Trial

Inasmuch as Hoffa's attorney, Z. T. Osborn, Jr., admitted his dealings with a juror, R. R. Vick, the major issue of the tampering case—moved from Nashville

---

[15]*New York Times,* 22 November 1962, p. 3:1.
[16]Ibid., 5 December 1962, p. 48:1.

to Chattanooga—was the governmental attempt to link Osborn (and others accused of similar efforts with other jurors) to Hoffa himself. Key to this line of evidence was Edward Partin, the government's star witness. Partin, a Teamster with a more than blemished record, had been drawn into Hoffa's entourage. Government blandishments—apparently both carrots and sticks were used—secured his cooperation. Partin divulged strategy on such matters as the alleged conspiracy to influence jurors—information he admitted having gathered by donning a miniature microphone. To the argument that Partin's presence was an intrusion upon privacy of counsel, the government replied there had never been a privilege in conspiracy to commit illegal acts. Even Hoffa's attorneys of record could not claim that extralegal right; they could, of course, keep normal legal consultations—even admissions of guilt—confidential. (As the Supreme Court's subsequent decision in the Osborn Case suggests, a conviction in the Test Fleet Case would probably have been reversed on the basis of Partin's activities. But in connection with jury tampering, the lawyers would be considered accomplices, not legal counsel.) Furthermore, the key Partin testimony related to matters not discussed with the lawyers. Since Partin had been admitted freely into the Hoffa circles there was, the Supreme Court decided, nothing involuntary or coerced in any sense.

Hoffa's attorneys attacked Partin's integrity and established both past criminality and perjury on his part. The irony of the situation was that Partin was emphatically the type of person the Department of Justice had condemned Hoffa for dealing with in the past. Now the department was using him, while Teamster forces were expressing dismay that anyone could deal with—and trust—so reprehensible a fellow. Furthermore, cross-examination developed the fact that although Partin denied being paid by the government, his wife was receiving government sums—though not in her maiden name.

Since the case followed closely upon the *Miranda* decision, the Hoffa attorneys also pressed the argument that no paid informants could be used by the police—or that such informants be obliged to inform the suspect, much as *Miranda* requires the police to act upon arrest. The Supreme Court eventually rejected both arguments, holding it no dereliction for police to continue to use informants, "countenanced . . . from time immemorial." As to the argument that once Hoffa was suspected, he had a right to be arrested and informed, the Court observed:

> Nothing in Massiah, in Escobedo, or in any other case that has come to our attention, even remotely suggests this novel and paradoxical constitutional doctrine, and we decline to adopt it now. There is no constitutional right to be arrested. The police are not required to guess at their peril the precise moment at which they have probable cause to arrest a suspect, risking a violation of the Fourth Amendment if they wait too long.[17]

The result of the trial was conviction for Hoffa, a sentence of eight years, a $10,000 fine, and a tongue-lashing from Judge Wilson on the consequences of

---

[17]*Hoffa v. United States*, 385 U.S. 293 (1966), 310.

jury tampering for the whole system of justice. Hoffa, he said, had tampered with the "soul of the nation." (Ironically, the maximum sentence for conviction in the Test Fleet Case would have been five years.)

Both Osborn and another attorney, Lawrence Medlin, were separately convicted of the same charge. Thus, three juries unanimously found the evidence (obviously somewhat different in each instance) convincing. The Osborn decision was also reviewed and sustained by the Supreme Court. When Hoffa's appeals in this case failed, he surrendered himself to the authorities. His instant reaction was to console his son and daughter. "He was," Murray Kempton wrote, "as he had always been, the best of family men and the worst of citizens."[18] Hoffa thus began a sentence from which he could become eligible for parole in 1969.

Once it became obvious he would be in no position to handle day-to-day affairs of the union, signs of opposition were discerned, with the possible candidacies of Einar Mohn and Harold Gibbons expected. During the months before going off to prison, Hoffa disarmed these opponents by introducing a rule that an individual could run for only one office at a convention. Mohn and Gibbons were thus presented with a situation where they could run for the top office only at the risk of their vice-presidencies and position on the executive committee. Hoffa also announced his own candidacy for reelection, and his support of vice-president Frank Fitzsimmons as interim president. Fitzsimmons was elected general vice-president, and assumed the functions of president when Hoffa went to jail. Without the strong regional base of either Mohn or Gibbons, he was less likely to emerge as a permanent Hoffa rival. While Fitzsimmons has been in office, the further deterioration of central power has been in evidence. The increased strength of the regional vice-presidents has not, however, resulted in any clear emergence of opposition to Hoffa control.

The Chicago Mail Fraud Case

Hoffa had entered into an agreement with the promoter and developer of Sun Valley in Florida. He helped Henry Lower promote the project with union members and placed $500,000 from a union local, interest free, in an Orlando bank to induce it to make a loan to Lower. As was later revealed, Hoffa had an option to buy forty-five percent of the enterprise at the original price; in effect, this made him a partner for profitable purposes but virtually guaranteed him no loss. (In the Chicago trial Hoffa was to deny his signature on the agreement.) Lower misused the loan for other purposes, letting Sun Valley go bankrupt.

After the original indictment in the case was set aside in 1961 (over the exclusion of Negroes from the jury), a new indictment was sought. This was set aside at government request in 1963, as the related Chicago Mail Fraud

[18]Kempton, "The Long Chase Through the Courts," New Republic, 14 March 1964, p. 7.

Case was deemed stronger. (Since simple fraud is a matter for local law enforcement authorities, emphasizing Hoffa's use of the mails to perpetrate his schemes converted such actions to alleged federal offenses, upon which government prosecutors could base their charges.)

Six weeks after the conviction of Hoffa for jury tampering in Chattanooga, the Chicago trial involving many of the issues of the Sun Valley Case and its ramifications came to a head. Hoffa contended this was deliberate timing to prejudice his case.

Basically the government charges were that Hoffa, after the financial disaster of Sun Valley, had been approached by Benjamin Dranow with a method of recouping the loss. The pension fund would make overgenerous loans when selected persons—notably Dranow and the Burrises—presented a proposition to the trustees. These individuals would receive "finders fees" from the grateful borrowers, who saved many times over that sum. The government's theory was that part of the "finders fee" was redistributed, ending up, eventually, in Hoffa's hands. He was accused of fraud perpetrated upon the trustees.

In their analysis of the trial, Ralph and Estelle James concluded that the trustees were not guilty of fraud, since the overall policy was so devoid of reason, the trustees themselves were acquiescing to—if not conniving at—corruption or something approximating it. Had Hoffa used this tack, they suggest, there would have been no case:

> In the context we have developed, the fraud indictment seems deceptive, and
> the resultant conviction both inadequate and unwarranted, for one cannot
> be legally defrauded unless one accepts the misrepresentation and acts in direct
> consequence thereof. A more pertinent description of the CSPF [pension
> fund] investment problem emerges from a study of the loans granted: the entire
> program appears ill-conceived by any standard of financial soundness, and
> the trustees from both sides of the table are responsible. In fact, Hoffa long
> believed that this would shield him from prosecution on the Pension Fund issue;
> to indict him, he thought, the government would have to indict others on the
> board, and Kennedy would not dare to cast his political net so wide. Had Hoffa
> more clearly revealed the CSPF investment policies at the trial, the judge
> would probably have thrown up his hands and directed a verdict of acquittal.
> Instead, Hoffa portrayed the Fund's investments in glowing terms, and the jury
> found him guilty.[19]

Hoffa had seized control of the fund right at the start. He had secured an even split in trustees with the Trucking Association, though most industries insist on their own control so as to assure fiscal responsibility. The truckers had expected this arrangement to result in a mutual veto situation with each group voting as a bloc. Hoffa smashed through to total control by insisting upon individual voting and the seating of a sixth "employer" trucker representing the "independents," an individual close to Hoffa interests. Hoffa obtained these concessions—and a replacement for Ben Miller, who had tried to

[19]James and James, *Hoffa and the Teamsters*, pp. 312–13.

organize the opposition among the trustees—by threatening the employers with harassment by means of extensive grievances:

> Representing the union, we will file a grievance against every carrier, every one, and we will take you out on strike, God damn it, until you do agree to draw up the proper kind of trust that we can live under. I can tell you that much, and I will, God damn it. Take that home, and see how you like it.[20]

Hoffa thereby established complete control over the fund—in violation of the spirit of Taft-Hartley, which, by requiring at least equal votes for employers, had sought to prevent union dominance. His control was then used to establish investment policies of the most incredible sort. Mad-hatter sessions took place at which the trustees argued with representatives of prospective borrowers that they must pay a lesser rate of interest than the borrower had proposed. On occasion, the trustees agreed and adjusted rates downward, without being asked to do so by the borrower. A surprising number—according to the James list, nineteen of the first eighty-nine recipients—went bankrupt or defaulted, one hotel within six months of receipt of a $2.75 million loan. In another case, the hotel involved went bankrupt before the loan could be made; it thus became one of the few ventures from which full recovery was made.

Since Hoffa in testimony took a sanguine view of the investment prospects, the trial necessarily degenerated into rather long and tedious accounts of the individual transactions. Judge Richard Austin, who presided, indicated in dismissing counts during the proceedings that the testimony was bewildering. Hoffa contended, throughout, that the conviction was obtained only because of the adverse atmosphere created by the jury tampering conviction (and this is by no means out of the question). Nonetheless, the government case was a solid one; the only dispute would seem to be whether the criminal case was proven "beyond a reasonable doubt," and judges have had no difficulty ruling it was a proper case to go to a jury verdict.

In a certain respect, the trial was admittedly tainted. On one occasion defendant S. George Burris had a conversation with Benjamin Sigelbaum, who was under electronic surveillance by the FBI at the time. The government belatedly acknowledged having listened to the two men, but claimed that no evidence used in the trial had been affected by the Burris incident, and that all information derived from the eavesdropping was already known to the government. In 1967 the Supreme Court held that the district judge should hold hearings as to whether any evidence was obtained against any defendant —not just Burris—through this device. In September, Judge Austin found that a close examination of the recording revealed nothing not previously known to the authorities.

Events have moved rapidly since October 1967, when the final appeal in the Chattanooga trial was completed. In January 1968 the Teamsters Union for-

---

[20] Ibid., p. 219.

mally agreed to stop spending its money to defend officers against allegations of personal wrongdoing or misuse of union funds. The agreement served to deny Hoffa access to any further legal defense funds and required him to repay $100,000 for past expenses. This action, in spite of the fact that Hoffa was reelected president of his home local in Detroit, seemed to indicate that perhaps he was finding it more difficult to maintain his control over dissident members from a jail cell. There still is little doubt, however, that Hoffa can win any fight in the union that he can personally direct.

There followed a year of charges and countercharges between Hoffa's lawyers and the Justice Department. In May a United States District Judge accused the Justice Department of a payoff because of its refusal to bring criminal charges against Edward Partin. Judge E. Gordon West rejected the department's motion to dismiss an embezzlement indictment against Partin. By the end of June, he had been indicted on five counts of conspiracy and extortion.

In August former Justice Department employee Walter J. Sheridan testified that Stephen E. Smith, Robert Kennedy's brother-in-law, provided a $3,000 "loan" to Robert Vick, the Nashville policeman who had been a key witness in Z. T. Osborn's jury tampering trial. Sheridan, former chief investigative official for the "Hoffa Squad," explained that the money had been returned two days later, apparently due to the realization that the transaction might be construed as "improper." The money was ostensibly lent to Vick on the grounds that he lost his job because he testified against the popular Osborn, and, as Sheridan put it, "it would be bad for law enforcement if people who testified for the Government were permitted to suffer for it."[21] In subsequent action District Judge Marion S. Boyd overruled a subpoena that would have forced Smith to testify at a hearing, on the grounds that the case did not justify bringing in witnesses from long distances. One week later Sheridan testified that the Teamsters Union had offered him one million dollars as part of "a concerted, intensive effort to bribe witnesses in the James Hoffa and Z. T. Osborn jury tampering cases."[22] He also testified that a similar proposition was made to Vick.

Hoffa has realized that effective utilization of appeals procedures adds a note of uncertainty to the effects of any jail sentence, and serves as a way of minimizing revolts in his union. Three times he appealed to the Supreme Court on various grounds (including one appeal based on the allegation that marshals in the district court had procured prostitutes to have sexual relations with the jurors during the trial and that the judge had said that Hoffa "would get what was coming to him")[23] and three times the Court declined to review the appeals. Hoffa, not easily discouraged, was to get yet another chance.

In late October 1968, the Justice Department disclosed that two of the defendants in the 1964 trial and three other men in Chattanooga had been overheard by federal agents who used illegal listening devices. The government contended that the conversations overheard were not relevant to the jury

[21]New York Times, 15 August 1968, p. 25:1.
[22]Ibid., 21 August 1968, p. 4:8.
[23]Ibid., 29 January 1968, p. 26.

tampering prosecution. Hoffa then accused the government of using illegal bugging to convict him of fraud in the use of teamster pension funds in 1964. Hoffa's attorneys contended, in spite of government denial, that the eavesdropping on S. George Burris tipped government prosecutors off to Hoffa's defense. Hoffa contended the Justice Department withheld the contents of the bugged conversation from the Supreme Court.

The Supreme Court responded on 10 March 1969, placing heavy penalties on illegal governmental eavesdropping with a ruling that a defendant and his lawyer (in espionage and racketeering cases) must be shown the transcripts of any electronic surveillance that violated the accused person's Fourth Amendment rights. On the basis of this decision, Hoffa appealed to the Supreme Court to reverse his conviction. The Court declined, but did send the case back to the district court for rehearing consistent with the wiretap ruling. Late in 1969 the United States District Court in Chattanooga ruled that Hoffa's Fourth Amendment rights had not been abridged. There was little likelihood, however, that this would be the last word on the matter.

ISSUES AND CONSEQUENCES

How one views Hoffa affects to some extent—but only to some extent—one's view of the labyrinthine proceedings against him. The reverse is also true. If the conviction for jury tampering was bona fide, only peripheral sympathy can be generated for one who rather wantonly moves against the processes of justice.

On the whole, the McClellan Committee's charges against Hoffa have stood up over time. He was accused of consorting with and abetting rather than controlling corrupt individuals; his characterization of Partin is something of a confession in avoidance. He was accused of misusing union funds for political and financial advantage. Here the conviction for mail fraud must be supplemented by the knowledge that Hoffa's behavior in the Test Fleet situation was sufficiently questionable that he himself felt a need to cover his tracks. He was accused of bending the law to suit his aims. Beyond the jury tampering conviction, the evidence of his ingenious distortion of law is striking. His ascendancy over the pension fund is, perhaps, a weak example of his agility, since it merely circumvented congressional intent. An even more questionable and relevant example is his use of what amounts to tertiary boycott tactics—threats to those who do business with the primary clients of Teamster target companies —to overcome the prohibition against secondary boycotts. Tertiary boycotts are more difficult to detect, involve almost no cost to the companies being pressured to act, and in many ways are more effective because of the subtlety of the pressures generated. Finally, there is Hoffa's use of union funds to foster his control even at obvious detriment to the well being of his membership.

In a sense Hoffa admits most of these charges, by the indirect process of not denying them, or doing so rather pro forma. He excuses himself by accusing the government of similar or worse tactics, and by suggesting tu quoque in two ways. Intensive scrutiny, he argues, will show technical faults in the conduct of any man, particularly one who attempts to get things done. This excessively minute scrutiny, plus the antagonism created by adverse publicity, resulted in improper convictions. Furthermore, improper governmental prosecution activity drove his loyal supporters to excessively zealous defense measures, according to Hoffa.

Certainly no one can avoid a sense of concern about the variety and extent of government activities directed against Hoffa in this case. Similar alarm developed following the Kennedy administration's handling of the steel price crisis in 1962. The criticized method then was principally the application of social and personal pressure—for example, the action of the FBI in awakening a reporter in the small hours of the morning gave rise to cries of Gestapo tactics.

It is clear that the government went well beyond this in the Hoffa case. Individuals were persuaded to cooperate by means of promises of leniency, exemptions from criminal charges, or threats of prosecution. An elaborate series of informers, ranging from bellhops to Partin himself, were clearly employed. Wiretapping there clearly was; the only argument being whether such tactics were authorized by Attorney General Kennedy or not. The interesting and highly acrimonious exchanges that developed between J. Edgar Hoover, Robert Kennedy, and Burke Marshall emphasize this point. Hearings on Internal Revenue surveillance and proceedings in court revealed fairly extensive use of taps and surveillance devices in the Hoffa cases. Such practices were defended on the ground that only *divulging* (not recording or obtaining) information was forbidden by the wiretap statute. Director Hoover announced such taps were authorized in a number of instances. When this was denied by Kennedy, the former attorney general, the director released a letter indicating that the senator had personally listened to such tapes. Kennedy replied that he had indeed listened but had not realized the tapes had been illegally obtained. It would appear, however, that he had not exhibited excessive curiosity either.

The manpower and the intensity of effort involved were also enormous. This, in itself, raises both the political problem—what would justify such an enormous expenditure?—and the moral problem—when does the relentless force of government massed against an individual assume a form so unfair, so unequal, that even an otherwise just result would be unjust?

As to the policy question, the Kennedys consistently denied the issue was their own attitude toward Hoffa. Rather, they suggested that the reputation of the rule of law and the perpetuation of honest unionism were the issues at stake. At times, Kennedy rhetoric went even further, suggesting that the fundamental issue was actual—not merely symbolic—civil war between the Teamsters and the authority of the United States. The Teamsters replied that Robert Kennedy was, next to the federal government, the most powerful force in our society.[24] In view of Hoffa's efforts to forge a coalition with the Long-

24*New York Times*, 27 March 1959, p. 15:s.

shoreman's Union and the ambitious program of his catch-all organizing local, the concern of the attorney general that Hoffa might have become the most powerful force in American labor does not seem wholly misplaced, although presented in exaggerated form. For several years, only George Meany's pre-eminence in the AFL-CIO prevented the Teamsters' return to the fold. His removal from the presidency through death or retirement would have brought forward a less domineering president—perhaps Walter Reuther—subject to Hoffa pressures and maneuvers. "He's blocking us now," Hoffa is supposed to have said of Meany, "but he can't live forever." In practical, political, and legal terms, including calculation of the effect upon other union leaders and their conformity with Taft-Hartley and Landrum-Griffin Acts, the attorney general's judgment that the Teamsters were a major concern seems quite reasonable, although expressed in exaggerated language.

The problem of power and pressure—the moral dimension—is rather more painful to contemplate. Comprehensive examination of almost anyone's career will perhaps expose culpable faults—"Use every man after his desert, and who should 'scape whipping?" Continuous pressure may, indeed, deepen faults and pressures, as in a Greek tragedy. When governmental officials engage in such a comprehensive scrutiny of a man's life are they not certain to condemn him?

But seen in perspective, a moral defense of Hoffa seems untenable. He was convicted not of relatively trivial offenses, such as running a traffic light or omitting a $25 windfall on an income tax return. Though we may be troubled by governmental intensity, it is difficult to exonerate a major crime. Even though the government might be estopped from punishment as a means of preventing bad police practice, this would not constitute moral exoneration of the criminal. Not everyone commits felonies with regularity, and even the fact that some individuals do cannot be license to others. Studies and polls do indicate fairly large percentages of the population admit to acts which would subject them to major sentences, but a very large percentage of these are within the currently unenforceable areas of sexual matters and drug consumption.

There are two aspects of Hoffa's position that make his conduct more culpable. In the first place his role was fiduciary, acting for his members, and in this respect, the Test Fleet and Sun Valley derelictions seem doubly serious. In the second place, his role was also quasi-official—he served as an exclusive agent, with license and authority granted by the government. Court decisions had early established the limitations of union officials to discriminate racially on precisely this theory of governmentally endowed power. The fiduciary relationship goes to the nature of Hoffa's responsibility and to the unique duty of the government. Having created the machinery of union leadership power, the government had a special responsibility to control it.

Where the Department of Justice seems at fault is in the size and intensity of its effort, and its overweening emphasis on results—on ends, rather than means. Under such conditions, due process was bound to be transgressed. In part, the apparent ruthlessness of the federal agents was justified on the grounds of Teamster chicanery, much as Teamster wiliness was justified on grounds of Department of Justice lawlessness. There is, indeed, escalation in the law enforcement area as well as in international relations.

Further, the department's motives display some curious and questionable aspects. The criminal process was activated (even hyperactivated) not primarily to enforce the law but to affect and control the leadership of a nominally private organization. Any charge that contributed to this end was treated seriously. In a restricted sense, then, there was verdict first, charges later. Whether this is in accordance with standard notions of the prosecutorial role is doubtful. In this quest for replacement of Hoffa, such actions have only been partly successful. Nominally, Hoffa remains in control, and will probably retain some measure of power for years to come. But his power has been channeled and restricted both outside his union and within. Instead of control continuously radiating toward the center—a probable consequence of his skills and energy—there has been, for half a decade, a trend to decentralization in the Teamsters: a direct and indirect consequence of federal efforts. Hoffa's removal from the day-to-day scene will continue to have consequences. Those years will never be replaced; estrangement from day-to-day activities will limit the power of one whose skill was not intellectual, but based in great measure upon mastery of detail.

Ironically, Hoffa's imprisonment facilitated the combining of the UAW and the Teamsters into the breakaway Alliance for Labor Action in 1968. The alliance of a union with so progressive a reputation as the Auto Workers with the Teamsters was one cemented by their leaders' hatred of Meany. But Walter Reuther no doubt found it easier—even face saving—to conclude arrangements with Fitzsimmons rather than with Hoffa. Somehow, too, this new amalgam, without Hoffa's active leadership, was also less threatening than the Teamsters would have been had they remained unaffiliated, with Hoffa still at their helm.

The government, then, has achieved a large measure of its goal. It has influenced the selection of the union's leaders by means of an institution—the criminal process—not created for this purpose nor primarily responsible for labor relations. I have indicated some sympathy for the notion of governmental responsibility for control of labor abuses, but even that does not justify random responsibility where specific individuals offend powerful officials. It remains to be seen whether welfare state regulation will generate sporadic incursions into social institutions, or will rather result in systematic visible and carefully responsive procedures for dealing with abuses in government-sponsored social agencies. This is no trivial question, but one of basic human values, a question raised by a spectrum of opinion from conservatives such as Von Hayek, in his *Road to Serfdom*, to humanistic communists, such as Djilas, in his *The New Class*. The specter invoked by the Kennedys in moving against Hoffa was that of *Imperium in Imperio*—a self-established personal government flaunting authority. The specter raised by the relentlessness of their response is the even more frightening one of *Behemoth*.

Such ultimate questions do not arise out of the actual trials of Hoffa, which were, by and large, well-conducted, despite the intrigues and extreme displays of emotion that accompanied them. But the pattern of pursuit—the trail of trials—is not without political overtones.

source note

The volume by the Jameses (*Hoffa and the Teamsters;* Princeton: Van Nostrand, 1965), although more a series of monographs than a book, is head and shoulders above any writing on the subject and will remain a classic in the labor field. The articles by A. H. Raskin in the *New York Times,* the *Reporter* and elsewhere (see for instance "Is Hoffa Finished" *Reporter,* 26 March 1966) are extremely insightful, and live up to Raskin's reputation in the field. Clark Mollenhoff's book (*Tentacles of Power;* Cleveland: World, 1965) is the most useful of the "exposé" attack literature, but McClellan's *Crime Without Punishment* (New York: Duell, Sloan and Pearce, 1962) and Kennedy's *The Enemy Within* (New York: Harper, 1960) have some useful information. There is abundant room for a full-scale unraveling of the practices of the Department of Justice in this instance, as well as its general prosecutory role. We also lack full-scale biographies of the two major protagonists in this case.

five:
a "political
trial"

KENNETH M. DOLBEARE

JOEL B. GROSSMAN*

11

LeROI JONES IN NEWARK

a political trial?

Few trials in recent American history have posed issues of the political use of the law as sharply as the 1968 prosecution of the militant black poet and author, LeRoi Jones, for alleged possession of two revolvers during the Newark ghetto riots of 1967.

To many blacks, all of the radical press, and to many "straight" or establishment media as well, the arrest, trial, and conviction of LeRoi Jones was the epitome of white establishment repression against the most prominent available symbol of black aspirations and independence. By contrast, officials of the city of Newark and many other observers insisted that the alleged repression was solely in the eyes of the beholders, and that except for the publicity attending the trial and its aftermath, this was but an ordinary felony prosecution, the characteristics of which all fell within the range of what is "normal" in criminal cases. Neither the defendant nor the circumstances were ordinary, of course. But, aside from the unusual publicity, this case seems to embody *both* repression *and* the more or less "normal" workings of the criminal law. As such, it poses the quite fundamental question of whether the concept of a "political trial" is a meaningful one or not.

The law and the courts are regularly employed to discourage reoccurrences of similar proscribed acts, particularly through well-publicized trial and thorough punishment of the most flagrant and visible transgressions. Most people recognize that the law and the courts are instruments of social con-

*The authors wish to express their gratitude to Stuart Scheingold of the University of Washington, Caleb Foote of the University of California Law School (Berkeley), Carl Auerbach of the University of Minnesota Law School, David Olson of Indiana University, and Matthew Holden of the University of Wisconsin for useful comments on earlier versions of this essay.

trol, the use of which is made with a view to efficiency in the application of prosecutorial resources and maximizing future obedience. Under what circumstances, then, can it be shown that any particular trial is so unusual as to be fairly termed a "political trial"?

The trial of LeRoi Jones offers a particularly good opportunity to examine in detail the utility of the concept "political trial." It is used here to refer to the use or misuse of the judicial process to achieve goals other than those usually associated with courts and judges: settlement of private civil disputes, challenges to the legality of government actions, prevention of further crime, punishment and rehabilitation (or both) of convicted criminals.[1] The existence of a "political trial" was not nearly so obvious to observers in the case of LeRoi Jones as it was in the even more widely publicized conviction of Dr. Spock and his fellow defendants for conspiring to aid and abet draft resistance to the Vietnam war. Nobody believes that Spock and company presented an ordinary case, with familiar facts and issues; all can recognize it as a unique and politically charged controversy which, for tactical reasons, was shifted to the courts.[2] But in the LeRoi Jones case we have employment of the law in a manner which the relevant authorities declare to be typical, nonpolitical, and routine, but which other observers find to be deliberately repressive, political, nonjudicious, and arbitrary. The Jones case allows us to investigate a far more usual situation; the authorities suddenly found in their legal custody a person whom they despised and, most probably, feared. In a context of great stress and publicity, could they conduct the trial within the "normal" range of idiosyncrasy and discretionary actions?

NEWARK: SUMMER 1967

Many other American cities suffered racial violence before the city of Newark erupted in July 1967. In retrospect, it seems as though such violence should have been predictable, although in almost every case it came as a great shock. Newark was no different. The statistics have meaning now, but the actions that developed out of conditions they describe have an even greater, perhaps symbolic meaning. In 1940 Newark's population was 429,750, of whom eleven percent were black. By 1968 Negroes constituted fifty-two percent of New Jersey's largest city, which had declined to a population of

[1]The leading work on this subject is, of course, Otto Kirchheimer's *Political Justice: The Use of Legal Procedure for Political Ends* (Princeton: Princeton University Press, 1961). His definition of a political trial, far more involved than ours, has three components: (1) "a trial involving a common crime committed for political purposes and conducted with a view to the political benefits which might ultimately accrue from successful prosecution"; (2) "the classic political trial: a regime's attempt to incriminate its foe's public behavior with a view toward evicting him from the political scene"; and (3) "the derivative political trial, where the weapons of defamation, perjury, and contempt are manipulated in an effort to bring disrepute upon a political foe."—p. 46. In general, the trial of LeRoi Jones falls closest to the second component, with some aspects of the third component involved as well.

[2]Reported in the *New York Times*, 15 June 1968. For a more detailed account, see Jessica Mitford, *The Trial of Dr. Spock* (New York: Knopf, 1969).

slightly less than 400,000.[3] In addition, another ten percent were Puerto Rican, making a total of more than sixty percent "nonwhite" citizens. These population proportions provide the base for a quick review of the sources of racial tensions in Newark.

In a 1967 police force of about 1,500 men, only 145 (less than ten percent) were Negroes. Of these, only 9 held a rank higher than patrolman and only 4 had any kind of command responsibilities. The Governor's Commission on Civil Disorders found also that Negroes on the force encountered unusual hostility from white officers and staff, and were subject to a high degree of internal discipline. The commission reported high levels of hostility toward the police on the part of Negroes—a product of perceptions of police brutality combined with inadequate protection. In the absence of a police review board, complaints against the police could be lodged with the county prosecutor or the FBI; but the chief magistrate of Newark declined to hear such a case in 1967, saying, "I've instructed my court not to take complaints against police officers. We're too busy."

The public schools of Newark present a comparable picture. By 1966, nearly seventy percent of the pupils were Negro, and the total "nonwhite" school population probably exceeded eighty percent. In addition to being overcrowded, the schools were run by whites: only one-fourth of the teachers were Negro, and a large proportion of these held only temporary or substitute certificates; two-thirds of the schools had Negro majorities, but there was not one Negro principal. Not surprisingly, Newark pupils scored substantially lower than the national average in performance tests.

In housing, employment, and welfare the situation was much the same. Negroes surveyed by the governor's commission felt that housing conditions were the most important cause of the riots. Newark's own Model Cities application characterized more than one-quarter of all the housing units in the city as dilapidated or substandard. Limited land availability led to high-rise public housing projects, perceived by tenants as laden with arbitrary restrictions and less hospitable than former "slum" dwellings; the scarcity of land also led to excessive tax assessments, which had the dual effects of speeding the exodus of whites and making it difficult for Negroes to become homeowners. Negro unemployment in Newark was twice as high as that of whites, and thirty-eight percent of all Negroes between the ages of 16 and 19 were unemployed. Blue-collar jobs were diminishing and the job training of Negroes in the critical 16–21 age bracket was increasingly obsolescent. But the capstone of discrimination in Newark, as in most large cities, was the operation of the welfare program. The product of the established combination of humiliating procedures and invasions of privacy—which no white American

[3]The demographic facts about the city of Newark and facts about the riot of 1967 which appear in the following paragraphs come primarily from three sources: *Report for Action,* A Report of the Governor's Select Commission on Civil Disorder, State of New Jersey (February 1968); Tom Hayden, *Rebellion in Newark: Official Violence and Ghetto Response* (New York: Vintage Books, 1967); and *Report of the National Advisory Commission on Civil Disorders* (New York: Bantam Books, 1968), hereinafter referred to as the *Kerner Commission Report.*

of means would tolerate—is the undermining of individual self-respect; as the President's Commission on Civil Disorders reported, "our present system of public welfare is designed to save money instead of people, and tragically ends up doing neither."

These conditions were exacerbated by the unrepresentativeness and unresponsiveness of Newark's city administration. In a city with a sixty-two percent nonwhite population, whites retained control of all the political machinery. The board of education for a system with eighty percent nonwhite students was eighty percent white, as was the city council. Negro residents continued to be represented largely by white Italian politicians, despite the historic rivalries and tensions between the two groups. *Life* magazine was surely correct in calling this "the predictable insurrection."[4] Almost anything could have sparked a riot, but it is fitting that the incident which touched off a week of looting and killing was the brutal beating of a Negro cab driver by two white policemen. When the carnage was over, twenty-four persons had been killed, thousands injured, and property damaged or destroyed to the total of millions of dollars. The gruesome details of this and other riots have been told many times, and there is little point in repeating them. But the arrest, trial, and sentencing of LeRoi Jones must be seen in the context of Newark's race relations situation and the resultant riot.

THE ARREST AND TRIAL OF LeROI JONES

At the height of the riot, at 2:30 A.M. on 14 July 1967, LeRoi Jones, wearing African dress, drove his Volkswagen microbus down one of the main streets of the riot area.[5] With him were two other black men, Charles McCray, a thirty-three-year-old accountant, and Barry Wynn, twenty-four, an actor. It is clear that Jones was arrested, taken to jail, and booked for illegal possession of two loaded revolvers and some ammunition, but practically all the rest of the facts of the case are in dispute. The accuracy of the charge and the behavior of the police are both the real and the controverted aspects of the case.

Jones emerged from the confrontation with a head wound requiring stitches; later, police alleged a bottle (thrown "from somewhere") had hit Jones during their arresting process. Jones's attorney, who saw him in jail several hours after the arrest, reports that he was bloody and battered and needed hospital attention. In any event, Jones was finally freed on $25,000 bail pending trial for illegal possession of firearms; McCray and Wynn, similarly charged, were released on lesser bail.

Jones's attorney was Irvin Booker, a flamboyant Negro lawyer from Newark.

---

[4]*Life*, 28 July 1967, p. 19 and on the cover.

[5]Sources for our description of the trial of LeRoi Jones include the trial record, newspaper and magazine accounts, and our interviews with the prosecuting and defense attorneys. Judge Kapp declined to be interviewed, but kindly supplied us with a verbatim copy of his sentencing speech.

His understandable request for a change of venue out of Newark was granted, and the trial was set in Morris County, a middle class suburb. To Booker's chagrin, both the prosecutor, Andrew Zazzali, and County Judge Leon Kapp followed the case to the Essex County Courthouse in Morristown. Judges accompany their cases less often than prosecutors (who often carry out their duties wherever the case is tried), and Booker had hoped for a non-Newark judge. The jury panel consisted exclusively of middle class whites, although when challenges excluded the first group of prospective members, the sheriff included three Negroes among those he rounded up from the streets; all were excused, however, and the jury ultimately was composed entirely of whites.

At the trial in November 1967, five policemen testified that they had stopped Jones's microbus because of previous reports of gunfire issuing from a similar vehicle, and that he had then assaulted them. They declared that the weapons, pearl-handled revolvers, had been found in the back of the bus. Other testimony identified a different vehicle as the one from which the previous shots had been fired, so that the entire issue before the jury was that of Jones's illegal possession of the weapons. (No records were produced to link them to Jones, but under New Jersey law the unlawful act was complete if they were carried in his vehicle, with or without his ownership or knowledge.)

Jones's version of the facts was completely at odds with that of the police. He related that after midnight of 14 July he and his companions were riding in his microbus, talking and listening to the radio. On their way home, as they reached the corner of South Orange Avenue, they were stopped by at least two carloads of police wearing riot helmets and carrying shotguns, and two detectives. The officers ordered the three men out of the bus. As Jones stepped down, he said, one officer, "whom I recognized as having once attended Barringer High School while I was there," started yelling that "we were the bastards" who had been shooting at them. Jones claimed to have replied that they had not been shooting at anyone, and that when he told the officer that he thought they had attended high school together, the officer "hit me in the face and threw me up against the side of the truck."

Jones said the detective then began to jab his pistol in Jones's stomach, asking, "Where are the guns?" When Jones replied that there were no guns, five or six officers began beating him up with nightsticks and fists and continued this assault when he fell to the ground. He alleged that one officer tried to kick him in the groin, and that the officers used various terms of verbal abuse. He was then put in the police wagon, where the beatings continued. When he arrived at the police station he asked the director of police who had ordered him beaten. According to Jones, the director replied "They got you, didn't they?" and smiled.

Taken to Newark City Hospital, Jones said he was dragged inside and handcuffed in a wheelchair. Eight or nine stitches were taken. One doctor shouted at Jones, "You're a poet, huh? Well, you won't be writing any poems for a long time now." Jones and his companions were returned to police headquarters, fingerprinted, and brought into the courtroom and arraigned. Bail was set at $25,000, as requested by the prosecutor. Jones was taken to the Essex County Jail and placed in solitary confinement, where he remained until released.

Despite Jones's personal account of what really happened, during the actual proceedings it was uncertain whether Jones was on trial for a stated or an implied charge—for having possessed the weapons, or for having been responsible, in some mysterious way, for the riots that had engulfed Newark. Judge Kapp made his own position clear through repeated intervention in the trial. He frequently took over the questioning of witnesses hostile to Jones, directing them to repeat damaging testimony in a loud voice for the benefit of the jury. At the end of the trial he charged the jury so as to leave no doubt of his belief that Jones was a liar and a scoundrel, and that the arresting officers were model policemen who had simply been doing their patriotic duty in difficult circumstances. The impression comes through clearly in his own words, and was shared by observers then present. Booker was convinced that the judge was prejudiced against Jones, and against Negroes in general. Jones himself did nothing to ease the tension. Garbed in African robes, he ignored the proceedings when he was not shouting at the judge, and ultimately received a thirty-day contempt-of-court sentence. Zazzali, perhaps seeing himself as representing the dominant Italian community in Newark, with which he had long associations, played the role of the abrasive, hands-in-pockets district attorney to the hilt. Between his summation and Judge Kapp's charge to the jury, little was left unsaid about Jones's guilt and responsibility for escalating the riot. The jury did not fail them, convicting all three men as charged.

But the sentencing stage of LeRoi Jones's trial is the point for which it has become most celebrated. The sentence was announced on 5 January 1968 in the old courthouse in Newark. Judge Kapp began his address by harking back to his days in the Navy and intoning "Now hear this . . ." in stentorian boatswain's mate style; his demeanor and tone were perceived by many of the Negroes in the packed courtroom as thoroughly racist and deliberately provocative. The two codefendants were sentenced, respectively, to twelve months in the county jail, six months' probation, and a fine of $500; and nine months in jail, nine months' probation, and a fine of $250.

The style in which Jones's sentence was delivered, however, was almost as spectacular as the sentence itself. The judge began by indicating that the basis for his action was one of a group of three poems by Jones which had been published in the *Evergreen Review* in December 1967, between the trial and the sentencing. Kapp read the poem aloud in the courtroom, substituting the word "blank" for certain "obscenities." The poem was as follows:

Black People!
  What about that bad short you saw last week on Frelinghuysen, or those stoves
and refrigerators, record players, shotguns, in Sears, Bambergers, Klein's, Hahnes',
Chase, and the smaller joosh enterprises? What about that bad jewelry, on

Washington Street, and those couple of shops on Springfield? You know how to get
it, you can get it, no money down, no money never, money dont grow on
trees no way, only whitey's got it, makes it with a machine, to control you you
cant steal nothin from a white man, he's already stole it he owes you anything you
want, even his life. All the stores will open if you will say the magic words. The
magic words are: Up against the wall mother fucker this is a stick up! Or:
Smash the window at night (these are magic actions) smash the windows daytime,
anytime, together, lets smash the window drag the shit from in there. No
money down. No time to pay. Just take what you want. The magic dance in the
street. Run up and down Broad Street niggers, take the shit you want. Take their
lives if need be, but get what you want what you need. Dance up and down
the streets, turn all the music up, run through the streets with music, beautiful
radios on Market Street, they are brought here especially for you. Our
brothers are moving all over, smashing at jellywhite faces. We must make
our own World, man, our own world, and we can not do this unless the white
man is dead. Let's get together and kill him my man, lets get to gather the fruit of
the sun, let's make a world we want black children to grow and learn in, do
not let your children when they grow look in your face and curse you by pitying
your tomish ways.[6]

Jones contributed to the tumult in the courtroom by laughing frequently
during the judge's rendition. Again dressed in flowing African robes, he
was the rhetorical equal of Kapp. When Kapp noted his failure to appear for
presentencing examination by the county psychiatrist, Jones filled in his sentence ". . . who needs treatment himself." When the judge then declared,
"You are sick and require medical attention," Jones shot back, "Not as sick
as you are!" He and Kapp then performed a duet:

" . . . you are in the vanguard of a group of extreme radicals who advocate
the destruction—"

"The destruction of unrighteousness!"

"—of our democratic way of life. . . . If the philosopher can make his own
law, so can the fool."

"We see that."

"The sentence of this court, on the basis of your conviction for the unlawful possession of two revolvers . . ."

"—and two poems!"

Kapp finally managed to sentence the unyielding defendant to two-and-a-
half to three years in the New Jersey State Penitentiary—virtually the maximum possible penalty; pronounced him unfit for probation; and fined him
$1,000.

After the sentencing, protests arose from some in the crowd. Two people,
including Jones's wife, were led out of the courtroom by bailiffs. Booker
sought mitigation of the sentence but was rejected. Jones began his authorized
statement: "You are not a righteous person, and you don't represent Almighty

[6]"Black People" by LeRoi Jones, from *Evergreen Review,* December 1967. Copyright ©
1967 by LeRoi Jones. Reprinted by permission of The Sterling Lord Agency.

God. You represent a crumbling structure. . . ." According to the *New York Times,* the judge then shouted at him to sit down; as Jones was led from the courtroom, he called back at Kapp: "The black people will judge me!"

WAS THIS A POLITICAL TRIAL?

Thus ended the first trial of LeRoi Jones. The question for analysis against this backdrop of events is whether or not the poorly defined boundary between the ordinary uses of the criminal law and the uses of the law for political reasons had been transgressed. In one sense, law and the courts are clearly and properly political. In most Western nations law has long been the means by which (political) aspirations and goals have been recognized and enforced. That courts make "political" decisions is hardly worth debating any longer. But the question which engages us here is whether we can create definitional categories, and then produce empirical analyses, which will enable us to specify *if* and *how* the courts have been used so arbitrarily and repressively as to constitute a political trial.

We will make three specific inquiries into the case of LeRoi Jones. First, what can be said about the behavior of the major actors in the case compared with their customary behavior in similar cases? Second, what were the actors' perceptions of the roles they were playing? Third, what was the public's view of the trial? Consideration of each of these questions is based on interviews with some of the protagonists, a scrutiny of the record of the case, and a survey of commentaries on the case in the mass media.

First, we ask whether the behavior of the protagonists differed substantially from the norms of behavior expected of such persons, or from their own previous personal behavior. The machinery of justice in American courts provides a ready forum for publicizing the heresies of defendants and a means of legitimizing sanctions against those whose political activities have passed the threshold of tolerance. It is a means of vindicating the prevailing regime, of showing "legally" that certain defendants are "un-American" or suffer from a similar social disease. But the prevailing liberal norms usually militate against any gross departures from accepted practices; the initiation of such departures usually proves dysfunctional for the authorities.

The use of more subtle deviations in official behavior is harder to identify and, hence, harder to combat. Most law enforcement officials and judges in the United States have sufficient discretion to permit large gradations of treatment of particular defendants. The discretionary authority of an arresting police officer is well known, as is the wide-ranging power of a public attorney to seek a conviction and severe sentence, or to plea-bargain with the defendant. Other studies have shown a positive relationship between the severity of sentences meted out to draft evaders and conscientious objectors both during war and during peacetime. It is not difficult to infer, from these and other studies, the broad discretionary authority of a trial judge, both in conducting a trial and in determining the sentence for a guilty defendant.[7]

Even a cursory look at the LeRoi Jones trial reveals a substantial number of instances in which the actors involved arguably behaved differently from what might be called the "norm." Granted that this norm is vague and indeterminate, it is not totally invisible, and some comparisons are possible. Besides the defendant himself there were three principal actors whose behavior can be analyzed: Judge Kapp, Prosecuting Attorney Zazzali, and Defense Attorney Booker.

Judge Kapp's behavior was the most flagrant and obvious. He accompanied the case to another county instead of relinquishing it to a judge there. He conducted interrogations of prosecution witnesses to insure that their damaging statements were clearly heard and understood by the jury. He delivered a prejudiced and inflammatory charge to the jury. He sentenced Jones to an unusually long term in prison. He allowed Jones's release only on a very high bail and sentenced him to thirty additional days in jail for contempt of court without allowing Jones or his attorney to contest the contempt citation. He accompanied his sentence of fine and imprisonment with a stern lecture on the morals of race relations, and based the sentence in part on matters completely extraneous to the trial—Jones's publication of several poems (after the trial) of allegedly obscene materials, his refusal to consult with a court-appointed psychiatrist, and in general his refusal to show the proper humility and make the proper obeisances before the court. These are neither legal errors nor atypical actions, though they appear to indicate prejudice in this context. And, finally, Kapp even refused to allow Jones to make a statement after sentencing merely because Jones began by attacking the "crumbling white power structure."

Each of these actions, taken alone, would not necessarily indicate either a prejudiced judge or a political trial, but in combination they represent an array of judicial maneuvers and tactics which hardly seems coincidental. To be sure, Jones himself was extremely provocative and, in the words of the sympathetic *New York Times* correspondent, Walter Waggoner, guilty of "unconscionable behavior" during the trial.[8] But it seemed to many witnesses that

[7]On the police, see, among others, David J. Bordua, *The Police* (New York: John Wiley & Sons, 1967); Paul Chevigny, *Police Power: Police Abuses in New York City* (New York: Pantheon, 1969); Arthur Niederhoffer, *Behind the Shield: The Police in Urban Society* (New York: Doubleday, 1967); President's Commission on Law Enforcement and Administration of Justice, *Task Force Report: The Police* (Washington, D.C.: U.S. Government Printing Office, 1967); and Jerome Skolnick, *Justice Without Trial* (New York: John Wiley & Sons, 1966). On the discretions of trial judges, see Jerome Frank, *Courts on Trial* (Princeton: Princeton University Press, 1950); Bernard Botein, *Trial Judge* (New York: Simon & Schuster, 1952); the *Kerner Commission Report*, chapter 13; and numerous journal articles. On prosecutorial discretion, see the aforementioned *Task Force Report: The Police*, and also *The Courts*; Abraham Blumberg, *Criminal Justice* (Chicago: Quadrangle Books, 1967); Arnold Trebach, *The Rationing of Justice* (New Brunswick: Rutgers University Press, 1964); Donald J. Newman, *Conviction: The Determination of Guilt or Innocence Without Trial* (Boston: Little, Brown, 1966); and Frank J. Remington, *Prosecution* (Boston: Little, Brown, forthcoming).

[8]Interview with authors.

Judge Kapp was holding Jones personally responsible for the riots and indeed for everything that was wrong with race relations in Newark.

If this had been just another trial, perhaps the judge would not have accompanied the case to another county. He might have let the prosecutor make his normal incidence of mistakes. He might have charged the jury on the state of the law only and not on the state of the city or the veracity and patriotism of the police. He might have given a convicted first offender a suspended or light sentence and a warning about the "technical" violation of keeping concealed weapons in his car. He might have released the defendant, a long-time Newark resident, on $1,000 or $5,000 bail. He would not know much about the defendant's life history, certainly would not have read any books the defendant had written; and, in any case, would (or should) have recognized that the defendant's books were not obscene according to the Supreme Court of the United States. Finally, he might have listened—perhaps even patiently—to the defendant's closing remarks.

The behavior of the prosecuting attorney is more difficult to compare with "norms," for he has if anything even greater discretion than a judge. Zazzali certainly made a great effort to convince the authors of his indifference to the results of the trial ("it was just another case"). He insisted that he had nothing to do with the sentence, that it was entirely the judge's prerogative, and that only the probation officer had communicated with the judge on this matter. Pressed further, he said that he thought the sentence was fair, that the judge was entitled to take a defendant's background into consideration in determining the sentence, and that in view of Jones's defiant attitude toward the courts and refusal to show any contrition or humility, it was proper for the judge to conclude that he was not a fit subject for probation or a reduced sentence.

On the question of selecting the jury, Zazzali denied that the absence of Negroes on the panel was his doing. He claimed he was willing to accept one of the three Negroes the sheriff brought in off the streets ("a colored girl"), but pointed out that she was later excused by the court. Nor was it his fault, obviously, that an "old Negro man" was excused by consent because of ill health, and a Negro domestic was "peremptoried" because she had no other means of support and "seemed dull, perhaps mentally deficient."

It is not unusual practice, nor is it unconstitutional per se, for a prosecuting attorney to peremptorily challenge a juror because of his race, without so stating; nor is it unconstitutional for a Negro to be tried by an all-white jury —or vice versa.[9] But in a case like this, which had originated in a city like Newark, it was something short of judgment by one's peers. Changes of venue can be a tactic which imposes certain costs of this kind.

The best clue to Zazzali's behavior in the case came from expert observations of his courtroom behavior and from his behavior regarding the role of the police in the brutal beating which Jones received. One veteran courtroom reporter asserted in an interview: "Zazzali was obviously involved in the case;

---

[9]See, among others, *Swain v. Alabama*, 380 U.S. 202 (1964), and cases cited therein.

it was simply not another case for him. He played the role of the tough D.A., pugnacious in tone and manner."

The unsolved mystery of the case is the array of circumstances and actions surrounding Jones's arrest. Jones claimed that the police were hounding him, were looking for him that night, and had planted the weapons to justify beating him up. Following the arrest, Jones had a head wound which required stitches; he later claimed that a tooth had been knocked loose. Records at the county hospital indicate that the tooth was pulled because of decay, but the head wound was confirmed. It was not until his summation that Zazzali conceded to the jury that Jones *may have* incurred some injuries while being arrested, but he attributed them to the fact that "all hell broke loose," and inferentially suggested that Jones himself bore some of the responsibility for his injuries. This, of course, was a very damaging admission, and Zazzali countered it with the statement that even if Jones *had* been beaten up by some policemen, it was not by the two arresting officers and therefore had no relevance to the issue of whether those officers "had it in for Jones." When asked in our interview if he had made any effort to identify and prosecute the perpetrators of the assault upon Jones, he responded that he had taken no action because it was impossible to find out which officers were present at the scene of the arrest or which officers took Jones into custody. His displeased reaction to our question was not accompanied by any sign of displeasure with the actions of the police in this case.

For Jones's attorney, Irvin Booker, this was a big case, perhaps the biggest in his legal career. It undoubtedly presented him with the opportunity to achieve high visibility within the Negro community and perhaps within the bar itself. One of the very few Negro lawyers in Newark, and perhaps the only one who would take a case like this, Booker knew that his defense of LeRoi Jones would be difficult under any circumstances.

Booker's preliminary tactics, for the most part, seemed conventional for cases of potential political import and visibility. He excused those veniremen from the jury who seemed potentially hostile but he was unable to get any blacks on the jury. He called witnesses to prove that Jones had been railroaded by the police, that the weapons had been planted in his vehicle, that he had been beaten by the police, and that he was innocent of any wrongdoing. The jury did not believe him even though Zazzali admitted in his summation that Jones may have been struck by the police. Booker moved for a new trial, then moved to suspend or reduce the sentence meted out by Judge Kapp. Finally, he filed a notice of appeal and turned the case over to two Jersey City lawyers—Raymond Brown and Irving Vogelman.

It is highly unlikely that any lawyer could have successfully defended LeRoi Jones in this case. Jones himself was the best witness for the prosecution before a middle class, all-white jury. His exotic dress and heated exchanges with the judge, expressing disdain and contempt for white people and their institutions, could not have won him any friends. Perhaps because of the nature of his client's behavior, Booker himself was perceived by observers as being wild and emotional rather than cool and subtle. The role of the defense lawyer, however, is like a work of art, of individual expression, and cannot be fitted into any mold.

Perhaps by such excess Booker sought to lessen the difference in the eyes of the jury between his own behavior and that of his client—to suggest that Jones's actions were not as extreme as they appeared. Perhaps by spending time attacking the trial and the judge, Booker was drawing attention away from the real evidence against Jones, demonstrating for the jury that an unfair trial was in progress. Whatever his reasons, it is clear that he chose not to proceed in a conservative, methodical manner.

Second, what were the actors' perceptions of their roles? One way of analyzing an event such as the LeRoi Jones trial is by reference to the roles which each of these actors was playing, or attempting to play, in contrast to the prescribed or expected roles each might have envisioned. The role played by an actor depends on the nature of the position he holds, the tradition and precedents of others who have held the same or similar positions, the public expectations which have defined the position, and the actor's own values and perceptions of what is expected of him.

The role of judge is often defined in Western culture, but there is consensus only concerning certain aspects of that role.[10] All would agree that a judge should be honest, fair, and impartial. But there is substantial disagreement over other facets. For example, should a trial judge interpret the facts for the jury and lead it to a "proper" verdict? Or should he content himself with a more passive role and let the skill of the attorneys and the presentation of evidence be the main influences on the jury? These two goals are not always in conflict, but it would seem that they were in conflict in LeRoi Jones's case. The law was quite clear and clearly constitutional and there was relatively little discretion vested in the judge. Where he had great discretion, however, was precisely in those matters where his behavior has been challenged and criticized. Was he fair and impartial? Was he honest? There seems to be considerable evidence for a negative answer to the first test.

It is hard to believe that LeRoi Jones was treated exactly like any other defendant charged with the same offense. Even allowing for the highly charged atmosphere and the tensions resulting from the multitude of riot trials, Jones was still singled out for particular attention for allegedly committing a minor offense. There was determination to convict in every recorded action of Judge Kapp, and his interpretations of evidence, charge to the jury, and sentencing speech were beyond recognition as fair and impartial judging —notwithstanding the fact that they may have been legally permissible.

The important question is the determination of why Judge Kapp chose to play the role of judge and prosecutor. Did he perceive that this was expected of him as a vindication of the established white community and a mark of its refusal to accept any responsibility for the riots? Did he consider LeRoi Jones a threat to the peace and tranquillity of the community and himself as the last bastion of defense? Did he think that making an example of LeRoi Jones would deter future rioters?

[10]See Botein, *Trial Judge,* and *Kerner Commission Report,* chapter 13.

The President's Commission on Civil Disorders reported that in many of the riot-torn cities, the administration of justice broke down, mass justice was substituted for individual treatment, and maximum sentences tended to be imposed on all persons accused of the same offense, regardless of the particular facts in the case or mitigating circumstances.[11] Yet the LeRoi Jones trial was not the product of mass hysteria or confused conditions; it was a carefully singled out, well-planned prosecution which took place long after calm had been restored to Newark. In part this was because Jones's lawyer immediately rushed to his assistance. But the point to be made is that the scenario of the Jones trial fits perfectly into a model of what a rational city administration might have planned in order to dramatize the severity of response to ghetto riots. Mass injustice, after all, is invisible justice (or injustice) and serves no function in educating the public. Perhaps it was absolutely necessary for Newark to produce a trial of this sort. That LeRoi Jones was the defendant was probably an accident only in the sense that he happened to be arrested at the height of the conflagration. It apparently was no accident that the Newark authorities, realizing the value of the prisoner in their custody, sought to maximize the educational value of such an event.

Whether or not Judge Kapp was a formal and planned participant in the production of this spectacle, or whether he simply played the role he did for personal, perhaps subconscious, reasons, is largely unimportant. Being a man of conservative values, Judge Kapp obviously looked upon the defendant with contempt, as a threat to organized society, as a purveyor of what Judge Kapp thought was obscene literature, and as a provocateur. It did not matter to him that Jones was certainly not a leader in the black community of Newark, though he was well known there; nor did it matter to Kapp that Jones was apparently not a looter nor a person engaged in physical violence. The fact that Jones was an "ungrateful" Negro who refused to humble himself before, as it were, "the ship's captain," seems to have been more important.

What is known of the role of public prosecutor in the United States suggests that, next to the police themselves, he is the most important determiner of "justice."[12] He decides whom to prosecute and on what charges. The prosecutory role is also a bargaining role, in which every attempt is made to avoid a trial by trading a reduction of charges against the defendant's confession. If a respectable white man had been stopped by the police under normal circumstances, and a weapon found concealed in his car, and if he had no prior convictions on his record, it is most likely that if the charge were not dismissed, it would be reduced to disorderly conduct and the defendant fined a small amount. The fact that the prosecutor refused to bargain in this case, and that he prosecuted with extreme diligence, might simply indicate unusual zeal, or it might indicate something else. While Zazzali's behavior in the case was within his lawful discretion, it seemed very much like a vengeful act—not against Jones so much as against what, in Zazzali's eyes, Jones represented. Except in the facts of the case, there was little difference between

---

[11]*Kerner Commission Report,* p. 343.

[12]See works by Blumberg, Trebach, Newman, and Remington cited in note 7 of this essay.

Zazzali's conduct and his likely conduct if the defendant had been a czar of organized crime.

In summary of these observations it can be said that both the judge and prosecutor operated in the margins of the roles that they could normally have been expected to play, that their behavior was characterized by what seemed to be a single-minded determination to convict and severely punish LeRoi Jones, and that this singlemindedness could not be explained with reference to the nature of the offense charged in open court, but rather only with reference to the defendant's role as a severe critic of white society.

Third, what was the public perception of the nature of the trial? Did the general public see the LeRoi Jones case as the majesty of the law in action? In lieu of evidence concerning public understanding of the nature of the trial, unobtainable except by advance planning and good fortune, we must speculate from the uncertain base of a review of press reports of the trial and sentence. In this instance, however, newspapers and news magazines were sufficiently in agreement to lend credence to the belief that most readers would find it very difficult to interpret this case as a routine example of mechanistic law enforcement.

Predictably, the left-wing press was outraged at Newark's brand of "justice." *Ramparts* may serve as a relatively moderate illustration: referring to Judge Kapp as "an example of the paranoid reality, the state of mind that has annexed America," its report suggested that white America had an obligation to impeach him "and others who have no conception of or respect for the law."[13] But sharp criticism was not limited to the left and liberal press. *Newsweek,* reporting the sentencing with the lead, "For Jones, . . . verse came quickly to worst," summed up the trial and sentencing in these words: "But for all his bellicose bluster [Jones] left serious questions behind him. His sentence was by far the longest yet imposed in a Newark riot trial; . . . It was plain that Kapp had indeed held Jones' poetry against him. . . ."[14] Even the *New York Times*'s news column reflected incredulity at the behavior of the judge. Highlighting the near maximum character of the sentence and comparing it with that meted out to Jones's codefendants, the news story describes the basis for the judge's sentencing with sober amazement and exhaustive detail. The inevitable implication of the story is one of prejudice and unfairness.[15]

The only distinctions in the image of the trial conveyed by the various media lay in the level of causation assigned. The left-wing press was more likely to interpret the events as an illustration of a repressive system at work, carrying out its racist propensities against a representative black man who dared to fight back. To *Ramparts,* for example, the issue of Jones's guilt or innocence, while important, was not crucial; its report conveyed doubt about Jones's guilt on several grounds, but went on to portray Jones as "guilty" of resisting white exploitation. In this view, Jones was "the right man on the

---

[13]Stephen Schneck, "LeRoi Jones or, Politics & Policemen, or, Trying Heart, Bleeding Heart," *Ramparts,* 29 June 1968, pp. 14–19.

[14]*Newsweek,* 15 January 1968, p. 24.

[15]*New York Times,* 5 January 1968.

wrong charge," and oppression the inevitable response by the system.[16] *News-week* tacitly laid the blame for an apparent misapplication of justice on a superenthusiastic judge, who, perhaps misguidedly, acted in the name of the Newark establishment. Its report concludes on a pragmatic note, citing with approval the ACLU comment that "actions of this kind tend only to exacerbate an already tense Negro community and do not serve the cause of justice."[17] Likewise, the account of the *New York Times,* while detailing every unusual aspect of the judge's behavior, never suggests that there is anything more to the incident than the idiosyncratic behavior of a single individual. Thus, if readers' understanding of the trial were shaped by the substance of these reports, they would not necessarily have been able to identify it as a "political trial" as such. But they could not fail to appreciate the distinctly unusual behavior of the judge, nor the special vindictiveness of the sentence for a crime which was, at best, a technical violation of the statutes if taken out of the context of the Newark riots.

CONCLUSIONS

In the day-to-day activities of an ongoing political system, the functions of law and legal institutions fall somewhere on a continuum between the mere rationalization of naked force, whimsically applied by dominant elites, and the living embodiment of community morality (or of a higher being) neutrally applied in a mechanical way. The precise location on the continuum is continually debated, but it is reasonably clear that such disparate types as scholars and revolutionaries have similar views on this subject at least. Both are inclined to believe that the operations of law and legal institutions in the United States fall somewhat nearer the former than the latter position. Both reject the more traditional view that the law and legal institutions are so infused with idealism that they stand above the conflicts of ordinary people and are immune to the temptations of personal bias and involvement. They see the facts differently—or different facts—than most of the practicing legal and political community.

Notwithstanding this unusual agreement between scholars and revolutionaries, there are substantial differences between them. Scholars tend to view the law and legal institutions as more or less rational attempts to create social order in a diverse society. The law is seen as the product of a sometimes bitter, always value-based, conflict among important segments of the society, with the state of the law determined both by tradition (precedent) and by the current interests of the majority. Most contemporary scholars conceive of the law and legal institutions as neither monolithic nor hierarchical. Rather, legal functions are said to be dispersed among a wide variety of legal and political institutions or actors, each of whom may bring to his legal role different ideas

---

[16]Schneck, "LeRoi Jones," *Ramparts,* 29 June 1968.
[17]*Newsweek,* 15 January 1968, p. 24.

and perspectives. The "rule of law" therefore is not (and cannot be) a uniform application of widely agreed-upon principles (though this may be the case on occasion). Instead, it is a highly complex process in which the social class, personality, and values of the legal actor, as well as the circumstances in which he acts, may produce widely divergent results—not the identical consequences which in theory follow from the implementation of a particular law or rule. Belying the famous slogan, "a government of law and not of men," the law is essentially a human institution, with all the imperfections and nonrational dimensions characteristic of human behavior everywhere.

Whereas the revolutionary may share the scholar's view of law as an attempt to impose social order, he comes to a parting of the ways due to his belief that there is also a conscious deliberation and conspiratorial aura to the repressiveness of the law. He finds coherent motivation behind the shaping of the law's substance, so that it becomes in effect the instrument by which one class or group establishes its values as dominant. He believes these values are maintained by the application of the law when feasible, or by harsher— sometimes extralegal—sanctions, including physical force, when necessary. Enforcement of the law is to the revolutionary wholly a political act. Repression of any form of deviant behavior, or resistance to even widely shared norms, is anticipated and even welcomed as a means of revealing the true class basis of the law. (Whether the dominant class is labeled "capitalist" or "white power structure" is irrelevant.) Instead of the diversity of purposes and the resolution of competing values which the scholar finds in the legal system, the revolutionary finds a single-minded, ideological purpose—to reduce and repress opposition to the legitimacy of the regime. High-minded enforcement of the law by policemen, lawyers, and judges becomes either an indication of conscious service to the ruling class or a tribute to the power and effectiveness of the promulgated ideology. The aforementioned slogan, "a government of law and not of men," is not merely an impossible—though perhaps commendable—ideal but a deliberate attempt to rationalize rule by the dominant group.

Neither the scholar nor the revolutionary should or could have been surprised by the outcome of the trial of LeRoi Jones. For the revolutionary it was simply the proof of the pudding; white society was acting toward a black leader precisely the way it was, in theory, supposed to be acting. For the scholar, however, evaluation is much more difficult. In many painfully obvious ways, our criteria indicate that this was the very *model* of a political trial. The actions of the public officials clearly implied the operation of extralegal factors and special motivations. It would be extremely difficult to show that the actions of the trial judge, the police, and the prosecuting attorney were consistent with the norms or role expectations of their positions. Their protestations to the contrary, it does not appear that any of them really perceived the apprehension and trial of LeRoi Jones as "just another case." Judge Kapp declined to be interviewed, but Zazzali, Booker, and veteran courtroom observers on the scene whom we did interview were quite aware of the uniqueness of the case and of the procedures followed. All of the reporting media emphasized the aberrational behavior of the judge and the retributional aura of the trial. We can conclude that at least insofar as our three empirical indicators can be tested by the sorts of evidence we have obtained, there are strong implications of the use of the trappings of a court and the "law" as a means of ritualistically applying force in behalf of dominant groups.

We are not quite prepared, however, simply to label this a "political trial." Not everything about the trial and sentencing was arbitrary or beyond the outer boundaries of the "norm," and in many respects, these events illustrate behavior within—but near—the outer limits of the normal workings of the law. The behavior of the key actors is better known in this case than in most others because of the intensive newspaper coverage of the trial of a famous person. We have little comparative evidence on which to base any characterization of how distinctively police and prosecutor acted in this case; only the judge's behavior seems on its face to be clearly unusual or in conflict with accepted norms. But even a trial judge has considerable discretion, and appellate courts in the United States are notoriously reluctant to reverse convictions because of erroneous judicial conduct; the higher courts are even more reluctant to reverse sentences imposed by the judge who actually heard the testimony and observed the behavior and demeanor of the defendant. Not even those attorneys who were handling Jones's case on appeal would predict a reversal on the facts in the record. Irving Vogelman, who helped prepare the brief on appeal, emphasized in an interview that neither the trial itself nor the sentencing behavior of Judge Kapp so violated established practices as to constitute an overwhelming case for reversal as an abuse of discretion. As the Epilogue will make clear, Vogelman was unduly pessimistic, but his caution is probably a good indicator of how much a judge can actually get away with and still not be reversed on appeal.

A similar problem exists with regard to the actors' perceptions. Not only do we have little comparative base from which to conclude that their self-images were less impersonal and more vindictive in this case than in others, but we also must give at least some credence to the fact that they insist that their actions were routine and in the name of the law. If they hold such convictions, that is what counts—not whether or not their beliefs appear to be empirically validated. Finally, public perception might be a product of the intensive media coverage of this particular trial. We suspect the existence of a substantial additional number of trials which, if covered with equal intensity, would acquire similar images of unfairness. The regrettable truth is that the LeRoi Jones case *is* probably an example of the "law" in action and may be only marginally a "political trial."

Our findings seem at first to go in two conflicting directions, but at a deeper level they are actually congruent. There is little news in the observation that law is an instrument of social control—but the significance of this commonplace may for that very reason be ignored. Just because law *does* serve to maintain an established pattern of status and power relationships, it can become an instrument of those who are dominant and a means whereby they insulate themselves from behavior which would modify the existing structure of the society, economy, and polity. What is the nature of the social reality that law preserves and protects? The scholar and the revolutionary tend to differ in their characterizations, but in both cases the law is the instrument of preserving that structure. It cannot be otherwise.

Those who administer the law are the agents of the dominant class. Whatever their actions, such actions are presumed to contribute to the general purpose of preserving the established order. At some points, individual agents may get carried away, and in their enthusiasm for their work may commit acts which embarrass those for whom they serve. On such occasions, some observers are ready with the label of "political trial," perhaps sincerely or perhaps as a means of excluding the more extreme illustrations of the basic purpose of law from analysis of the role of law in society. Such occasions do not differ qualitatively from the everyday function of law within the social order, but only in degree and perhaps in visibility. The law is *always* a means by which the dominant obtain their ends and protect their gains, and it seems ingenuous if not downright misleading to take special note of the overzealousness of some agents by raising such actions to the level of a new and aberrational category.

Perhaps we should modify our definition to say that a "political trial" is merely one which is marked by one or more of the authoritative actors failing to perform the social control ritual within the range of "norms" for such behavior. The difference is in the style and procedure, not in the substance of what is being done, and this is the real distinguishing feature of political justice. At this fundamental level, perhaps LeRoi Jones was convicted by essentially standard means for failure to acquiesce in the established order of things in the United States. Some of the agents were indeed unusually enthusiastic about their job, but perhaps this should be seen as a relatively minor embellishment upon the basic process.

EPILOGUE

On 28 December 1968 the Superior Court of New Jersey, Appellate Division, unanimously reversed the conviction of LeRoi Jones for unlawful possession of two revolvers, and at the same time also reversed the contempt-of-court conviction unilaterally meted out by Judge Kapp at the conclusion of the trial.[18] A new trial was ordered for Jones and his codefendants, Barry Wynn and Charles McCray.

The opinion of the court dealt exclusively with the unfairness of the judge's charge to the jury. Having found grounds for reversal here, it declined to consider any of the other grounds for appeal advanced by Jones's attorney: that the arrest and search of the defendants was without probable cause and

[18]*New Jersey v. Jones, et al.,* 104 N.J. Supr. 57 (1968).

was conducted with excessive force, that the weapons, if they were found at all, were improperly seized, that the bias of the trial judge so pervaded the entire courtroom as to make a fair trial impossible, and that the sentences were excessive.

Superior Court Judge Gaulkin found, much as we had observed earlier (and written before the appeal was decided), that the judge's charge to the jury, and by inference his very behavior as a judge, unfairly led the jury to believe the testimony of the police officers and cast doubts and aspersions on the credibility of the defendant's own account. (Judge Kapp extolled the police officers as "these five men in blue," and admonished the jury that "the police officer is the shield of the community against the use of violence and other lawless acts.")

The court took further exception to Judge Kapp's derogatory remark about the conduct of Jones's defense, speaking of "the mass of trivia which unfortunately has crept into this trial," and which obviously referred in the context of the trial to Jones's claim that he had been beaten by the police. No one—certainly not a juror—could have mistaken Judge Kapp's words and manner, nor fail to answer his rhetorical questions as intended: "You saw and heard each of these officers testify. The defendants would have you believe that they are prevaricators and that they committed the most flagrant kind of perjury when they stated under oath the manner in which they found and removed the two loaded revolvers." And: "Did they appear to you to be evilly disposed and wicked men who would resort to such calumny?"

In reversing the contempt citation against Jones, the appeals court also ruled that "if defendant did do and say what he was charged with doing and saying, it constituted contempt." But because he was not advised of the contempt charge nor given an opportunity to be heard before the judge found him guilty and sentenced him, the citation was held invalid.

Both decisions of the superior court, appellate division, were appealed to the Supreme Court of New Jersey, that state's highest court. The supreme court reversed the superior court to the extent of ordering a new trial on the contempt charge, but refused the state leave to appeal the guns possession decision. Thus, both charges against LeRoi Jones remained open if the state wished to press them—and it did.

A new trial on the weapons charge was held, but this time before a different judge, and in the Essex County Courtroom in Newark. The jury consisted of eight whites and four blacks, a ratio more nearly consistent with—but not a mirror image of—the racial distribution of the people of Newark. The proceedings before Judge Melvin P. Antell seemed much closer to those normally found in a courtroom. The testimony for both sides was substantially the same, although Judge Antell did not participate in the questioning of prosecution witnesses. The defense lodged the additional claim that the police had concocted the weapons possession charges only after they had arrested and beaten Jones and Wynn and allegedly needed a cover for these extralegal actions. Reversing the position of Judge Kapp, Antell even allowed jury inspection of the vehicle in which the three men had been apprehended. Finally, the charge to the jury was scrupulously limited to the law and not the judge's interpretation of the facts in the case.

On 2 July 1969, nearly two years after the alleged events took place, LeRoi Jones and his codefendants were acquitted of the charge that they unlawfully had in their possession two revolvers.[19] Several months earlier, another Essex County judge had found Jones guilty of contempt of Judge Kapp, for calling those earlier proceedings a "kangaroo court." But his sentence of a $200 fine and no imprisonment was so lenient and so indisputedly a tacit admission of the truth of the statement that Jones's lawyer, Booker, considered this to be a victory as well. The fine was quickly paid.

The political trial of LeRoi Jones ended in defeat and humiliation for the authorities, and it would certainly be satisfying to end this account with the observation that justice had, in the long run, triumphed. But several corollary events point instead to a continuing trial of LeRoi Jones, a trial of patience, fortitude, financial and legal resources, and political strategy. Twice since his original conviction Jones has been rearrested by the Newark police, in circumstances which suggest that whatever the verdict of the second trial, they still consider him a dangerous and undesirable person to be roaming the streets.

On 4 October 1968 Jones was arrested in a bank on a charge of using loud and abusive language and resisting arrest, and other charges which included a traffic offense and receiving stolen goods. Two of his friends were also arrested on a charge of interfering with a police officer.[20] On 27 November Jones was convicted of the first two of these charges. As the story came out in court, Jones exchanged words and then insults with a detective who had entered the bank on a "special bank detail." Jones admitted calling the detective a "punk," but denied using abusive language and claimed that he had been provoked by the officer. The judge ruled against him, citing a case in which the word "punk" was found to be offensive, and because he thought Jones had used it intentionally to be offensive. For calling a police officer a "punk" Jones was sentenced to sixty days in jail and a fine of $100.[21] Two months later this conviction was also overturned by a superior court judge because of lack of evidence.[22]

There were two charges of receiving stolen property. The first involved a stolen duplicating machine, valued at just under $2,000, which was found "in a building used by Jones."[23] The second charge involved the same two revolvers found in Jones's microbus the night of his first arrest. Jones was acquitted of the first charge, while the second has never been pursued by the Newark authorities and will, presumably, expire when the statute of limitations runs out. But the pattern of police harassment seems clear enough. The irony is that, had the arresting officers, the prosecutor, and Judge Kapp been able to

[19] New York Times, 3 July 1969.
[20] Ibid., 4 October 1968.
[21] Ibid., 27 November 1968.
[22] Ibid., 17 January 1969.
[23] Ibid., 18 March 1969.

disguise their enthusiasm at finding LeRoi Jones in their custody two years earlier, and had they been able to control the hostility which they had for him and for what he represents, he would in all probability be residing in the penitentiary today.

It is not at all impossible to believe—at least not for two white political scientists who were not present at the original trial—that Jones was at least technically guilty of the offense charged against him; it is certainly possible to doubt some parts of his story, as his insistence that at 11:30 P.M., at the height of the Newark riots, he was taking driving lessons. Likewise, knowing his explosive temper and hatred of whites (policemen especially), it is not hard to believe that he reacted so violently even to being stopped by the police that force was needed to subdue him simply in order to question him, or that his provocative behavior in the courtroom contributed to the behavior of the judge and prosecuting attorney. There is surely no excuse for their actions, but the onus of conducting a "political trial" is not entirely theirs. A political trial is the result of a combination of forces, and in this case LeRoi Jones willingly provided the material for a spontaneous combustion of events.

As these final words are written, LeRoi Jones is not in jail. His "thing" is not violence but organizing a variety of welfare, cultural, and civic activities for the black community in Newark, including a highly successful voter registration drive. Above all he is not the political activist or violent anarchist who bore the brunt of the authorities' retribution for the riots. He was and is, above all, a poet, a writer, and an activist of letters, and it is in those relatively peaceful capacities that he is in fact far more dangerous to the continued white domination of Newark. The irony of this trial is that its exposure of the hatred and bad temper of a black poet was far less damaging to Jones than its exposure of the workings of political justice was damaging to the very same political rule which it was meant to uphold.

index